D1168807

Entrances
Gregorian Chant in Daily Life

Entrances

Gregorian Chant in Daily Life

*To Betty Hudson.
In gratitude for
many years of encouragement
and support.*
Rembert
1.1.2000

Rembert Herbert

*Enter his gates with thanksgiving;
go into his courts with praise.*
—Psalm 100

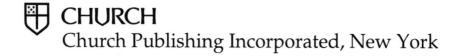

CHURCH
Church Publishing Incorporated, New York

Copyright ©1999 by Rembert Herbert
All rights reserved.

Figures 1, 8 (see Chapter Three) and Figures II, III (see "The Uses and Users of Books")—from the collection of the Music Division, Library of Congress; photographs by Horace Groves. Used by permission.

Figure I (see "The Uses and Users of Books")—from the Christian-Weise-Bibliothek Zittau, Wissenschaftlicher und Heimatgeschichtlicher Altbestand, Missale A IV, Zittau um 1450, Blatt 1 Initale V. Used by permission.

Most of the music with Latin texts found in the appendices has been derived from editions compiled by the Abbaye St. Pierre de Solesmes and used by permission as follows:
    —from *Graduale Sacrosanctae Romanae Ecclesiae*: the Marialis Kyrie, Sanctus, and Agnus Dei of the "Marialis" Ordinary (Appendix 6); the Introit, Kyrie (transcribed into modern notation by author), Alleluia, Tract, Offertory, Sanctus, Agnus Dei, and Communion Antiphon of the Eucharist in Honor of the Holy Spirit (Appendix 11);
    —from *Antiphonale Monasticum Pro Diurnis Horis*: the *Salva regina* of Compline (Appendix 10); the music with Latin text of First Vespers for the Third Sunday of Advent (Appendix 8), except *Rorate caeli*;
    —from *Liber Usualis*: the simple Latin Gloria (Appendix 6); the *Rorate caeli* of First Vespers (Appendix 8);
    —from *Officium Majoris Hebdomadae et Octavae Paschae*: the Latin responsories of Tenebrae for Wednesday Evening of Holy Week (Appendix 9).

Every effort has been made to trace the owner or holder of the copyright for every previously published musical setting used in this book. If any rights have been inadvertently infringed upon, the Publishers ask that the omission be excused and agree to make the necessary corrections in subsequent editions.

Portions of the appendices of this book may be reproduced by a congregation or choir for its own use. Commercial or large-scale reproduction, or reproduction for sale, of any portion of this book or of the book as a whole, without the written permission of Church Publishing Incorporated, is prohibited.

LIBRARY OF CONGRESS CATALOGING-IN-PUBLICATION DATA

Herbert, Rembert.
    Entrances : Gregorian chant in daily life / by Rembert Herbert.
        p.   cm.
    Includes bibliographical references.
    ISBN 0-89869-315-2
    1. Chants (Plain, Gregorian, etc.)--Study and teaching.
        2. Contemplation.
    I. Title.
            MT860 .H47 1999
            26'.2--dc21   99-045497

Church Publishing Incorporated
445 Fifth Avenue
New York NY 10016

5 4 3 2 1

For my parents

R. Bryce Herbert

Mary Motte Anderson Herbert

Contents

ENTRANCES

Contents

Acknowledgments

This book would not have been possible without my years of liturgical performance with the Schola Cantorum of New York, which I have directed since 1986, and without the advice and collaboration of my assistant in the Schola, Karl Peterson. Many of the ideas contained in these pages surfaced during weekly Schola rehearsals between 1986 and 1998. The members' faithfulness and dedication have been exceptional. I also would like to thank the clergy who have supported the Schola's efforts over the years, especially the Rev. Richard Downing, the Rev. Betty Hudson, the Rt. Rev. Catherine Roskam, and the Rev. Norman Catir. For training in paleography and chant performance, I am indebted to Prof. Ruth Steiner and Prof. Theodore Marier, both of Catholic University. For their support and insight, I owe a special debt to several monastics and spiritual leaders, especially Paul Reynard, the Rev. Chrysogonus Waddell, and Sr. Mary Frances Wynne, and the Community of the Holy Spirit in New York City. For the opportunity to explore all the ideas of this book with a large group of exceptional spirits, I am indebted to The Friends of St. Benedict and The Benedictine Experience of New Harmony, Indiana, especially the Rev. Benedict Reid, Jane Owen, the Rev. Milo Coerper, and Elizabeth Swenson.

The book could not have been written without the initiative of Marilyn Haskel and the editorial skills of Frank Tedeschi and Johnny Ross, all of Church Publishing Incorporated, and without the ongoing support of Dr. Anthony Miserandino, formerly of Hunter College High School in New York City. And finally, the text would be unintelligible to all but me except for the extraordinary editorial eye of my wife, Rebecca.

Introduction

In the spring of 1975 I first visited St. James's Episcopal Church, a small parish in Washington, D.C., where Gregorian chant was sung every week and had been for many years. The entire congregation took part. I knew very little about this music, but the choir needed singers and was eager to share their skill. I was working then in the Music Division of the Library of Congress, and another tenor from the choir worked elsewhere in the library. Shortly before the Feast of Corpus Christi in 1975, this generous singer made regular lunchtime trips to the Music Division to teach me the service. I remember following him through the narrow, labyrinthine library stacks, rows of books high above our heads to left and right, to a corner where we could spend a few minutes each day poring over *The English Gradual* and Winfred Douglas's ubiquitous green *Kyrial*.

I soon became Cantor at St. James's and remained in that position for the next ten years. It was in that role, guided by the rector, the Rev. Richard Downing, that I came to experience again and again the peculiarly affecting power of the Gregorian liturgies—the Mass, Lauds, Vespers, and Tenebrae most especially. It was also during those years, as I became more familiar with the history and technical aspects of the chant, that questions began to form in my mind about its special quality. Nowhere in my musical or literary training had I been given language to describe what it seemed to me the music was fundamentally about. Even though, historically, chant was the source from which all Western classical music derived, it was, I felt, different in its purpose even from other sacred music which came after it, even from the magnificent works of Palestrina, Handel, and Bach.

These questions stayed with me until, by chance, I found myself several years later in the bookstore of Catholic University in Washington. I pulled from the shelf a volume of St. Bernard's sermons on The Song of Songs and, as I read, began to hear a familiar sound. Even though Bernard had nothing whatever to say about music, I thought I heard in his prose an echo akin to the underlying voice of the chant.

The present book began in that moment of recognition. I soon discovered that, among both Anglican and Roman Catholic monastics even today, a close connection between the chant and certain "fathers of the Church," including Bernard, is accepted as a matter of course. But nowhere had those relationships been set down in detail. Nowhere in the published literature had an attempt been made to develop a method of teaching the chant which would acknowledge that relationship and use it as a guide to help singers enter fully into the contemplative world the chant inhabits. For most modern Christians outside monastic life, that world is quite new.

This book is an attempt to place the study of the chant in this larger context of traditional monastic thought. It is also an attempt to present a method of teaching and singing which will support the aims and character of that tradition. Since inner harmony and consistency are two of its salient characteristics, there should be in this approach to the chant no dichotomy between the technical and the spiritual. Every technical exercise must have both a musical and a contemplative purpose.

This book is primarily, then, for those who are already singing Gregorian chant or would like to begin, but it is also for those who may not be singers but have been stirred by the chant's special quality. There is, however, no recording planned as a companion to the book. A basic thesis here is that Gregorian chant is for those who sing it. Bernard of Clairvaux in the twelfth century wrote of inner realities that "in matters of this kind, understanding can follow only where experience leads" (*Bern/SS* 2: 15). Only physical participation, as a singer or active listener, can provide that experience. If you can carry a tune and have the urge, find a choir or organize one, and sing. If you can't carry a tune and have the urge, find a church or monastery where the chant is in use and participate by being present with your disciplined listening.

Chapters Two and Three contain as much musical instruction as should be necessary to begin a new choir. The remaining chapters explain how the experience of singing the chant can be understood within the context of traditional monastic teaching about the contemplative life. The twelve appendices include four complete liturgies. All of this material can be put to use in a broad range of ways, from the parish choir, which simply wants to refine its skills at chanting psalms, to the specialized chant choir, or "schola," which plans to explore the contemplative possibilities of the chant in detail. Chapter Six describes a few of these options.

A second thesis of the book is that the chant is essentially about listening and silence. By disciplining our wandering thoughts to rest attentively with the sound of the voices, we are able to find within ourselves mental and emotional stillness and, with that, order and intelligence. According to monastic tradition, a "quiet mind" allows a deeper intelligence to be heard which is able to interpret the will of God for one's life, and is able to perceive the inner voice of scripture. Chanting is, thus, more a form of prayer and meditation on scripture than it is music in the conventional sense. It offers an entrance into silent worlds within ourselves and into worlds that lie beneath or within the literal meanings of scripture.

Throughout the Middle Ages, Christian culture was sustained and fed by the strength of this silent, inner vision. Although these centuries have been called the "Dark Ages," what is striking in the contemplative literature of the time is the pervasive imagery of light, a vision which was given tangible shape near the end of that age in the extraordinary stained glass of the cathedrals. Amidst the confusion and materialism of our own day, there would seem to be a compelling need to seek out these pure sources. It is my hope that this small book may contribute to that effort.

Advent 1998

Abbreviations

All quotations in this book are followed by a source citation in parenthesis. Most source citations follow immediately after the quoted material; a few follow after the last in a series of quotes from the same source. Source titles are abbreviated (see key below).

Except for books of the Bible and translations of the Bible, all titles listed below also are listed in the Bibliography.

TRANSLATIONS OF THE BIBLE:
DR   Douay-Rheims
KJV   King James Version
NEB   New English Bible
RSV   Revised Standard Version

BOOKS OF THE BIBLE:

Acts	Acts of the Apostles	Gal	Galatians
1 Chr	1 Chronicles	Gn	Genesis
Col	Colossians	Habak	Habakkuk
1 Cor	1 Corinthians	Heb	Hebrews
2 Cor	2 Corinthians	Hos	Hosea
Dt	Deuteronomy	Is	Isaiah
Eccl	Ecclesiastes	Jer	Jeremiah
Ecclus	Ecclesiasticus	Job	Job
Eph	Ephesians	Jn	John
Ex	Exodus	Jon	Jonah
Ezek	Ezekiel	1 Kg	1 Kings

ENTRANCES

Lk	Luke	Ps	Psalms
Mk	Mark	Rev	Revelation
Mt	Matthew	Sg	The Song of Songs
Mic	Micah	Titus	Titus
Num	Numbers	Wis	The Book of Wisdom
1 Pet	1 Peter	Zech	Zechariah
Phil	Philippians	Zeph	Zephaniah
Prov	Proverbs		

WORKS OF THE CONTEMPLATIVE TRADITION
  (fathers of the church and others):

A/Conf	The Confessions of Saint Augustine
A/LF	Expositions on the Book of Psalms, by Augustine, A Library of the Fathers of the Holy Catholic Church
A/ACW	On the Psalms, by Augustine, Ancient Christian Writers Series
Amad	Magnificat: Homilies in Praise of the Blessed Virgin Mary, Homily IV, by Amadeus of Lausanne
Athan	The Letter to Marcellinus, by Athanasius Classics of Western Spirituality
Bern/SS	On the Song of Songs, by Bernard of Clairvaux
Cass/CWS	Conferences, by John Cassian, Classics of Western Spirituality
Cass/SL	The Conferences, by John Cassian, A Select Library of Nicene and Post-Nicene Fathers of the Christian Church
Clim	The Ladder of Divine Ascent, by John Climacus, Classics of Western Spirituality
Evag	The Praktikos and Chapters on Prayer, by Evagrius Ponticus
G/HHP	Homiliae in Hiezechihelem Prophetam, by Gregory the Great
G/LPR	In Librum Primum Regum, by Gregory the Great
G/MBJ	Morals on the Book of Job, by Gregory the Great, A Library of the Fathers of the Holy Catholic Church

Guid   Source Readings in Music History; "Preface" to his Antiphoner, by Guido of Arezzo

Guig   The Ladder of Monks and Twelve Meditations, by Guigo II

Hesy   "Hesychius of Jerusalem" from Writings from the Philokalia on Prayer of the Heart

Max   The Church, the Liturgy and the Soul of Man: The Mystagogia of St. Maximus the Confessor

Nyssa   The Life of Moses, by Gregory of Nyssa, Classics of Western Spirituality

Orig/CWS On First Principles Book IV (pp. 171–216); Prologue to the Commentary on The Song of Songs (pp. 217–244); Homily XXVII on Numbers (pp. 245–269), by Origen, Classics of Western Spirituality

Orig/SS   The Song of Songs: Commentary and Homilies, by Origen, Ancient Christian Writers Series

Rich   The Twelve Patriarchs (pp. 53–147); The Mystical Ark (151–370); Book Three of the Trinity (373–397), by Richard of St. Victor, Classics of Western Spirituality

Ter   The Interior Castle, by Teresa of Avila, Classics of Western Spirituality

OTHER WORKS:

BCP   The Book of Common Prayer of the Episcopal Church

Bread   Bread in the Wilderness, by Thomas Merton

Brev   The Roman Breviary

Hours   The Liturgy of the Hours East and West: The Origins of the Divine Office and Its Meaning for Today, by Robert Taft

Learning The Love of Learning and the Desire for God: A Study of Monastic Culture, by Henri Leclerq

Melodies Les mélodies grégoriennes, by Joseph Pothier

Papal   The Papal Encyclicals, 1878–1903, edited by Clauria Carlen Ihm

Prayer   Prayer, by Henri Le Saux

Entrances
Gregorian Chant in Daily Life

Chapter One

Gregorian Chant in Context

MONASTIC CULTURE AND THE "FATHERS OF THE CHURCH"

Gregorian chant is the traditional music of Western Christianity. For several hundred years, until the late Middle Ages, it was the only music allowed in Christian services. The repertory includes thousands of melodies for nine services each day. It is sung in unison, without accompaniment, to Latin texts largely from the Bible. It is ancient, and its history abounds in puzzles and enigmas. The music notation we use today was invented (probably in the Frankish empire, somewhere around the ninth century) in order to write down the chant and preserve it. But no one knows when the music itself was composed. Current scholarship is rife with speculation as to the places, times, and manner of its origin, but little can be said with certainty.

St. Gregory the Great, whose name became identified with the chant at least as early as the eighth century, died in 604, about 200 years before music notation was invented. We do not know what music was used in services in Gregory's day, though we do know that services were sung. Could the chant, which consists of hundreds of melodies, have been transmitted orally for centuries? Could it be even older than Gregory? No one can be sure.

Intriguing as these historical questions are, the important mystery has more to do with what Gregorian chant is than with where it came from, as is clear to any sensitive listener today. That

1

essential mystery lies in the unmistakable sacred quality of the music, a quality which can touch almost anyone with a reminder of something beyond the ordinary.

If we are to understand the chant, it is this sacred quality we must try to understand, and here we encounter a problem. There is little in modern aesthetic theory that can help us articulate what we feel in this ancient music. More surprisingly, we find little help in medieval treatises on music, either. But if we turn to medieval writings on scripture and immerse ourselves in these works, especially those of Gregory the Great himself, we begin to realize that we are in the presence of sacred qualities reminiscent of the chant. Even though Gregory seldom mentions music, his commentaries are sister works to the chant. The chant is a musical commentary on its scriptural text just as Gregory's is a verbal one, and the aim of the two commentaries is the same. Both arts, verbal and musical, are concerned with bringing about a meeting between text and person, a meeting based on prayer. When we recall that the commentaries and related monastic writings on prayer are products of exactly the same setting as the chant—the early medieval monastery—we find this common concern less surprising. The study of scripture was the foundation of monastic life, and "to study" meant to grow into a living relation to the text.

Perhaps we should pause to consider the significance of this monastic culture of which the chant was a part. If Gregorian chant were simply beautiful music with which to grace a service, its potential value to the church today would be far less than it is. But the chant carries in that music the sound of an entire religious culture, one with an understanding that was far-reaching, centered on God and—within itself—balanced, coherent, and unified. The chant speaks of a Western Christianity many of us do not know ever existed, of a "Middle Ages" which might deserve that name, not because it fell "between" the glories of the ancient world and the glories of the Renaissance, but because it understood every nuance of the concept of a "middle"—a center, the heart of things, the point of balance. These "Dark Ages" are obscured from us by their many periods of political chaos, their apparent brutality, disease, their strange "superstitious" mind, and so on, but their religious literature is filled with imagery, not of darkness, but of light; Gregory's "incorporeal light [that fills] the inner parts" (*G/MBJ* 3: 262) or, five hundred years later, St. Bernard's "infusion of light that illuminates the intellect" (*Bern/SS* 3: 102); the same light of which ancient craftsmen left us a vivid reminder in the glass of their cathedrals.

The language of this medieval world was Latin. Although the Bible, the product of a Middle Eastern culture, existed originally in Hebrew and Greek, it was in Latin, over many centuries, that Western Christianity absorbed the scriptures' meaning. And so it is within the Latin tradition that we find an ancient, sophisticated, and, indeed, adequate body of teaching about how to come to terms with this strange Middle-Eastern faith and its sacred book. Perhaps most importantly, this tradition contains concepts of human nature and the nature of a sacred text which might reasonably claim to be universal and, indeed, have much in common with the teachings of other religious traditions.

Our purpose is to search out the origins of this mysterious call we hear sounded in the ancient Latin chant and, if we can, find some way to give this mystery a place in our lives. Our effort must be at the same time historical, theological, musical, imaginative, and—most of all—practical. Clearly, there can be no point in trying to relive a past age. But if the monastic tradition contains a "teaching" that is itself practical, unified, and universal in its view of human nature and the nature of scripture, it should be possible to bring that teaching into the contemporary world, translated where necessary into contemporary forms. Indeed, the time may be right for just such an effort. Many antagonisms of the past which separated Christian groups are fading. In a sense, the Reformation has just begun to end. The time may be right today for all Christians with an interest in the contemplative life—Catholic and Protestant —to reclaim their entire heritage, including, for Protestants, those centuries which may have been rejected as "Catholic."

Having begun the discussion with an impression of the chant itself, we must now move on to these early writers whom scholars call the "fathers of the church." (The study of this literature is sometimes called "patristics," from "pater," the Latin word for "father.") It is here that, if we cannot explain the chant's mysterious sacred quality, we may at least discover a context within which that quality seems at home. So our first question is: Who are these fathers?

In a word, the "fathers" are exactly what their name implies, those writers from roughly the second through the twelfth centuries whose ideas played a crucial role in defining the character and direction of the early church. They were often bishops, sometimes scholars, sometimes monks. Some of the names may be familiar— St. Augustine, who was Bishop of Hippo in North Africa in the fourth and fifth centuries; St. Jerome, author/compiler of the Latin Bible, who died in 420; St. Benedict, author of the sixth-century *Rule for Monks* that virtually defined monasticism in the West; St. Gregory the Great, biographer of St. Benedict, early supporter of Benedictine monasticism, and the first of the popes to become a major force in secular politics; and finally St. Bernard, abbot of the huge and influential monastery of Clairvaux in France in the twelfth century.

Bernard (d. 1153) has been called "the last of the fathers." There were many important spiritual writers after him, of course, but it is true that something fundamental in the tradition changes after about 1200. In this book I will draw sporadically on later authors, particularly St. Teresa of Avila (sixteenth century). But the consistent and unified tradition that is most closely connected to the chant stretches from the end of the second century through Bernard in the twelfth; thereafter, the tradition becomes diffuse. Even within this time period, not all the fathers were concerned primarily with the study of scripture and the inner life; not all were closely tied to monasteries. We are concerned here with those who were, and with other lesser monastic writers of the period who might not be classed as "fathers" in importance but have still recorded valuable ideas. Within that tradition, stretching across the roughly 1,000 years just outlined, the teachings which concern us were maintained with extraordinary consistency.

Two qualities stand out in writers of this tradition, separating them from later monastic authors. One is a distinct preference for scriptural commentary as their primary form of expression. Origen, Gregory, and Bernard all have in common the fact that their most profound insights into the inner life are offered as if in passing, as part of their interpretation of passages of scripture. As a result, what Gregory, for example, has to say about the "quiet mind" cannot be found gathered together in a chapter of abstract treatise but must be absorbed piecemeal over many hundreds of pages of scriptural commentary. (This method of presentation is itself significant, as we shall see in Chapter Five.)

The second quality is what we might call "reticence," or what Bernard himself calls "discretion." Bernard observes that one who has understood the inner life will choose "to hide in modest silence what he has perceived in silence" (*Bern/SS* 3: 100) unless, like Bernard himself, he is a teacher whose responsibility it is to speak, one "who may not be silent." Like other writers in this tradition, Bernard discusses the most exalted of spiritual experiences in understated, almost technical terms. His insights could only be the product of personal experience, and he speaks of the necessity for personal experience, but he rarely speaks from a personal point of view. Like others before him, he seems to speak from a life filled with such experience at many levels over many years. While he is obligated to lead others toward such a life, the actual events are rarely to be spoken of directly, even to the monks in his charge: "I may have been granted this experience [of the Word], but I do not speak of it. I have made allowance in what I have said, so that you could understand me." The limitations and dangers of language must be respected: "Do you suppose if I were granted that experience [of the Word], that I could describe to you what is beyond description?" (*Bern/SS* 4: 210). Bernard, like others in the tradition, assumes that his readers will know what he is speaking of, either because of

5

what they have seen in themselves or because of what they will see as they grow in the spiritual life.

The effect of this reticence is to present inner experience as available to anyone who takes on the discipline. It is available as a way of life, a way of existing in the workaday world, rather than as extraordinary "visions" such as might come only to great saints once in a lifetime. As Bernard puts it: "With a certain boldness I also maintain that the soul of any one of us here, if it keeps a similar vigil, will similarly be greeted as friend, consoled as the dove, embraced as a beauty" (*Bern/SS* 3: 105). I have therefore chosen to call these writers "contemplative" rather than "mystical," considering that in common use the word "mystical" is associated with the visionary and the exceptional. The contemplative tradition, by contrast, is concerned with one's experience of life on a moment-to-moment, day-by-day basis, and with the regular, daily discipline necessary to deepen that experience of life.

The tradition which is our focus is defined by Origen, John Cassian, Benedict, Gregory the Great, and Bernard of Clairvaux, though it includes many other figures. Within this group of five, Origen and Bernard form a beginning and an end, and Cassian, Benedict, and Gregory belong together in the middle. Over the centuries, Origen has been one of the most influential and controversial of all the fathers. He was a wealthy, educated man, born in Egypt about the year 185. He became a biblical scholar and teacher of formidable reputation, but harbored a passionate sense of his own shortcomings and a deep desire for perfection in the spiritual life. The church in Origen's day was young and in formation, and some of Origen's theological speculations got him into trouble with authorities in the church even during his lifetime. Throughout the centuries, however, the powerful inner quality of his commentaries on scripture have endeared Origen to monastics in the Eastern and Western churches alike.

Bernard was born around 1090 of a noble family in what is now France. He joined the strict order of Cistercian monks in 1112 and, three years later, led a group of Cistercians who founded a new abbey at Clairvaux, where Bernard remained as abbot his entire life. It was an extraordinary life. He was famous for his sanctity, the eloquence of his speaking and writing, his concern for the poor, and his political wisdom. He was the close advisor of kings and popes, and responsible for the foundation of more than sixty new monasteries.

Bernard's Cistercians were the most severely ascetic branch of the tradition of Western monasticism begun by St. Benedict in the sixth century. But the Benedictine tradition can be said to begin, not with Benedict himself, but with his predecessor, John Cassian. Cassian was born about 365 in what is now Romania. As a young man he traveled with his friend Germanus into the Egyptian desert in search of inner wisdom. There he met and shared in the teachings of a group of Christian hermits whose sanctity had become legendary even in their own day, a group known to later centuries as "the desert fathers." Cassian then took what he had learned in the desert and traveled into what is now France, where he founded a monastery at Marseilles. He recorded his earlier experiences in Egypt in two books, the *Conferences* and the *Institutes*. Benedict, in his *Rule for Monks* a generation later, referred to these two works of Cassian as among those teachings that will lead the aspiring monk to "the very heights of perfection." Benedict modestly describes his own work as a "little rule written for beginners." Gregory the Great, a younger contemporary of Benedict, put the *Rule* to a practical test in monasteries he established in Rome in the late 570s. He accepted election as pope in 590 with great reluctance but used his office with powerful effect to maintain order amidst the chaos left by the collapsing Roman Empire.

THE MESSAGE OF THE FATHERS AND THE EXPERIENCE OF SINGERS
These five "saints"—Origen, Cassian, Benedict, Gregory the Great, and Bernard of Clairvaux—are our primary figures of interest. But our next questions are more challenging: What do these writers have to say that is so important, and how are we to make practical use of it today? Indeed, for modern temperaments, their world is not easily entered. If we approach their writings without preparation, we may

find them as alien and impenetrable as the chant is mysterious. Preparation is the key. As Bernard puts it, "In matters of this kind, understanding can follow only where experience leads" (*Bern/SS* 2: 15). But where and how are we to gain this particular kind of inner experience? Bernard is not talking about anything we could learn from psychoanalysis or introspection. In fact, very little in our modern world leads us to experience ourselves in a way that would resonate with the fathers' descriptions; the singing of the chant, however, does (or at least under certain conditions, it can). Drawing on the experience of singing, we gradually find ourselves able to recognize in the fathers' writings a wide-ranging and systematic understanding of the inner life of a human being in search of the divine. In this search, we discover forces within ourselves which are intensely personal but at the same time, we suspect, universal— at work in everyone. We find that we are the same as the fathers were, if we "walk in their way" and accept a similar discipline. It is to this way that the chant can be a guide, and within the context of this way that its special, sacred quality is felt to be entirely at home.

Let us take a concrete example. In his *Conferences*, Cassian describes how monks "while singing psalms and kneeling in prayer . . . have their thoughts filled with human figures, or conversations, or business, or unnecessary actions" (*Cass/SL* 528). Anyone who has recited psalms in the lengthy liturgy of Matins using Gregorian melodies has some idea of what he means. The quiet, repetitious character of the music allows the instability of the mind and emotions to become clearly visible. The moment we believe we're attending to the chant, we find, like Cassian, that our minds are, in fact, wandering among memories, among "figures and conversations." By seeing in ourselves, through the stillness of the music, something of what Cassian saw, we are able to follow his descriptions with better understanding and considerably more interest.

As we become more attentive to the experience of singing, our understanding of the fathers' descriptions of our own inner life deepens. We see, for example, that the instability of mind which Cassian describes is due to the fact that we have taken the outer world into ourselves. We have become attached to opinions, ideas, emotions, and images of ourselves and the world which have very little substance. As Augustine puts it, "All these seeming sources of worldly happiness are the dreams of sleepers" (*A/LF* 6: 95). In fact, if we have glimpsed the image of God which we are seeking in ourselves, we may suspect that, by comparison with that image, even our deepest feelings, our best ideas, have very little substance. And we find, once again, that the fathers have been here before us and have both described this experience and explained its consequences. Gregory calls these images "fantasies of the worldly imagination" and writes: "While the delighted mind wholly precipitates itself into these [images of visible things], it waxes gross [and] loses the fineness of the inward sense" (*G/MBJ* 1: 288).

Much to our disadvantage, we take this lightweight "inner" material as the truth, as a reflection of our real selves. We attach ourselves to this material and define ourselves by it. Gregory in another passage calls this lightweight material the "water of the world" which must be resisted by an "ardent striving" within (*G/MBJ* 2: 43). Ecclesiastes calls it "vanity," meaning "emptiness," suggesting this paradox: we are full of this material, in fact, so full that there is room for little else, and, therefore, we are empty. Gregory explains that, for this reason, according to scripture, only the "poor" or "hungry," those who are empty in a different sense, can be filled with the Holy Spirit.

To be filled with the spirit of the sacred text, then, we must prepare ourselves by resisting our attachments to images, thoughts, and feelings. We must restrain the aimless mental wandering which these attachments cause in us. The chant, the stillness of which began to show us our inner condition in the first place, now becomes our means of resisting this attachment as it makes more extreme demands on our attention. To maintain the still, unison character of the music, we must listen and focus our listening without interruption on the sound of the music. But the more we try, the more we discover again, as Cassian did, that the mind "insensibly returns to its previous wandering thoughts" or "slips from the inmost recesses of the heart swifter than a snake" (*Cass/SL* 362). Our recourse is simple but demanding: to bring the listening attention back to the sound of the music.

As this exercise of constantly calling the mind back to listening is continued, gradually something in us begins to ease and change. Even the physical body begins to open, slowly, to the sound, so that the sound penetrates more fully; one draws closer to it. One finds also that, as the attention is called back to the sound, an additional quiet watchfulness appears inside, so that one can actually see one's listening disappear and return. St. John Climacus advises: "Sit in a high place and keep watch if you can, and you will see the thieves come, and you will discover how they come, when and from where, how many and what kind they are as they steal your clusters of grapes" (*Clim* 263). Grapes—the watchful attention—are the raw materials of wine, which in the fathers' imagery represents spiritual understanding. To be drunk is to be opened to that greater intelligence. In the medieval Latin Bible, Psalm 23 reads: "Your cup, making me drunk, how wonderful it is!" (Ps 23:4).

As this individual discipline becomes more serious with each singer, an openness appears in the sound of the group, so that impulses or inflections of meaning can move through the choir almost instantaneously. It becomes possible for the choir, through its singing, to touch the text with a new immediacy and to discover what Gregory called the "voice of psalmody directed by the intention of the heart," by which "a way to the heart is prepared for almighty God, so that he may pour into the attentive mind the mystery of prophecy or the grace of compunction" (*G/HHP* 12). In this condition of receptive quiet, the spirit of the sacred text may begin to stir toward the singer's awakening intelligence, not as an idea or interpretation but as an action. Origen compares its movement to the divine Lover in The Song of Songs, "leaping upon the mountains, skipping over the hills" (*Orig/SS* 209–210). Other writers speak of a "sudden brightness" or an "aroma" or "taste." By sensing the mystery, the heart intuits the divine source and nature of the text and is able, for a short time, to rest in that nourishing presence, or, as Cassian put it, to "gaze on the mysteries" (*Cass/SL* 245).

One purpose of Gregorian chant is to teach us to speak the sacred text in such a way that we perceive its divine source and nature. The "schola cantorum" (Latin for "school of singers"), which is the traditional name for a chant choir, teaches not so much "singing" as "sacred speaking." Music brings the "ear of the heart" very close to the divine word in order to hear it directly. The singer learns to let the sacred text speak "in its own voice," without interference from his own emotions or ideas. The sound of this pure but simple speech nourishes both the singer, who hears it within, often without being fully aware of it, and those listening, who hear a special quality in the sound even if they do not understand the words. The sacred character of the chant, then, is based on a threefold relationship—not just words and music, but words, music, and the inner condition of the singer. When we include all three elements, we see clearly that, when we consider the special quality the chant conveys, we are dealing, not with an aesthetic phenomenon, but a spiritual one. The discipline of the chant allows this "triad" to close, so that the three elements become one—text, singer, and song.

Considering the chant in context, then, we see that its purpose is to allow a special interaction to take place, by means of music, between the divine text and a deeper intelligence within a person. The chant begins to live when this triad begins to live, when its parts become absorbed in a larger unity. To learn to sing the chant is to learn to allow that process to take place. And in the course of learning, one encounters other, related triads, one of which is of special importance. It lies at the heart of the chant and of many other aspects of traditional monastic life as well. The first two "sides" of this triad may be familiar, "action" and "contemplation." The third, which makes its appearance only when there is a perfect balance between the first two, is described by Gregory as "blessed." We need to look at this important triad more closely.

Monastic life was sometimes called the "way of perfection," from the Latin word "perfectus" which means, not "without flaw," but "made whole" or "completed." According to the fathers, the life of anyone who takes up the "way of perfection" is double—active and contemplative. At its simplest, this duality corresponds to a practical division of activity into work and prayer. But the same duality was also understood in more subtle ways. Prayer itself, for example, has its active and contemplative aspects, its giving and receiving, doing and waiting. But at all levels, the contemplative aspect is the more valuable. Gregory writes: "The active [life] struggles in the manner of our ordinary efforts, but the contemplative indeed savors now, by means of a deep inner taste, the rest to come" (G/HHP 37).

Among traditional writers the most common symbol for these two lives is the story of Mary and Martha in the Gospel of Luke. When Jesus comes as a guest into the house, one sister, Martha, keeps busy in the kitchen serving the guests, while the second sister, Mary, "sitting also at the Lord's feet, heard his word" (Lk 10:39, DR). Martha is irritated because she's been left to do all the work, and she complains to Jesus. He answers: "Martha, Martha, thou art careful, and art troubled about many things. But one thing is necessary. Mary has chosen the best part, which shall not be taken away from her" (Lk 10:39–42). Of the incident, Gregory writes:

> So one was attentive to work, the other to contemplation. One was serving the active by a more external ministry, the other the contemplative by suspension of the heart into the Word. And however good the active work might be, the contemplative nonetheless is better, because the first dies with this mortal life, but the second truly grows more complete in the life of immortality. Hence it is said, "Mary has chosen the best part, which shall not be taken from her. . . ." For even though by action we accomplish something good, nevertheless by contemplation we awake to the desire for heaven. (G/HHP 37–38)

The fathers believed that contemplative prayer was essential in the life of a monk. But perfection—wholeness—did not lie in leaving the active life behind. Pure contemplation was not considered possible in this world. Perfection lay in finding the proper relationship or balance between the two, and from that balance arose the third condition which Gregory describes as "blessed." This balance can never be permanent, and so one must continually search for and rediscover it. When the balance is located, the third element appears; when the balance is disturbed, it disappears. So this triad is always in a sense in motion, dynamic.

One could describe the chant as an exercise in the search for this balance. The musical material of the chant contains both elements of speech (activity) and elements of quiet (contemplation). The elements of quiet are found both within the music itself and in the pauses which the music requires regularly, especially in the recitation of psalms. Where chant is concerned, the silence is actually part of the music, and—as we will discuss in detail in Chapter Two—one must learn to handle the silence just as one must handle melodies and rhythms.

In general, we can understand the articulation of the text as the "active" life of the singer, and careful listening and watchfulness during that recitation, as well as during pauses, as the "contemplative." For singers who have been trained to be sensitive to this process, there is no mistaking these two different directions. The contemplative direction has the feel of gathering in toward oneself, what monastics call "recollection." (St. Teresa of Avila described it as a turtle pulling into its shell.) The active direction, the recitation of the text with enough lightness and freedom to be responsive to its meaning, is clearly outward. It demands energy. Singers must learn how to find that energy, where in oneself it comes from, and how it is released.

Singers discover further that each of these directions depends on the other. The feeling of recollection—a sense of life in the silence—doesn't appear until a certain freedom of recitation is sustained. As long as the recitation drags, or rushes nervously, or sinks under excess vocal weight, the silences between phrases will appear to be no more than the chance to grab a breath. Likewise, even if the recitation is light, quick, and natural, but the choir ignores or rushes through the pauses, the opportunities for attending to silence, the

13

feeling of a gently nourishing energy will never appear in the verses. But when the balance of recitation and silence is achieved, singers discover that here, too, the contemplative element is the more precious: the key to the life of the chant lies in attention to silence.

The third element of the triad, which Gregory called "blessed-ness," is unmistakable when it is present in the choir, when the perfect balance is found between silence and speech, action and contemplation, giving and receiving. This third element, however, cannot be controlled. Its appearance is a gift, but a gift for which we must prepare. It is, the fathers would say, a movement of the Holy Spirit. It is by this movement that the larger intelligence of the singer can open and the text speak with its active, symbolic voice. It is then that the singer is able, at least for an instant, to speak the sacred text "in its own voice," with the "eyes of the heart" open.

Singing the chant invites us to approach our inner selves in this new way, with an emphasis on the listening attention and watch-fulness. We do not analyze what we see; we do not talk about it; we do not even form opinions about it. We simply try as consistently as we can to be attentive, to listen and watch. As illustrated in our discussion so far, time spent in this attitude can bring us observa-tions about ourselves which we find described in page after page of monastic writing. Through these writings we begin to see that these same inner realities are being described in symbolic terms on page after page of scripture. And as we follow the chant into older forms of liturgy, we discover that the forms of the liturgy support our growth in exactly these inner directions. By this process we begin to appreciate the order and consistency of this ancient teaching.

As a part of this consistent teaching, the chant is different in character and purpose from all other Western music. First, it is intended primarily for the spiritual benefit of the singers, not for those who listen. Upon reflection, we see that this conclusion should not be surprising. The longest service of the monastic day was chanted between two and four in the morning, when no one but the monks could be expected to be present. We also begin to grasp a second essential fact about the chant: it is not intended to express emotion as other music may do. Its purpose is the opposite —to *quiet* both emotion and thought; not to "suppress" either of these, but to help them slowly evaporate. We may find ourselves deeply sobered as we observe how noisily these emotions and thoughts insist upon themselves in our minds, but how easily they then disappear without a trace.

A TRADITIONAL UNDERSTANDING OF HUMAN NATURE

In our discussion so far, two important concepts have begun to emerge which we may now develop in more detail: a concept of human nature and a concept of the nature of a sacred text. Both are important if we are to explore in greater depth the demands the chant makes on singers and the uses the chant makes of scriptural passages. Both concepts, too, will help us anticipate why we ourselves might consider the serious study of Gregorian chant, what possibilities it may offer us.

Already we have begun to see that the fathers put great emphasis on the natural, everyday tendency of the mind to wander. We have heard John Cassian on this subject. Here is Gregory:

> We do many earthly things every day, and after these we return to prayer. The mind is fired to compunction, but images of those things we have done are turned over in the mind, and hamper the intention of compunction in prayer, and what we did willingly outwardly, inwardly we allow still to be entertained, so that certain fantasies of thought spread through the mind by means of the fleshly imagination, so the mind does not collect itself closely into a unity in prayer. This is the voice of the flesh. (G/HHP 108)

We may be surprised that the fathers go so far as to identify this tendency in the mind with original sin. Cassian observes that "it is from no fault of our own but from a *fault of our nature* that these wanderings of the mind are found in mankind" (Cass/SL 362, emphasis mine). What seems at first a trivial matter becomes more serious as we look into it. By means of this "trivial" shifting movement of the mind, an entire world of inner experience, to which we are entitled by our humanity, may be lost. Let's assume that what the fathers say is true: that only a quiet mind, free of attachments, is capable of immediate experience of the reality of the divine image within us. The submersion of that intelligence, then, leaves us adrift in a world of abstract possibilities, a world of "maybe this and maybe that, maybe yes and maybe no," a world in which we hear conversation about what is right and what is wrong, what is our true nature and what is destructive to it, but we have no firsthand knowledge of these realities. In such a state, we are easy prey, as scripture says, for those influences which like "a roaring lion walk about, seeking someone to devour" (1 Pet 5:8). Even experiences we may have had earlier in our lives of a powerful sense of presence, of the magnitude and scale of creation, are set aside or forgotten, as if they never happened, because the intelligence which was capable of such experiences has been smothered. The distractions to which we attach ourselves most fiercely may indeed be our strongest "virtues"—our talents, even our religious opinions. Unconsciously, we are betrayed by our best qualities, as the psalmist says, "Even my best friend, whom I trusted, who broke bread with me, has lifted up his heel and turned against me" (Ps 41:9).

Sin is our affection for the forces which submerge real intelligence in us. In traditional teaching, daily concerns are sinful only to the extent that we attach ourselves to them. Extremes of sin—lying, betrayal, murder—are the result of an extreme forgetfulness. But even in such cases, healing remembrance is possible. Such moments of return are given special importance in monastic teaching, and scripture provides numerous examples. Peter, when he hears the cock crow, is pierced with remorse as he remembers who he "is"— the faithful disciple—and sees what he has become, "betrayed" by his own fear. This experience of a sudden, immediate appearance of painful self-knowledge is called "compunction" in monastic tradition, from the Latin root "punctus," meaning "pierced." The experience was considered a gift of grace, and is often accompanied by what the fathers called "the gift of tears." The older liturgies, which encourage recollection, tend as well to encourage this experience of healing return.

In Jonah's case it is not his "self" which he forgets, but rather his perception of the reality of God within him. Trapped in the belly of his fear and near death, Jonah *thinks* of God but does not "remember" him, and this thinking does him no good: "I am cast out from thy presence; how shall I again look upon thy holy temple? The waters closed in over me. . . . I went down to the land whose bars closed upon me for ever" (Jon 2:4–6). But at this crucial moment, something happens within Jonah which is a preparation for grace; something gives way, "faints," and with that "fainting" comes the healing remembrance that is the reality of God's presence: "When my soul fainted within me, I remembered the Lord; and my prayer came to thee, into thy holy temple" (Jon 2:7, RSV).

Both Peter and Jonah discover depths within themselves which they had not believed existed. Jesus shows Peter just how easily his sense of self can slip away from him, and how completely his outlook on the world changes when that happens. Jonah discovers that his real sense of self lies only in his awareness of the presence of God, and finds that, not only his outlook, but his physical survival depends on this intelligence. Both figures experience a dramatic transformation of mind. Neither would have believed the transformation possible before it happened, so compelling was the sense of "reality" which their ordinary, daily intelligence provided. Both, we must assume, are left with a new skepticism about that ordinary sense of "reality." This kind of self-knowledge, the awareness of different levels or modes of being within oneself, was thought essential by the fathers. Bernard writes that "knowledge of God and of self are basic and must come first, for as I have already shown, they are essential for salvation" (*Bern/SS* 2: 182). Four hundred years later, Teresa of Avila writes, "Knowing ourselves is something so important that I wouldn't want any relaxation ever in this regard" (*Ter* 43).

In recent years experiences such as those of Peter and Jonah have been called "conversion," whose root meaning is "turned," from the Latin "versum." The term is used by the fathers but in a different sense. In modern Christian discussion the model for this term is the experience of St. Paul, a single experience which changes a life. The fathers saw conversion as a process of growing toward wholeness, "perfection," a state in which the ordinary, "worldly" mind is not split off in fragments from the deeper intelligence.

As we have seen, "forgetfulness" is a sign of our fragmented, divided inner condition, but there is one kind of division which is so fundamental it deserves special attention: the division between flesh and spirit. In the fathers' view, a person is a kind of battleground on which these two forces are at war. According to tradition, the incarnation of Christ effects the reconciliation of this warfare, but this reconciliation does not mean the victory of the spirit over the flesh, or a compromise in which both remain essentially the same. It means the emergence of a new being which is both spirit and flesh, and this new being has a different intelligence; it sees with "the mind of Christ." Once again, this process should be understood in practical, not abstract, terms. One who is "wise," in the traditional use of the term, has had firsthand experience of this transformation.

Most of us are unaware of this duality in ourselves most of the time. We don't feel like a battleground. Except at special moments, often moments of trauma, our spiritual nature—if we believe we have any—seems remote. Or our sense of something lacking in our lives, of something wrong, is gnawing but indistinct and vague. The fathers' explanation is that we experience only one world because we have taken the outer world inside ourselves. In a real sense, we have no inner existence. When we close our eyes—when we try to pray, for example—all we're aware of is a stream of wandering thoughts and emotions. The outer world has invaded our inner world and taken it over. When we try to look for what scripture calls "the inner being," we can't find it. For this reason, quite rightly, many people in our secular culture feel that, to ease their minds, to "pray," they must engage in some special activity such as a hobby or a sport, which may relieve the oppressive babbling of this superficial mind for a time and allow them to feel the smallest hint of the greater intelligence that lies hidden within.

Consequently they feel better, reassured, more at ease. But these are small, compromise measures; virtually nowhere in our culture is there a clear understanding of how to move into the inner quiet of the self in a more deliberate and disciplined way.

The ideas and emotions which we do find within ourselves are what the fathers call "the flesh," as we saw in the passage from Gregory quoted earlier. These are not ideas about sexual lust, but ideas and desires that are of the nature and quality of the outer world. Our most outwardly important insights or what we believe are our deepest feelings may fall into this category, as we've seen. The discipline which the chant offers invites us to become skeptical of what we thought we knew about ourselves, what we thought was important.

This deeper intelligence which lies within us is never lost. Bernard observes: "The soul [in its everyday state] has not in fact put off its original form, but it has put on one foreign to it. This latter is an addition; the former has not been lost" (*Bern/SS* 4: 172). And its reappearance does not happen all at once and is not permanent. Herein lies considerable reassurance. Most of us, in almost any occasion of quiet, will begin to see the world slightly differently. We will remember important insights we had forgotten, or see our way out of some tight spot, or remember some small good thing we had meant to do. Likewise, those for whom the discipline of the chant is congenial will feel the effects of a more quiet mind at once, in small ways. We must indeed be "born again," and to do that, certain forces in us must "die," but this process takes place again and again, and at many depths.

According to the fathers, the mysteries of scripture and the faith can only be approached through this deeper intelligence. Richard of St. Victor, in the twelfth century, wrote: "Let one who eagerly strives for contemplation of celestial things, who sighs for knowledge of divine things, learn to assemble the dispersed Israelites—let him endeavor to restrain the wanderings of the mind" (*Rich* 142). More specifically, the "natural" mind is not able to grasp the true meanings of scripture, that is, is not able to grasp its divine origin. Gregory writes:

19

> For when the mind is at rest from outward employments, the weight
> of the Divine precepts is more fully discerned. It is then that the
> mind penetrates, in a more lively manner, the words of God, when
> it refuses to admit within the tumult of worldly cares. . . . For the
> crowd of earthly thoughts, when it clamors around, closes the ear of
> the mind. (*G/MBJ* 3: 32)

But when the person is prepared inwardly, so that the deeper
intelligence begins to operate, that mind interacts with the sacred
word, and a person is changed: "And it happens that as you
perceive the words of sacred scripture to be of a celestial nature, so
you yourself, illuminated by the grace of contemplation, are raised
to the level of celestial nature" (*G/HHP* 87).

As one means of access to this deeper intelligence, the fathers
stress the importance of listening. As we have seen already,
listening is at the heart of the discipline of the chant. The fathers
also point out that the first commandment of the old covenant
begins with listening: "Hear, O Israel . . . "; that the thief on the
cross next to Jesus was saved by what he heard spoken by the
Savior; that the princess—the soul—in the psalms is admonished,
"Hear, O daughter; consider and listen closely" (Ps 45:11). Benedict
begins his *Rule* with "Listen carefully, my son, to the master's
instructions, and attend to them with the ear of your heart," echoing
Proverbs: "My son, hear the instruction of thy father" (Prov 1:8).

From very early times, the psalms were considered an important
means for exercising the ear and quieting the mind to prepare the
monk to understand the scriptures. (It may be for this reason that
each of the services of the Daily Office, designed to be chanted as
an interruption to one's ordinary activity, begins with a series of
psalms.) Basil the Great, in the fourth century, observed: "Rising up
from the prayers, the monks begin the psalmody. And now,
dividing into two sections, they chant alternately with one another,
thus reinforcing the study of the scriptural passages, and at the
same time producing for themselves attentiveness and an undistracted heart" (*Hours* 39).

THE NATURE OF A SACRED TEXT

When the mind is quiet and the scriptures begin to open their inner meanings, the real "study of the scriptural passages" begins. In this living relationship between the person and the Word is the heart of the tradition's concept of the nature of a sacred text. It is alive. Scripture, like human intelligence, functions on many levels, referred to in simplified imagery as "body" and "spirit." The body is the literal meaning—which speaks to the natural mind—and the "spirit" is the symbolic meaning, which speaks to the deeper intelligence. Consider this passage from the vision of Ezekiel:

> As I looked at the living creatures, I saw wheels on the ground, one beside each of the four . . . and the rims of the wheels were full of eyes all round. When the living creatures moved, the wheels moved beside them; when the creatures rose from the ground, the wheels rose; they moved in whatever direction the spirit would go; and the wheels rose together with them, for the spirit of the living creatures was in the wheels. When the one moved, the other moved; when the one halted, the other halted; when the creatures rose from the ground, the wheels rose together with them, for the spirit of the creatures was in the wheels. (Ezek 1:15–21, NEB)

Gregory explains that scripture is telling us about its own nature. Like the wheels, the Word follows us (we, of course, are the "creatures") wherever our understanding goes. If our minds are literal and move along the ground, scripture provides a meaning that follows us; if we rise through disciplined prayer to a higher intelligence, likewise the mystical wheels of the Word meet us there with a more profound meaning, for the "spirit of the creatures," the Holy Spirit, is "in the wheels," in the Word.

When this meeting of the Word and the awakened intelligence takes place at a high level, the words of scripture are found to be symbols. It is as if symbolism is the language of the spirit, in the way that mathematics is the language of physics. The spirit speaks "in tongues," the inner meaning of which is communicated even where the literal sense is obscure. Through the power of the spirit, for example, the tradition has understood that, when God tells

Moses to remove his shoes before the burning bush because the ground under his feet is holy (Ex 3:5), we as readers are meant to know that we are to remove the "covering" of our minds, since "sandaled feet cannot ascend the height where the light of truth is seen" (*Nyssa* 59). What we are being told is beyond the capacity of ordinary literal thinking. We are being told to attend "barefoot" to the spirit's voice, to be in direct contact with the "earth," the body.

When the moment of insight has passed, the mind in its natural state will, of course, be able to see a certain superficial logic to the symbols. Anyone can see that the soles of shoes are "dead skin" which should not be placed between the living person and the living spirit of holy ground. But the natural mind is not able to know directly that the symbolic meaning is the true one, the meaning "intended by the author"—as modern textual critics say —except that the "author" here is understood to be the Holy Spirit. The natural mind cannot, so to speak, hear the voice of the spirit directly. Only a larger, spiritual intelligence can work on such a level. As Origen put it: "For of a truth nobody can perceive and know how great is the splendor of the Word, until he receives dove's eyes—that is, a spiritual understanding" (*Orig/SS* 172). To perceive the "splendor of the Word" is to perceive its divine source.

The fathers were, of course, deeply concerned with the literal meaning of the words. Origen was one of the most learned biblical scholars of his day and created the first comparative edition of the versions of the Bible then in existence. But they were also perfectly clear about their priorities, as Gregory illustrates in a particularly apt metaphor:

> Whereas when ships carry fruits, they mix chaff with them, in order that they may transport them to land without injury, the days of the Fathers of yore are rightly described [Job 9:26] as like to ships bearing fruits, for in that the sayings of the Ancients tell of the mysteries of the spiritual life, they preserve these by means of the intermingled chaff of the narrative, and they bring down to us the

fruit of the Spirit under a covering, when they speak to us of carnal things. For often whilst they relate circumstances proper to themselves, they are exalted in the secrets of the divine nature. (G/*MBJ* 1: 528–529)

The central idea behind the symbolic use of the Bible is that all of scripture speaks a consistent message in a consistent language. The message lies on a plane above the historical context of any given passage and is constant throughout the centuries. From the point of view of the true author, the Holy Spirit, writings which seem to us many centuries apart are simultaneous, one sentence right with another, Old and New Testaments created "together," in a timeless present. All these writings speak of transcendent and unchanging realities—the laws and being of God, the inner nature of the human person reaching for God, the mysteries of Christ and his church. From a point of view outside of time, we aren't so surprised that the image of Moses lifting up a bronze serpent before Israel should be meant to tell us of the lifting up of the Savior on the cross. Or that the cool shadow of the beloved, under which the bride rests in The Song of Songs, would be that same "shadow" which is promised to Mary when the angel says to her, "The power of the Highest shall overshadow thee." The message *and* the language are consistent, even in translation.

Paradoxically, this unity of scripture expresses itself in diversity. A wonderful virtue of the Word is its ability to speak differently to each believer, according to the occasion and the need. Any passage or image may have multiple meanings. As Gregory puts it: "The Word of God is manna and gives, in truth, that taste in the mouth of the eater which the wish of him who partakes it rightly deserves" (G/*MBJ* 3: 448). Or again, "The Divine Word, being at the same time suited to all minds, yet never at variance with itself, condescends to the kind and character of its hearers" (G/*MBJ* 1: 328).

It is also true that the fathers believed passionately that every word of scripture is inspired and significant. Origen expresses this conviction clearly: "Holy Scripture never uses any word haphazard and without a purpose" (*Orig/SS* 280), and Bernard concurs when he writes: "In the sacred and precious writing there is no slightest detail which is without significance" (*Bern/SS* 4: 69). But the subtleties of their approaches did not allow them to draw rigid conclusions from this conviction. Every detail in the narrative is critical, yes, but—since the meaning of those details is symbolic and multiple—there is wide latitude and freedom in understanding them. After explaining a particular phrase, the writer will feel completely at ease remarking, "I realize I interpreted this phrase differently in my last sermon. You pick the one you like." Behind this attitude is the image quoted above: the Word as "manna" which feeds each person according to his or her need.

At its most profound, the speaking of the Word to an awakening intelligence in the individual is beyond "multiple meanings," in fact beyond discursive meaning of any kind. It is compatible only with silence. The mind opens to the Word in silence and that opening, in turn, deepens the quiet. As the Word speaks within, it carries the heart into an entirely new dimension, where the Almighty "speaks by Himself [and] the heart is instructed in his Word, without words and syllables" (*G/MBJ* 3: 262).

But the experience of the mind awakening to the Word comes in "multiple" forms, some more intense than others. One prototype is found in the last chapter of the Gospel of Luke, when Christ, after his resurrection, appears to two of his disciples on the road to Emmaus: "And beginning at Moses and all the prophets, he expounded to them in all the scriptures, the things that were concerning him." Later, when the disciples realize that they had been speaking to Jesus, they remember the feeling they shared of an awakening mind: "Was not our heart burning within us, whilst he spoke in the way, and opened to us the scriptures?" (Lk 24:27, 32). And when Jesus appears a second time shortly thereafter, "He opened their inner minds, that they might understand the scriptures" (Lk 24:45). The experience, then, is not one of lights and voices but an inner warmth, an "opening" of the understanding by which the truth of the symbolic message of scripture is known directly.

A second prototype, just mentioned, is the feeding of the Israelites

24

in the wilderness. Following The Book of Wisdom (Wis 16), the fathers identified the Word with the qualities of the manna: that it was a "new" food, could not be stored, was always in sufficient quantity, and nourished everyone exactly as was necessary for each of them. Likewise, when the Word speaks within, it appears as something new and unexpected; gives a nourishment which is good only in that moment of experience and which can't be "stored"; and speaks exactly as the individual needs to be spoken to at that moment.

According to Gregory, Christ's first miracle, the changing of water into wine at a marriage at Cana in Galilee, is a symbol of this inner speaking of the Word:

> [Our Lord] commanded that the jars be filled with water because first, by means of the narrative of sacred reading, our hearts are filled [with holy scripture]. And he turns water to wine in us, when that same narrative, by means of the mystery of allegory, is changed in us into spiritual understanding. (*G/HHP* 70)

As we've seen, the two levels of scripture, the literal and the symbolic or allegorical, correspond to a tiered structure of human understanding, the natural mind and the spiritual intelligence. But we should add that the image of two discrete levels is an approximation, not entirely adequate. Both the fathers in their interpretations of scripture and we in our own experience acknowledge that the mind can shift in many small gradations of perception or understanding. It would seem that the "spiritual intelligence" can be more or less awakened. We could say that the sacred text can reveal to the mind a glimpse of its inner meaning, or it can reward the mind with a more complete view. At the same time, there is substance in the original idea that the levels of perception are discrete. We discover that even a small glimpse of the inner meaning of scripture strikes us inwardly with a quality of an entirely uncommon order, as if even this small glimpse comes from and appeals to a level of understanding discretely "other," qualitatively different from our ordinary perceptions.

According to the fathers, obscurities and inconsistencies have been written into the literal narrative of scripture on purpose in order to turn the mind to this higher plane. The apparent absurdity of God's command to Ezekiel, for example, "Eat this book" (Ezek 3:1), must not be explained away. In a real sense, the echo of a higher meaning is in the apparent absurdity itself. According to Origen, it is by this means that the Holy Spirit:

> . . . denies a way and an access to the common understanding; and when we are shut out and hurled back, it calls us back to the beginning of another way, so that by gaining a higher and loftier road through entering a narrow footpath it may open for us the immense breadth of divine knowledge. (*Orig/CWS* 187–188)

The "speaking" of the active Word to the awakened intelligence in contemplation is an individual experience, but the individual would not have this experience without the preparation provided by the tradition of monastic teaching. Accepted interpretations were passed from generation to generation. Augustine and Bernard, seven hundred years apart, read important symbols in the same way. This accepted "vocabulary" of symbolic readings acted as a guide for future generations. Individuals confirmed for themselves the divine origin of the allegories and the divine character of the symbolic level. They might make their own contributions to the "vocabulary" of generally accepted readings but would also learn to know when a symbolic "speaking" of the text in prayer was meant by the spirit for themselves alone and was not to be shared with others. Reticence and discretion in matters of the spirit are part of the tradition.

In this way individuals would join themselves to those who had gone before, and so the tradition would be passed on. Gregory makes this point in his commentary on the story of Jacob's struggle with an angel (Gn 32:24–32). The struggle, according to Gregory, is a figure of the life of contemplative prayer. Gregory observes that Jacob met the angel as he journeyed back to "the land of his parents." He continues: "If we, therefore, return to our parents, that is, to our spiritual fathers, we may grasp an angel in the way, so that by a deep inner sweetness we may apprehend God" (*G/HHP* 234). The way of angels is the way of "our spiritual parents," the way of tradition.

THE WAY OF WISDOM

We have before us now concepts of human nature and the nature of a sacred text which are complementary. A sacred text is one which is capable of evolving into higher forms within the mind, body, spirit, and soul of a human being, beginning with its own literal meaning but going far beyond that. It is sacred because of the particular aspects of human nature which it calls into play and nourishes as it evolves. At its highest levels, it acts within the soul of the person as pure energy, as action. It closes itself to anyone who does not respect its nature. And again and again, as in the manna, the wheels of Ezekiel, and the transformation of water into wine, it contains stories and images in which it tries to tell us about itself, about its own nature, and helps us find our way into its evolving life. In powerful images from The Song of Songs, it appears to the soul as a bridegroom, a marriage partner, a leaping gazelle, for whom the soul longs and searches in the night, whose odor is of ointments and spices, whose taste is honey and milk, whose sound is the voice of the turtledove heard across the flowering land, who watches sharp-eyed, partially obscured, from beyond the lattice.

According to tradition, the aim of the way of perfection was to live in contact with this spiritual force, a force which was identified both with Christ himself, following John's gospel—"In the beginning was the Word . . ." (Jn 1:1)—and with the active, powerful Spirit of Wisdom in the Old Testament, clearly identified in Proverbs, The Book of Wisdom, and Ecclesiasticus as female:

> For in her is the spirit of understanding: holy, one, manifold, subtle, eloquent, active, undefiled, sure, sweet, loving that which is good, quick, which nothing hindereth, beneficent, gentle, kind, steadfast, assured, secure, having all power, overseeing all things, and con-

taining all spirits, intelligible, pure, subtle. For Wisdom is more active than all active things and reacheth everywhere by reason of her purity. For she is a vapor of the power of God, and a certain pure emanation of the glory of the almighty God, and therefore no defiled thing cometh into her. For she is the brightness of eternal light, and the unspotted mirror of God's majesty, and the image of his goodness. And being but one, she can do all things, and remaining in herself the same, she reneweth all things, and through nations conveyeth herself into holy souls, she maketh them friends of God and prophets. (Wis 7:22–27, DR)

The indwelling of this spirit was understood to be the same as the indwelling of Christ of which St. Paul speaks. The way of perfection was, thus, also called the way of Wisdom, with the word "Wisdom" meaning something more exact than we normally mean by it today:

The "Way" of Wisdom may be taken as that actual thing that comes into the mind, and infuses itself into us in the interior. And the "Place" of Wisdom is the heart in which She thus abides. Of this Her Way it is said, "The voice of one crying in the wilderness, Prepare ye the way of the Lord." That is, open in your hearts an entrance to Wisdom at Her coming." (G/MBJ 2: 398)

To become "wise" meant to become one in whom the Spirit of Wisdom dwells. It is clear from monastic writings that in traditional environments Wisdom visited many and dwelled powerfully in more than a few. St. Maximus the Confessor, in the seventh century, described a certain holy man whose

mind was illumined with the radiance of divine light; hence he could straightway see things not visible to the majority of men . . . like a mirror stained by no spots of passion, he was able to pick up without interference, and transmit, things imperceptible to others. (Max 62–63)

Bernard has left us a particularly striking description of the external appearance of such a person:

But when this beauty and brightness has filled the inmost part of the heart, it must become outwardly visible, and not be like a lamp hidden under a bushel, but be a light shining in darkness, which cannot be hidden. It shines out, and by the brightness of its rays it makes the body a mirror of the mind, spreading through the limbs and senses so that every action, every word, look, movement and even laugh (if there should be laughter) radiates gravity and honor. (*Bern/SS* 4: 207)

It has been our purpose in this first chapter to consider seriously the distinctive sound that so many listeners today and throughout the centuries have heard in the ancient chant of the Western church, and to follow that sound back to its origins, into an environment of thought and feeling within which this distinctive sacred quality seems at home. This environment depends, we have seen, on assumptions about human nature and the nature of sacred scripture which are in some cases surprising and in some cases contrary to the mindset of our own secular culture. But it is these very assumptions which have helped produce the riches of "the way of Wisdom"for generations of monastics in the past and which might, under the right conditions, continue to guide active "seekers" today. It now remains for us to become more practical and see how the serious study of Gregorian chant might offer our skeptical world a means of entrance into that tradition.

Chapter Two

Chanting the Psalms

The Way of Wisdom just described can be thought of as a disciplined, long-term exploration of the sacred, within oneself and in the scriptures. The problem we face today is that its language and ways of thinking are products of a different world, a different culture. And yet none of what was said in Chapter One matters if it cannot be made part of our own immediate experience. So we must adjust our sights sufficiently that we are able to understand the language, and we must participate somehow in the life to which that language refers.

One modern scholar and monk, Jean Leclercq, puts the problem of language and experience this way: "There are terms which he [Bernard of Clairvaux] and other monastic authors use, as the Fathers formerly before them, to describe with precision experiences and realities for which ordinary language has no exact equivalent." Leclercq goes on to call this terminology a "traditional technical vocabulary" the terms for which were taken "from the language in general use and from a book intended for all: the Bible" (*Learning* 201). These "experiences and realities" of which Leclercq speaks are largely interior, and the "technical vocabulary," being symbolic, would seem to most of us to be anything but precise. Our ready response to symbolic language is often, "That interpretation is arbitrary; you can make the passage mean anything you want." So we need to consider this problem further.

We can understand part of what Leclercq means by "precise" if we recall a time, perhaps from adolescence or young adulthood, when we first read in a book or heard in a song a phrase that captured *exactly* a personal experience which, until that moment, we had felt no one in the world had ever shared. It is the precision of our response which makes it memorable: that is *precisely* what I felt.

Perhaps we can remember a moment in which that phrase was not an explanation but an image. Near the end of Norman McLean's popular novel, *A River Runs Through It*, is the line that gives the book its title, "Eventually, all things merge into one, and a river runs through it." If we share a response to that image of a river and all it suggests, then we are closer still to the fathers' world, whose language speaks most often in images taken from scripture.

Precision of this kind—the immediate, inner conviction of a correspondence between what is read and what has been felt—is the starting point, but there is more. St. Gregory says that in passages of scripture we are informed "by the posture of the body . . . by the temperature of the air . . . by the character of the time" (*G/MBJ* 1: 68). In other words, every detail of the symbol is significant. When the psalmist says, "He shall come down like rain upon the mown field, like showers that water the earth" (Ps 72:6), it is important that the rain descends upon a field and that the field is "mown." Why is it important? That, we can only know for certain if the spirit reveals it to us. The meaning of those details for me today might not be the same as it will be next year, and may be different for you than for me. But perhaps it is a field because the spirit descends only where there is life, something growing, and perhaps only where care has been taken and preparations such as mowing have been made.

If we've done some reading about the psalms as Hebrew poetry, we know that "rain," repeated as "showers," is a Hebrew poetic device. The psalms often repeat an idea or image in slightly different language. But the fact that it is a familiar device does not mean that we should ignore the difference in meaning between the two terms. The shift of meaning from "rain" to "showers" is also important, and the "precision" of the symbol invites us to open our inner minds to that difference. It is, say the fathers, only the inner mind which will hear what the spirit may say to us by means of the difference. We must listen with what Gregory calls the "ear of the heart" or see with Origen's "dove's eyes," faculties which open only in deep silence.

So the language is symbolic but also precise, and its subject is inner experience. Where is the difficulty here? We all have "inner experience," certainly. The difficulty lies in the fact that the fathers are not talking about the normal joys and sorrows, fears and hopes of human lives. Their "technical language" is not primarily concerned with being in love or having ambitions to be a partner in the law firm. Their language is concerned with experiences which I definitely have had but which I probably have not noticed, not registered as significant. Or, if I noticed them, I didn't have any frame of reference within which to understand their significance.

Near the beginning of his long series of sermons on The Song of Songs, Bernard calls his monks' attention to the line, "Let him kiss me with the kiss of his mouth," with what may seem to us a novel, even shocking proposition:

> Today the text we are to study is the book of our own experience. You must therefore turn your attention inwards, each one must take note of his own particular awareness of the things I am about to discuss. I am attempting to discover if any of you has been privileged to say from his heart: "Let him kiss me with the kiss of his mouth." (*Bern/SS* 1: 16)

Since Bernard is not speaking of desire for a human lover, we are faced with the obvious fact that he is referring to a realm of experience which is foreign to most of us. How then, in the face of such a gap of experience, can we profit from anything he has to say?

The key may lie in the phrase, "turn your attention inwards." Most of our associations with this phrase are vaguely negative. We think of brooding, introspection, self-centeredness, and so on— nothing we'd want to be involved with. So to give blessed Bernard the benefit of the doubt, we assume that none of these is what he had in mind, and we close the book in respectful puzzlement. But it may be exactly here that the chant can help us, or where, to be more specific, psalmody can help us. Rarely in our ordinary lives do we have occasion to "turn our attention inwards" simply to listen and be watchful, as psalmody requires us to do. Not to think, not to brood or worry, but simply to *be*, in complete stillness—open, alert, and quiet—for an extended period of time. What the fathers promise is that, after returning regularly over long periods of time to this experience, to what they call its "sweetness" of "taste," we will see many things within us and in the scriptures which we would otherwise overlook or not see at all: not visions of angels, but small truths, small "grapes" for our "chewing"—as Guigo II put it in the twelfth century—which are able to nourish our souls and hearts in an unaccustomed way. And for some of us, perhaps visions of angels as well. As Hesychius of Jerusalem put it in the fifth century: "Silence of the heart, practiced with wisdom, will see a lofty depth; and the ear of the silent mind will hear untold wonders" (*Hesy* 306).

It must be acknowledged here that the contemplative life from which these fathers speak was based on an intense, many-faceted discipline defined by centuries of tradition. Anyone would be foolish to claim that a few months spent singing Gregorian chant or anything else will lead even the most ready soul to dramatic mystical visions. And this book makes no such claim, exactly. What it does claim is that, even in the fragmented form in which we find it today, the tradition offers us a lifetime of very real, small visions— a means of entering the world in which such a life is possible. The key to this guiding force within even the fragments of the tradition is the inner consistency of the teaching. Scripture, as we've seen, was thought to be like the manna in the wilderness, and also like the consecrated bread of the Eucharist, in that its entire nature is entirely present in every fragment. In a mystical sense, all of scripture is contained in every word of it. In a more immediate and practical sense, it is true that to begin to practice the chant seriously, to obtain even a small morsel of authentic experience of its true nature, is to gain entrance into, to have access to an intuition of, the entire world of which it is a part. The chant is capable of becoming a door through which one may indeed enter a very different experience of the Christian life. And the study of the chant begins with psalmody.

MUSICAL FUNDAMENTALS

From a strictly musical point of view, "Gregorian psalmody"—chanting the psalms in Gregorian style—is simple. A single musical formula is repeated for each verse of the psalm. But despite its simplicity, psalmody is at the heart of the discipline of the chant. The daily cycle of medieval monastic services consists primarily of psalms, a witness to the importance the fathers gave to this activity. The study of the chant must begin with the psalms, but it also ends there. Those who have gained an understanding of the art through years of practice never stop returning to the psalms with deepening affection and gratitude.

Ideally, neither psalms nor longer chants should be accompanied or conducted. The most important aspect of the chant discipline is listening, and that demand will be compromised by an organ or a conductor's hands. Any uniformity imposed from the outside will weaken the pressure on the group to develop forms of unison from the inside by listening. However, not every parish choir will be able to devote time to serious chant study, and all forms of the chant are, after all, beautiful music. There is a place in almost every parish music program for both accompanying and conducting this repertoire. We'll return to the problem of integrating chant into a parish music program in Chapter Six.

The medieval monastic liturgy included nine services each day—the Eucharist and eight prayer services called "Offices," from the Latin "officium," which means "obligation." Priests and monastics were required by the church to "say the Office" (all eight services) every day. As a group, these services are also called the "liturgy of the hours" and are assigned to specific times of the day: Lauds, just before sunrise; Prime, at the "first" hour (or about six o'clock); Terce, at the third hour (or nine o'clock); Sext, the sixth hour, (at noon); None, the ninth hour (at three o'clock); Vespers at about sunset; Compline just before bed; and Matins, usually about two in the morning. This arrangement of the Office is at least as old as St. Benedict's *Rule for Monks* in the early sixth century. Two verses from Psalm 119 account for the traditional division of the Office into seven "Day Hours" and one "Night Office" (Matins): "Seven times a day do I praise you" (Ps 114:164); and "At midnight I will rise to give you thanks" (Ps 114:62). Of these eight hours, the longest by far is Matins, which on a feast day could last more than three hours. Next in order of importance are Lauds, Vespers, and Compline, which in altered forms are in use in many churches today. Prime, Terce, Sext, and None are known as the "little hours" and will not be discussed here. During the Reformation, the Anglican church created Morning Prayer from Matins, Lauds, and Prime and combined parts of Vespers and Compline to form Evening Prayer. The most recent edition of the American church's Book of Common Prayer has restored Compline as a separate service.

Each of the traditional hours of the Office includes a group of psalms placed near the beginning. Before and after each psalm a short melody called an "antiphon" is sung which serves to highlight an idea or image within the psalm and connect the psalm to the feast of the day and, in some cases, the time of day. An antiphon text may come from the psalm itself or from other parts of scripture, or may be a "free" text, a composition based on scripture or the theme of the day. The psalm is recited using a short musical formula called a "psalm tone." There are eight tones for the Daily Office, one for each of the eight "modes" or scales on which the chant melodies are based.[§] (See the Appendices 2 and 3 for all eight tones and for a brief explanation of the modes.) The psalm tones are commonly referred to by number, and the tone which must be used for any particular psalm is determined by the mode of the psalm's antiphon. The antiphon and psalm must match—an antiphon in mode 1 calls for psalm tone 1, and so on. A psalm without an antiphon may be chanted on any convenient tone. There is no

---

[§]There is no connection between the fact that there are eight tones and the fact that there are eight Office hours.

thematic significance to the tones themselves, although each does seem to have its own emotional coloring. Most tones have several alternative endings. An ending is assigned which will allow a smooth musical transition from the end of the psalm tone back to the beginning of the antiphon, since the antiphon is repeated at the psalm's conclusion.

To begin our study of psalmody, we will choose the most frequently used of the psalm tones, tone 8, with its simplest ending:

Figure 1

The first two notes are called the "intonation." They are sung only by the person leading the chant (called the "cantor," Latin for "singer") on the first two syllables of the psalm verse. The cantor then sings the entire first verse alone in order to set the pitch and establish the sound of the psalm tone for the choir. The pitch should be comfortable. For most choirs that means a reciting note somewhere between F♯ and A♮, although A♮ may begin to feel high for low voices.

To illustrate the use of psalm tones, figure 2 shows two verses of Psalm 88 with tone 8 written out for each verse (in actual practice it is not necessary to write out each verse with its music).

When the choir joins at verse 2, they begin singing with the "reciting note," (sometimes called a reciting "tone"). The first half of the psalm tone, to the full vertical bar, is used with the first half of the psalm verse, up to the asterisk. The second half of the tone is used for the second half of the verse, after the asterisk, and has its own reciting note. In the eight standard tones, the reciting note is the same pitch in both halves of the tone. All the words of the first half-verse of the psalm are recited on this first reciting note until it is time to conclude the half-verse with a short melodic turn. This

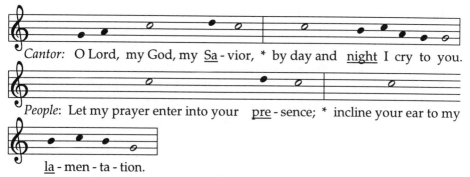

Cantor: O Lord, my God, my <u>Sa</u> - vior, * by day and <u>night</u> I cry to you.

People: Let my prayer enter into your <u>pre</u> - sence; * incline your ear to my

<u>la</u> - men - ta - tion.

Figure 2

turn at the end of the first half of the verse is called the "media-tion." After the mediation, the second half of the psalm verse is sung on the second reciting note, the same pitch as the first, which concludes with a second melodic turn called the "ending." The psalm tone is then repeated in exactly the same way for every verse of the psalm. There is never a change from one psalm tone to another within a single psalm. Near the end of each half-verse of the psalm, one syllable will usually be underlined or marked in a manner that tells the singers when to leave the reciting note and begin the mediation or ending. The process of marking these syllables is called "pointing" the psalm, which we'll discuss in detail at the end of this chapter. Careful pointing is necessary to allow for natural recitation of every verse[§] The notes in parentheses in the psalm tone (fig. 1) are used when necessary for extra syllables at the mediation or ending. For example, the black note in parenthe-sis at the mediation of tone 8 is not needed in the two verses in figure 2, but it would be needed in verse 8 of the same psalm where the first half-verse ends with "<u>heav</u>ily." The second syllable ("-vi-") would be sung on the black note. At the ending of the cantor's verse, the extra black note is used for "to."

Very often in English the mediation ends on a stressed syllable, usually a monosyllable such as "Lord" or "God." The marking in

[§]For pointing examples, see the section,"An Introduction to Pointing," later in this chapter, especially the mediation formulae for classes 2 and 3.

37

figure 1 suggests that such a mediation should end on the pitch D, one step above the reciting tone. The last note of the mediation, the white note on C, is unnecessary in these verses and is therefore in parenthesis. Some musicians feel that the mediation should always "resolve," that is, return to the C. There are compelling reasons to prefer the "unresolved" method suggested here, reasons we will discuss at the end of this chapter when we return to the problems of pointing.

Once the cantor has finished the first verse, the choir and congregation join and sing together for the entire psalm. This technique is called "direct" psalmody or, in Latin, psalmody "in directum." The explanations which follow will assume this approach. More experienced groups may wish to try "antiphonal" psalmody, in which the singers are divided into two groups and each group sings one or two verses alone, alternating. Many parishes today use "responsorial" psalmody, in which a cantor sings the verses of the psalm and the congregation sings a simple antiphon after each verse or group of verses.

One last musical characteristic of the psalm tones must now be examined. If the first half of a psalm verse is particularly long, it can be divided with what is called a "flex." The voice drops a whole tone or a minor third, depending on the tone, and then resumes on the same reciting tone it just left:

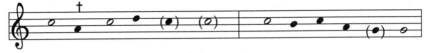

Figure 3

The flex is usually indicated with a cross (†) both in the music and in the psalm text. If the phrase ends on a monosyllable, the voice drops on that syllable, as in the word "forth" in this example:

> Before the mountains were brought <u>forth</u>,†
> or the land and the earth were <u>born</u>, *
> from age to <u>age</u> you are God.

If the phrase ends on a word of two or three syllables, as in the example below, the voice drops on "-wind," *after* the last accented syllable "whirl-":

> The sound of your thunder was in the whirl<u>wind</u>;†
>> your lightening lit up the <u>world</u>; *
>> the earth <u>trem</u>bled and shook.

The flex is used only in the first half of the verse, never in the second, and never on the first verse of the psalm. The pause after the flex should be very short.

GREGORIAN PSALMODY AND MONASTIC TEACHING

These are the musical fundamentals of Gregorian psalmody. They are simple and widely understood, and frequently constitute a formula for disaster. As often as not, choirs and congregations who attempt Gregorian psalmody give it up in frustration and opt for alternative, more modern methods of singing the psalms which are widely available and popular today. Several of these methods are easier for a congregation to manage on Sunday morning, but few make the demands or offer the inner rewards of the Gregorian tones.

Our goals are clear. Without a conductor's guiding hand, we must listen attentively and speak simply, in perfect unison. Both actions are related and are aspects of the fundamental monastic symbol we met in Chapter One, the apparent duality of the active and contemplative lives. Where psalmody is concerned, the active life is our recitation of the text, and the contemplative is our attentive listening during brief silences after each half-verse. According to Gregory, the active life "comes before the contemplative," even though the contemplative is more important: "The lives of holy prophets are double, obviously active and contemplative, but the active comes before the contemplative because a person is stretched from good works toward contemplation. But the contemplative is greater in merit than the active, because the active labors in the manner of our ordinary efforts, but the contemplative indeed savors now, by means of a deep inner taste, the rest to come" (*G/HHP* 37). So we must give attention first to the active life and then see how we might "stretch" toward contemplation. That is, we must first concern ourselves with recitation. It is a question of energy. The text must be recited with a quality of very light energy, an energy which does not tire the singers, before we can hear any meaning in the silences between phrases. The recitation must find simplicity and lightness which are compatible with silence, capable of establishing a relationship with it. One could say that learning to sing Gregorian chant is a matter of learning to make silence a part of the music. Silence is the guide and source. It is, very literally, by listening to silences between phrases that the choir discovers the real voice of the psalm, allows the text, as Gregory says, to speak "in its own voice." We are shown how we are to sing by what we hear when we are listening to "nothing." In the final analysis, we are guided by the silence. As Gregory puts it: "The censure of silence is a kind of nourishment of the word. . . . We ought not to learn silence by speaking, but rather by keeping silence we must learn to speak" (*G/HHP* 170).

But before we can receive this guidance from stillness, our recitation of the text must reach a certain level of ease and simplicity. The first obstacle we encounter is our ingrained tendency to even out verbal rhythms and syllable lengths when we sing. Long vowels are shortened, short vowels are lengthened; unaccented syllables are stressed, and accented syllables are weakened. As a result, we sing much more slowly than we speak, and we sing in rhythmic patterns which would sound flat and silly if spoken. In English speech, there is what we might call a "rhythm of meaning" which is precise and delicate. Meaning is conveyed by the most minute shifts of emphasis, that is, of accent and therefore of rhythm. It is rhythm at this level which a choir must learn to articulate. Once again, the chant is aimed primarily at the singers themselves, and so they must recite lines of the psalm with a subtlety of rhythm that is accepted as meaningful by the inner ear of each singer. To do so is more demanding than the usual choral challenge of articulating text clearly enough to convey its literal sense to an audience. The inner ear of an individual is more discriminating than the mind of a crowd, and that ear is, in addition, the gateway to the heart, which will not be moved except by what the ear has accepted as meaningful. Once the choir begins to chant in this style, their chanting will be felt as a collective probing of the psalm, searching out the possibilities of its meaning.

As a choir begins to shift from their old patterns to a more radically natural recitation, there may be some panic. Natural English rhythms are disturbingly uneven. When soldiers wish to march exactly together, they adopt a stride; everyone conforms; short legs stretch, long legs pull back. How could a crowd of individuals walk in unison? Likewise with a choir. When the uniform verbal "stride" is abandoned, there's a feeling that it will not be possible to stay together; there's quiet resistance, and then panic. With the panic, however, comes a great benefit—a new level of listening attention from every individual which, in the end, will prove far more effective than a common stride. As we will see momentarily, the chant requires a depth of "unison" which can't be reached by lockstep conformity. This deeper unison is really a series of unisons—of pitch, volume, pace, word accent, vowel sound, and more—some of which may appear spontaneously as the choir begins to perceive the common goal of meaningful speech.

As recitation begins to be free, there may also be complaints from singers of being too preoccupied to "think about the words," but this uneasiness too will pass as singers feel a new, more visceral relationship developing with the text, based on the physical rhythm of the words more than on their literal sense. If we hear people speaking in a distant room, we can tell whether they are angry or sad by the tone, without understanding the sense of the words at all. Likewise, meaningful rhythms chanted in the psalms speak directly to the feelings whether we follow the sense or not, and single words and images or short phrases are able to strike a mind that is open and quiet with a force that is beyond the reach of more elaborate syntax. Meaning, in this situation, is communicated first as physical movement, as rhythm, and, in the mind, as action (as with Origen's leaping stag or the refreshing grape of Guigo).

FREE RECITATION

Our first challenge is to break old habits and locate the sources of heaviness and weight in our handling of words. The psalm tones were of course created for Latin, but they work remarkably well in English, partly because medieval Latin relied, as English does, on accent to convey meaning. Accent patterns in English, however, are far more irregular than in Latin, as are vowel lengths. If you are fluent in both Latin and English, chanting will flow more smoothly in Latin. (We will look more closely at this question of Latin versus English in Chapter Three.) But with some effort and daring from the singers, English psalmody can become radiant.

Let us examine, for starters, verse 3 of Psalm 4 from Compline:

> Know that the LORD does wonders for the <u>faith</u>ful; *
> when I call upon the LORD <u>he</u> will hear me.

Most singers who chant this verse will distort the first line in predictable ways. "Know" will be unnaturally shortened, while "that the" and "for the" will be drawn out. We will probably also be treated to a ringing "-ers" at the end of "wonders" and, no doubt, a resounding "-ful" at the end of "faithful." No one in the group would do any of this if they spoke the line, even if the group spoke it together. In speech, the most heavily accented syllables in the line are as follows: Knòw that the Lòrd does wònders for the fàithful. The accented words—Know, Lord, wonders, faithful—are the important words, and in natural speech they stand out. But when the line is sung, "Lord" will usually be masked by excessive emphasis on "the" and, likewise, "faithful" by "the." By freeing the rhythm, we allow the important words to emerge.

The first step in the choir's training must be guided practice in "dropping" words and syllables which, as in the examples above, are getting unnatural emphasis. Remember always that our goal is to recite simply and naturally. "Dropping" a syllable in this context does not mean leaving it out, but reducing its exaggerated verbal emphasis. Prepositional phrases with short prepositions are good candidates for drill: "in the Name of the Lord," "to the King," "of hosts," "in the land," "with a shout," "like a flock," and so on. In all such phrases, the preposition and article must be dropped, in order to allow the noun to be heard with the emphasis of natural speech. Also good candidates are important words preceded by: monosyllabic articles (the Lord); interjections (O Lord); and pronouns (your Name). These phrases should be lifted out of the psalms and practiced alone; it may help to speak them several times first, then sing them, then sing an entire line, then a verse. The choir may wish to put small check marks over troublesome syllables as reminders.

Even as the phrases begin to become more natural, the choir may continue to have trouble at the mediation of the psalm tone and at its ending. At both places, the choir may tend to slow down unnecessarily and may tend to overemphasize syllables that should go unstressed. With some encouragement, the group can easily "speak through" the changing pitches at a natural pace. Throughout this drill, the leader must be relentless and settle for no less than rhythmic perfection. If he or she does so, the rewards for the choir can be immediate. Suddenly, perhaps for the first time, singers will hear meaningful phrases. This experience is the quiet beginning of a major change of orientation, since the kind of light energy we are seeking is to some extent the energy of meaning itself. But this energy will not be felt by singers until the phrases are precisely accurate—the key must not simply fit into the lock, but turn it as well. On the other hand, the director must use judgment in the beginning to avoid trampling the singers' enthusiasm with this drill. Mastery of this approach may take months, depending on the choir, and their skill at articulating meaningful rhythm will deepen over many years.

As the choir begins to "drop" syllables effectively, they will be able to recite comfortably at a faster pace. Eventually, they will be able to recite freely at any pace, very fast or very slow, but in the beginning a moderately fast pace will help the learning process along. At some point, however, two related problems may arise which the director must watch for. Longer vowel sounds such as "know," "sleep," "dwell," and "good," and diphthongs (two sounds spoken almost as one) such as "ate" and "like" will begin to be clipped short. As short syllables are dropped, there will again be a tendency toward uniformity, toward making *all* syllables short. The director must be sure that every word is given the exact time necessary for it to "speak" (again, without trampling enthusiasm). A dash placed over a "long" syllable as a reminder may be helpful.

The second tendency which may appear is the tendency to rush, so that the chanting seems to acquire a momentum of its own. The choir will feel the force of that momentum urging the recitation along and must resist it. The chant should be completely relaxed, giving both singers and listeners the impression that it could cease at any moment, that it is not rushing ahead or dragging. The most powerful antidote to both the rushing and the clipping of longer syllables is active listening, which is always the most important aspect of the discipline of psalmody. The importance of active listening should be made clear in the beginning, but it is not until this intermediate stage in the choir's learning that the truth of its importance will become apparent.

USING SILENCE

Listening is key for both practical and spiritual reasons. The chant is designed to discipline our inner attention, and our first access to that attention is the ear. St. Bernard says that we "merit the beatific vision by our constancy in listening.... The hearing, if it be loving, alert, and faithful, will restore the [inner] sight" (*Bern/SS* 2: 92, 94). But if we are attentive as we try to listen, we find our minds filled with competing thoughts. We observe that we are actively listening only a portion of the time. St. John Climacus tells us exactly what to do: "Fight always with your thoughts and call them back when they wander away.... Do not lose heart when your thoughts are stolen away. Just remain calm, and constantly call your mind back" (*Clim* 112).

It will take time for singers to realize that St. John's words—
"fight always . . . constantly call your mind back"—are urging a
level of inner activity which is foreign to almost all of us. But at
least, as singers, we are familiar with the idea that good musicians
listen to each other. What we must add now is the novel idea that,
more important even than listening to each other, is listening to the
silence between the phrases of the psalms. There are primarily two
such moments, one at the asterisk in the middle of each verse and
another between verses. The two should be treated differently.

At the asterisk in the middle of the verse there is a pause. We
breathe but, more importantly, we are attentive to that short silence
before beginning the second half of the psalm. We listen actively
but without any expectations. Especially in the beginning, we are
not sure what we are listening for, and it is certain that we will not
know whether we have received it, not until we have had years of
experience. And even in that long run, we become aware of only a
small part of what we receive. We must listen in faith until we
begin to sense a kind of gentle refreshment in that moment.

The pause at the asterisk must not be too long, or the living
quality in the silence will disappear. But its length must not be
rigidly controlled by anyone in the choir, including the leader, once
the choir has begun to recite freely enough to feel some attraction
in that still moment. A good rule is that no one person should break
the silence—lead in with the next phrase—twice in a row. A unison
of initiative is necessary at this point. Everyone must lead in some
of the time. If everyone takes part, the silence will find a length that
is appropriate, and that length will change as the feeling of the
psalm changes. Often singers are very unconscious of themselves
at this moment, and frequently one person will lead in again and
again, persistently imposing his or her will on the group. Often this
is a person who finds the silences uncomfortable, or one who is
accustomed to being a "leader" as a singer. The director must
respond to such a person, first by general reminders to the whole
group, and then by speaking with the person privately. This
seemingly small matter can touch very deep nerves, and singers

may leave the group over it. The group must accept that possibility. But one voice cannot be allowed to dominate the choir's experience of silence. Here, as in many ways, the chant requires sacrifice of the ego. I learn to be skeptical of my own judgments of how fast or slow, good or bad, the group is singing. I learn to be skeptical of my judgments in general, and, during the chant, to try to turn them all loose by refusing to listen to their insistent voices, but turning my listening attention, again and again, back to the chant.

Of the two major points of rest in the psalm tone—at the asterisk and between verses—the asterisk represents the "contemplative moment." The choir's movement between verses is different; it should be active. The choir should consciously, intentionally, infuse the psalmody with energetic movement into the new verse. The pause between verses therefore should be short, only as long as is necessary for breath. Here again is a formidable demand on the choir's attention. The temptation is to allow the pause at the asterisk and the pause between verses to become the same. The group must remember to move between verses with a quick energy while still listening to the silence that is there, and to wait more deliberately at the asterisk. There is a rhythm which can be set up between verses, which is in a sense broken at every asterisk and must be constantly reestablished. The active movement between verses also helps quiet the breath; the length of that pause should allow for an unhurried breath from the diaphragm, but no more.

The silence of the pauses in the psalms represents the "contemplative" aspect of psalmody. But, as Gregory established for us in Chapter One, there can be no substance to the contemplative aspect unless the "active" dimension—recitation of the text—has reached a certain level of simplicity and freedom. And so we return now to the crucial balance between action and contemplation, between these two energies which, according to Gregory, support each other: "Blessed ["pie" in Latin] is the mind which, the higher it is drawn in divine contemplation, the more devotedly it exerts itself in holy work" (G/LPR 95). Evidence of this balance in the choir is a deep, harmonious quiet once the psalm is over. Having come to this state by their "constancy in listening," singers may find that their own minds have also become more still, and that they are aware of themselves, each other, and the texts in a different way. The doves' eyes of the spiritual intellect have begun to open. Our surroundings appear in somewhat finer detail, and we are able, as Origen says, to "examine the meaning of things with more acute perception" (*Orig/SS* 79). In this condition, listening itself becomes easier because the mind is quieter and more open. If the choir members can sing while maintaining this inner listening, they are more likely to allow the psalms to speak simply, "in their own voice." This kind of speaking while listening within, Gregory explains, feeds both those who speak and those who hear. He is speaking of prophets, but his words apply equally well to singers:

> In that which they [holy prophets] both hear and speak, they feed ["reficiunt"] others and at the same time are fed. They feed their hearers when they make the Word known in its own voice; they themselves are fed when that Word, which they make known, is made known to them by divine revelation. . . . And so they nourish ["pascunt"] others by speaking who are themselves nourished by listening to what they speak. (*G/LPR* 358–359)

When the choir has reached this level of experience, their chanting of the psalms should be both devotionally effective and musically appealing. Their efforts to maintain listening attention will have provided inner experiences which are recognizable in the fathers' writings and which thus provide a gateway into this aspect of monastic spirituality. The singers have begun to join themselves to the ancient contemplative tradition, to struggle with Jacob's angel as they return to the land of "our spiritual fathers."

As St. Bernard points out, faithful listening leads naturally to strengthened inner vision—not mystical experience, but a state of gentle awareness of one's inner condition. When the choir has begun to chant consistently with the kind of simplicity, freedom, and balance we have been discussing, a condition of inner watchfulness will appear by itself in some singers. It should be encouraged. It is possible to be aware of the chant almost physically filling the body, and this awareness encourages greater openness. Tradition puts the sharp admonition from the First Letter of Peter at the beginning of Compline: "Be sober, be watchful" (1 Pet 5:8). In Mark (and elsewhere) Jesus is likewise emphatic: "And what I say to you, I say to all: Watch" (Mk 13:37). Inner watchfulness is a favorite theme of the fathers. We heard from St. John Climacus on the subject in Chapter One. Evagrius, in the fourth century, advised that the monk who wished to advance in the monastic art should

> keep careful watch over his thoughts. Let him observe their inten-
> sity, their periods of decline and follow them as they rise and fall. Let
> him note well the complexity of his thoughts, their periodicity, the
> demons which cause them, with the order of their succession and the
> nature of their associations. Then let him ask from Christ the
> explanation of these data he has observed. (*Evag* 29–30)

Watchfulness and listening attention can be strengthened if each singer is urged to search for a sense of contact, by means of the sound, with the larger group. The sound of the larger group in an individual singer's head becomes a point of attraction for the attention, and there can be a sense of reassurance in resting there, in maintaining that sense of connection with the group. At times, a feeling of exchange can arise by means of that contact; if I hear the group speak with an especially subtle energy, I find that I myself begin to sing with that same energy simply because I have heard it in others. When that connection to the group is present, singers standing next to each other may feel a kind of transparency in each other's sound, as if each voice is permeable to others. When a singer is *not* listening, not maintaining this connection, a singer next to him may feel an intangible wall separating him from his fellow singer.

FOUR EXERCISES

To conclude our discussion of psalmody, four exercises follow which may be helpful. Discuss with the choir the idea that the chant is an exercise of the community. It is important that no one "lead," and that the group sing in unison. As has been said, there are several different kinds of unison—of pitch, volume, vowel sound, consonant treatment, initiative, and intention, to name six. "Singing together" does not mean that every voice is forced into the exact same mold. Rather, every voice finds its place in a balanced whole. Stronger voices continue to be stronger, but weaker voices are heard. A useful image of what "unison" should mean is the rose window of a medieval cathedral. Here many shapes and colors combine to form a harmonious, unified pattern. Each shape and color contributes to the whole, to the unison, by finding its proper relationship to the others.

1) To encourage "unison of initiative," have the choir sit in a circle. Prepare to chant a psalm, and explain that the purpose of the exercise is to encourage each person at regular intervals to "lead in" after a half-verse, either after the asterisk or between verses. The leader will begin the psalm and sing the first verse alone as the cantor normally does. The leader asks a person known to be musically confidant to begin the second verse. The lead-in responsibility then moves clockwise around the circle. After verse 2 is begun, the next person leads in after the asterisk, the next person begins verse 3, the next leads in after the third verse asterisk, and so on. Throughout the exercise, no one sings until the designated person begins. Everyone then joins immediately. If a voice begins before the designated person, no one else should follow. To insure that the group continues to listen for the cue, the designated person should vary the time he or she takes to begin, never allowing a long pause. This exercise is excellent when the group is first introduced to the idea of a "unison of initiative" and can be profitably brought back from time to time when the psalmody begins to be dominated by two or three voices.

2) Once a choir has begun to chant with some confidence, the next exercise can be effective at strengthening the group's attention. It can be used in either of two ways. Explain to the choir that distractions during the psalmody are not necessarily a bad thing. Sirens outside, babies crying in church, people moving about—all these tend to draw our attention away from the psalm. Because these distracting forces are external and obvious, they can be useful

for building stronger attention if we deliberately turn our listening attention from them to the psalm. Warn the choir that during the next psalm they are to continue singing no matter what happens. The simplest form of this exercise is then to allow the choir to begin singing a long psalm and to proceed for a few verses to establish recitation. The leader then begins banging a book on a pew, rattling metal chairs, stomping on the floor—doing whatever is handy to create noise. At the first eruptions of clatter, the group may need to be reminded to "keep singing," but once they do that, the strength of the psalmody should increase immediately.

The second way to try this exercise is to begin the psalm as before, having had the same discussion, and begin to make small but very obvious musical or textual mistakes. The effect is similar, once people recover from their shock and tendency to laugh. There is a further point in this second version. Real "mistakes" in the psalmody itself, even during a service, are not necessarily a bad thing, but can provide a useful jolt that wakes up everyone.

At the outset, the choir should be asked to find a volume level which allows each person to hear his own voice and the larger voice of the group at the same time. Many singers will be inexperienced in listening for this kind of balance, and some will be accustomed by years of habit to the sound of a drastic imbalance in their own ear. Most of us give the bulk of our attention to our own voices. But over time and with guidance, each singer can be drawn more powerfully to the sound of the other voices, without losing track of his own. This contact with others through the ear becomes a kind of lifeline and a source of increasingly intense interest. The other voices can be examined with increasing attention, searched out for fresh impulses. This relationship of each singer to the group by means of the sound will begin to strengthen only if the sounds of the choir and the individual are balanced in every ear.

3) The following exercise can help everyone understand this "unison of volume" in a similar way. The entire exercise is explained beforehand, and the exercise should be done with women's voices alone, men's voices alone, and with mixed voices. With the

choir seated in a circle, the leader sings a random, comfortable tone using any convenient vowel. The group is asked to join and to simply hold that pitch for a considerable length of time at a moderate volume. Singers should drop out for breath and reenter as necessary to maintain a solid body of sound. As the pitch is held, each person is asked to be keenly aware of her listening attention, keeping it resting on the unison sound as long as possible, bringing it quickly back to the sound when she notices that the mind has wandered. Once the tone is established, the group maintains a constant volume while the leader gradually gets louder and louder until, in her own ear, she hears primarily her own voice, not that of the group. She then gets gradually softer until her voice is inaudible. She repeats this process, fairly quickly, two or three times. Each time she observes carefully in her own ear the changing relationship of sound between her own voice and that of the group. Each person in the circle then repeats the process the leader has just demonstrated, and the exercise is repeated, using women only, then men, and then mixed voices.

4) This final exercise can be used even with a very experienced choir to begin every rehearsal. It is an exercise for the attention, not the voice. The leader begins a tone, as in the previous exercise, and everyone joins. The tone is simply held for a considerable length of time—several minutes, with singers again dropping out for breath and reentering as necessary. The "exercise" here lies in simply waking up when one's mind wanders and bringing its attention back to the sound. As a variation specifically to encourage listening, the leader may make changes as the pitch is held—change the volume, vowel sound, or pitch—and ask everyone to follow the changes. The exercise should conclude with an extended period of sustained listening.

AN INTRODUCTION TO POINTING

As we've seen earlier in this chapter, each of the eight Gregorian tones contains two reciting notes, one for each half of the psalm verse. The first reciting note leads to the "mediation," concluding the first half of the tone, and the second leads to the "ending" and the conclusion of the tone. The process of marking exactly where to move away from the reciting note is called "pointing."

In the following discussion of pointing, the eight psalm tones have been divided into three classes. A director who wishes to learn to point should begin with the tones in class 1 only, and read the following comments in that section before beginning.[§] The discussion of the tones in classes 2 and 3 is intended for those who have had some experience with the process. All eight of the simple psalm tones are given in Appendix 2 with a selection of their most common endings. More elaborate tones—those intended for use at the Eucharist, for feast days, and for gospel canticles—do exist in the repertoire, but we will deal here only with the simple tones (which also may be used in all the above liturgical situations in place of their festal counterparts).

As with every other "technical" aspect of chant study, the pointing of the psalms should be understood in terms consistent with the overall purpose of psalmody. The first principle of pointing should be to mark the psalms in such a way that they are as logical as possible to the ears of the singers. The pointing should promote listening attention in the choir, strengthen the singers' shared (unison) understanding of the rhythmic logic of each tone, and encourage closer attention from each singer to the natural rhythms of the words. The long-term goal of the pointing system must be to make itself obsolete. The system should not build up in the choir a feeling of dependence on the editor's marks but, rather, should present each psalm tone in such a way that the more experienced the choir becomes, the more the singers feel the pointing to be unnecessary. A choir that sings together regularly over a long period of time, in fact, can learn to sing the psalms straight from the Prayer Book without marks of any kind.

[§]Directors who have never pointed psalms may wish to avoid the problem altogether. The psalms included in this book have been pointed already, and the entire psalter, pointed and with antiphons, is available from Church Publishing Incorporated (*The Plainsong Psalter*, James Litton, ed.).

Mediation Formulae, Class 1:
One accent, no preparatory notes (Psalm Tones 2, 8, and 5)

In the discussion which follows we will use a system of classifying the tones which is common and useful but can lead to awkward and "editor-dependent" pointing if used rigidly. The confusion results from the fact that the tones as they function in English are far more flexible than the system would indicate, as will shortly become apparent. In each of the eight psalm tones, at both the mediation and the final, there are notes which tend to supply stress or accent to syllables sung to them. For example, if I am reciting a text on a single pitch, let us say as indicated by #1 in the staff below (fig. 4), and I sing a higher note (#2), and then return to the original pitch (#4), whatever text syllable I sing at the higher pitch (#2) will tend to be emphasized or accented. Thus, this little two-note melody, by its shape, tends to supply an accent at this one point to a text sung with it. The mediation patterns of the eight psalm tones create similar musical accents using this shape and others slightly more intricate and melodic. The ideal in pointing is to have a naturally accented syllable in the text fall at such an accented point in the melody. What causes confusion and needs to be acknowledged is that some melodic shapes can supply a text accent or not, as the text requires, if the singer pays attention to natural recitation of the text.

Several of the eight tones are said to supply two accents at the mediation, and in some cases the note which normally supplies the first accent does not immediately follow the reciting note. Pitches leading from the reciting note to the accent are called "preparatory notes," and the syllables assigned to them are "preparatory syllables." The simplest form of mediation among the eight tones, however, has no preparatory notes and supplies only one accent. It requires only two syllables in its most common form and will resolve in some cases with only one syllable. We find this pattern in psalm tones 2, 5, and 8. In fact the mediation patterns in these three tones are identical (although tone 2 is placed at a different pitch):

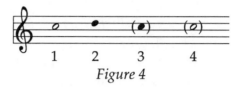

Figure 4

This formula's simplest case is a line of the psalm ending in an accented syllable followed by one unaccented syllable (the under-line marks the first syllable to move away from the reciting note):

They make known the glory of your <u>king</u>dom.

"King-" is sung on the black D (#2); the black C in parenthesis (#3) is omitted; and "-dom" is sung on the white final (#4). The pointing is the same if the last two syllables are separate words:

He fulfills the desire of those who <u>fear</u> him.

or

The Lord is near to those who call up<u>on</u> him.

If the accent is followed by two unaccented syllables, the optional black note (#3) is used:

If I forget you, O Je<u>ru</u>salem.

or

For my brethren and com<u>pan</u>ions' sake.

The principle is simple and obvious to the ear: the last accent of the line is sung on the D. In order to maintain its immediate logic to the ear, this principle must be allowed to hold even if *three* extra syllables are needed after the last accent:

Judah became God's <u>sanc</u>tuary

and even if *no* syllables are needed (a very frequent occurrence):

Give praise, you servants of the <u>Lord</u>.

Here, only the D (#2) is sung, leaving the mediation unresolved on that pitch. Recitation then returns to the reciting note C for the second half of the verse. If our goal is to make pointing unnecessary, leaving the choir to rely only on their listening, then the necessity for this unresolved choice should be clear if we consider the alternative. In the line just given, there can be no question in the choir that the final accent should be on "Lord." But if the mediation must resolve by moving back down to the C, how far back should the underline fall? On "the" or "of"? The ear can make no clear choice between these two, leaving the group dependent on an editor's choice. Going all the way back to "ser-" would begin to distort the basic structure of the tone, unnecessarily. One could of course sing two notes on "Lord," both D and the resolving C. But this ploy violates a fundamental principle of the chant, namely, that only as much sound is to be used as is necessary to articulate the words—no excess. Simplicity is essential.

Mediation Formulae, Class 2:
One accent with preparatory notes (Psalm Tones 4 and 6)
The second class of mediation formulae, found in tones 4 and 6, is usually said to supply one accent but add one (tone 6) or two (tone 4) preparatory notes. The simplest form of tone 4 requires four syllables to complete the mediation, and tone 6 requires three. With this tone class, we first encounter the limitations of the classification system itself, since both tones frequently supply two accents. In the following examples, the usual accent notes are marked "a" and the preparatory notes "p":

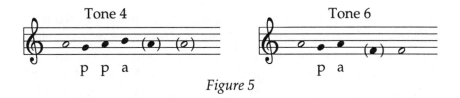

Figure 5

Theoretically, the accent in tone 4 should always fall at "a," but, in fact, the first preparatory note can also supply an accent, or not, as the text requires. For example, both of the following lines flow naturally over the tone. In the first, the accent falls as theory says it should and the G is preparatory:

He caused the east wind to blow <u>in</u> the hèavens.

But in this next line, the first accent, on "side," is supplied by the supposedly preparatory G:

The Lord is at my <u>sìde</u> to hèlp me.

In the first example, the G easily can be "dropped" in emphasis in order not to overemphasize "in," or the G can supply an accent if the text requires it. The tone is flexible. When the preparatory note supplies an accent, as on "side," the tone has two accents. This "confusion" makes perfect sense to the ear, however, and causes no trouble once it is acknowledged and allowed. Difficulty arises when an editor feels the need to rigidly enforce a single accent (designated "a" in the two examples of figure 5) and, consequently, supplies an idiosyncratic pointing solution in order to make that happen, a solution which would never appeal immediately to the ears of a group singing the psalm.

Finally, as in class 1 formulae, tone 4 must be allowed to end on the accented note B when the line ends in a stressed syllable:

The mountains <u>skìpped</u> like ràms.

or

I was pressed so hard that I <u>àl</u>most fèll.

The ear will omit the concluding notes spontaneously once the tone is learned. The same is not true of tone 6, however. It never should be necessary to end tone 6 on the normally accented A, because the ear readily accepts an accent on the final F, with two preparatory notes, once the choir has been trained to sing the two preparatory syllables very quickly with little emphasis:

> Turn again to your rest, O̱ my sòul.
> It is better to rely o̱n the Lòrd.

Alternatively, the first "preparatory" note can supply an accent, with an unstressed syllable falling on the supposedly accented A. A second accent is supplied by the final F, again creating a tone of two accents:

> Give thanks to the Lord, for he̱ is gòod.
> Let Israel no̱w proclàim.

This alternative is very common when reciting on tone 6 and is immediately understandable to the ear.

Mediation Formulae, Class 3:
Two accents (Psalm Tones 1, 3, and 7)
All three of these mediation formulae are generally said to move directly from the reciting note to an accented syllable, with no preparatory notes. That is the ideal pattern when it can be followed with ease. But, again, the formulae are flexible in ways which should be acknowledged in order to avoid excessively complicated pointing. All require four syllables in their simplest forms to complete the mediation, but each of the three presents its peculiar problems. These must be handled consistently if the collective ear of the choir is to be trained and not confused. Let's look first at tone 1:

Figure 6

The first accented syllable should be placed on the B♭ if convenient, but it is quite possible for a choir to sing the B♭ with reduced stress and throw the first accent onto the following A (#1), as in:

> He will not let yo̱ur fòot be mòved.

In the interests of simplicity, this choice is preferable to the second possibility, singing the B♭ on "let" and placing an extra syllable at

#4. Frequently the choice between these two depends simply on the weight of the syllables. For example, a well-trained choir would probably sing,

All the ungòd-ly‿en-còm-pass‿me,[§]

rather than,

All the ungodly encompass me,

which would appear to be parallel to "He will not let your foot be moved." But the ear hears at once that the first choice avoids excessive emphasis on "me" and allows "encompass" to speak more naturally.

The second accented syllable is customarily said to fall on G (#3), but here again the G can be accented or not, as the text requires. The second accent may actually fall on the final note (#6), as in:

I will lift up my eỳes to the hìlls.

Here, no optional notes are needed, and both the A and the G can be dropped easily in emphasis to give natural accents on "eyes" and "hills."

An important consideration in pointing tone 1 is the placing of extra syllables. Consider:

There is a sound of exultàtion and vìctory.

Both the syllable "-tion" and the syllable "and" should be sung on A (#1 and #2), in order to allow the second accented syllable ("vic-") to fall naturally on the G (#3). The question arises over what to do next. In published pointing one frequently sees the first extra syllable "-to-" also placed on the G, but to do so throws an unnatural accent on "-ry" as it is sung on the final A (#6) alone. This choice is illogical to the ear. The more natural alternative is to leave "vic-" alone on the G to receive a full accent and place the rest of the

[§]The tie (‿) symbol indicates that the tied syllables are sung on the same note. Untied syllables are always on different notes of the tone. If two syllables are untied, it is assumed that each new syllable moves to the next note of the tone. In this example, "com-" is sung on G and "pass‿me" on A.

word, "-tory," on the A. This is a choice which, if consistently called for by an editor in her markings, will quickly become logical to the choir's ear and will no longer require marking. Until that happens, choices of this kind can be indicated to the choir by tying the syllables which are to fall on the same note. For clarity, it may help to separate the syllables that fall on different pitches and tie those which fall on the same pitch:

There is a sound of exal<u>ta</u>-tion‿and vic-to‿ry.

One should not, however, form a rigid rule that extra syllables after the second accent are always sung on the final A (as in the previous example). If the line ends in a stressed syllable, the extra syllables should be sung on the G (#4):

The Lord is <u>faith</u>-ful‿in all‿his words.

"Words," being the accented word, must be sounded alone on its own pitch. The ear will make this distinction spontaneously in order to hear more meaningful phrases.

Tone 3 exists in two versions. *The Plainsong Psalter* gives the reciting tone on C, a simpler medieval form. The *Antiphonale Monasticum*, used by many Benedictine monastic communities around the world, gives the slightly more challenging form of tone 3 with the reciting tone on B. We will use the *Antiphonale* form in what follows. Here is the mediation:

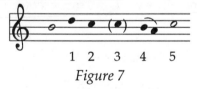

Figure 7

The ideal arrangement is to allow accented syllables to fall at #1 and #4, as in:

The Lord is at my <u>sìde</u> to hèlp me.

But the tone will accommodate a number of other possibilities and still give a natural rhythm. For example, the D (#1) may become a preparatory syllable, with the accented syllable falling at #2:

Again and again <u>they</u> tèmpted God.

This solution will often present itself for short lines:

This is <u>the</u> Lòrd's doing.

The challenge is to avoid excessive and unnatural emphasis on the final syllable, "-ing." This difficulty can never be entirely overcome.

Tone 3 also will function with a second accented syllable on the final note (#5):

Blessed is he who comes in the <u>nàme</u> of the Lòrd.

The general idea when reciting on tone 3 is to place any extra syllables at #3 and recite the next-to-last syllable of the line, accented or not, at #4. The tied notes at #4 always should be sung on a single syllable, as the tie is part of the musical structure of the tone.

Tone 7 is the trickiest of the eight. Here is its mediation:

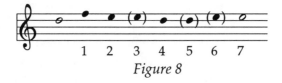

Figure 8

This formula is generally said to call for accented syllables at #1 and #4, which is preferable:

He gives food to <u>thòse</u> who fèar him.

But other configurations are common. Like tone 1, this formula can provide an accent at #2 and allow #1 to be de-emphasized as a preparatory note. Accented syllables may then fall on #2 and #7:

When they breathe their last, they <u>retùrn</u> to eàrth.

It is also common for the first accented syllable to fall at #1 and the second at #7, with the intervening pitches de-emphasized:

The Lord opens the e̲y̲e̲s̲ of the blìnd.

or

He is not impressed by the m̲ì̲g̲h̲t̲ of a hòrse.

Extra syllables are placed in ways reminiscent of tone 1. More than one syllable can be placed at #3 if necessary to allow the next accented syllable to fall on #4:

His work is full of m̲à̲j̲-es‿ty‿and splèndor.

or

He commanded his c̲ò̲v̲-e‿nant‿for èver.

As in tone 1, extra syllables at the end of the formula are placed at #5 if an accented syllable is needed at #7:

Their descendants will be m̲ì̲g̲h̲ty in‿the lànd.§

On the other hand, extra syllables at the end of the formula are placed at #6 if an accent is needed at #5:

On those who k̲è̲e̲p̲ his còv-e‿nant.

or

The Lord è̲x̲-e‿cutes rìgh-teous‿ness.

or

Offer the ap̲p̲ò̲i̲n̲t̲-ed sà-cri‿fi‿ces.

or

Turn, O L̲ò̲r̲d̲, and‿de-lì-ver‿me.

These rules for added syllables appear to the mind as maddeningly detailed, but to the ear they readily become spontaneous, because they allow the words to speak in meaningful rhythms. Even the most experienced choir, however, will "disagree" occa-

---

§This line is sung as marked rather than: " ... m̲i̲g̲h̲ty‿in the land," according to a general rule which holds for all tones: move one pitch per syllable unless there is reason, audible to the hear, to place more than one syllable on a pitch.

sionally when singing without pointing. There are always a few phrases which make sense to the ear in more than one way. But these phrases are remarkably rare, and the group's response should depend on the situation. If the choir is preparing a public liturgy, then those places can be easily agreed upon and marked in rehearsal. However, if the choir is chanting psalms for its own purposes, everyone should understand that these occasional moments of disagreement, like any other distraction, can be taken as small jolts to awaken everyone's attention. The singers may notice that for a few lines after such a moment, the choir's unison is likely to be near perfect, due to the sudden intensity of listening. In general, though, a choir which is able to chant the psalms effectively without pointing has by definition internalized the rhythms of the tones and is listening carefully to each other and to the rhythms of the text. Such a group, even with occasional moments of "difference," is far more deeply unified than another group which never makes a "mistake" because everything has been marked for them and drilled in rehearsal.

All the tones except 2 and 6 have several commonly used endings. It is not possible or necessary here to discuss all those possibilities. The principles explained above can be applied just as well to the endings. To summarize: 1) the pointing should be applied in such a way as to reveal to the choir the inner rhythmic logic of the tone and thus gradually make pointing unnecessary; 2) the tones are rhythmically flexible at many crucial points and will accept word accents or not as required, if the choir makes a disciplined effort to speak naturally; 3) in English, unlike Latin, three or even four syllables may be required on a single pitch; 4) extra syllables, particularly at the end of a formula, should be placed so as not to mask an important word or accented syllable by preceding or following it on the same pitch.

Chapter Three

Exploring the Gregorian Repertory

ORIGINS

Our understanding of the history of Gregorian chant is dependent on our study of the music in early, written form and, so, is dependent on the development of music notation. The earliest notation system we know of in the West developed in the ninth century, possibly among the Franks. The first complete manuscripts of chants for the Mass and the Daily Office which have survived date from the tenth century, so that, as soon as it was possible to write down music, the entire repertory was put down almost at once. We can thus be virtually certain that the earliest repertory of the chant, thousands of melodies, pre-existed the notation and had been preserved by memorization. No one can say for how long. It is tempting to imagine that the chant grew out of the music of the Jewish temple, but, due to the absence of music manuscripts from the pre-Christian era, this link cannot be established.[§] Recent scholarship has regarded the chant as a European phenomenon, with its development centered in Rome and in what is now France.

We have been speaking in these pages of "Gregorian" chant, but, from his death in 604 C.E. until the middle of the ninth century, there is no mention in surviving records of any connection between

---

[§]The best-known attempt to make a connection with the music of the Jewish tradition was Eric Werner's *The Sacred Bridge: The Interdependence of Liturgy and Music in Synagogue and Church During the First Millennium.*

St. Gregory the Great and the chant which now bears his name.[§] Beginning in the ninth century, however, the tradition connecting Gregory both to an original "antiphoner," or book of chants, and to the first "schola cantorum," or school for singers, is very strong, supported even by a surviving papal letter. The name receives general acceptance today because of the strength of this later tradition, but because of the uncertain early connection, some scholars have preferred to use the term "plainchant" or "plainsong," instead of "Gregorian chant." "Plainsong" comes from a later medieval phrase, "cantus planus," or "level song," which may describe either its even rhythm or the narrow melodic range of certain kinds of chant. "Plainsong" and "plainchant" are interchangeable translations of "cantus planus." "Gregorian chant" and "plainsong" are not exactly equivalent, however. "Gregorian" chant refers to that repertory of plainsong which was in general use throughout Western Christendom in the middle ages. There are other branches of Western plainsong which sound like "Gregorian" chant but are classified differently, largely because their use was restricted to certain geographical areas. They were not part of the body of chant available to the entire Western church. Two of the best known of these specialized branches are "Ambrosian" chant, specific to the cathedral of Milan, Italy, and Spanish "Mozarabic" chant.

Although music notation first appeared in the ninth century, these early forms did not specify exact levels of pitch. Figure 1 below shows half of a tenth-century page of music from the collections of the Library of Congress. At the top of the page are three antiphons for Vespers of the third week of Advent, followed by Matins for the Feast of St. Lucy (December 13). The name of the feast is visible five lines down from the top in larger letters: "In Nativitate Scae Luciae Virginis" (On the birthday of the Holy Virgin Lucy). The music is indicated by the marks above the syllables. In the right margin are three sets of the letters "e u o u a e a," with musical notes indicated above each letter. These sets indicate which

[§]See Peter Wagner, *Introduction to the Gregorian Melodies: A Handbook of Plainsong*, 172–173.

psalm tone ending belongs with each of the three antiphons given in the body of the text. (At the far left margin by each antiphon is the letter "A" for "antiphona.") These same letters are used for exactly the same purpose in editions of chant today. The first five letters represent the last syllables of the Latin words "sEcUlOrUm AmEn." These are the final words of the Latin Glory to the Father: "Gloria patri et filio et spiritui sancto. . . . in secula seculorum amen" (Glory to the Father and to the Son and to the Holy Spirit. . . . in the age of ages amen). Since the Gloria concludes each psalm in the Office, as we explained in Chapter Two, this set of letters will always represent the final syllables which are sung to the psalm tone, whatever the psalm. The final letter in the set, "a," indicates that the antiphon is repeated after the psalm is finished.

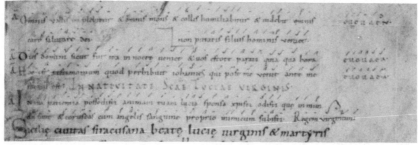

Figure 1

If this manuscript were all we had of the music for St. Lucy's Day, we would not be able to sing the liturgy. A tenth-century monk would have used this copy only for reference, as a reminder of details of rhythm for a melody which he had already memorized. As we will see later in the chapter, a practical system for indicating exact pitches (basically the same system of staff lines which we use today) was invented in the early eleventh century and quickly adopted across Western Europe. Because these later, pitch-specific manuscripts have survived, we can turn to a liturgy contained in them, look for a chant with the same text in the same liturgical position as the chant in the earlier manuscript, and compare the two. Figure 2 shows two notation styles for the first three words of a familiar Magnificat antiphon for Advent, "O radix Jesse" (O root of Jesse): an early, "staffless" notation and a later English-style manuscript which indicates exact pitches with a four-line staff. The letter at the far left of the staff which looks like an "f" is exactly that. It indicates that the second line down from the top is the note "fa" on the scale. Simply by comparing the shapes of the note forms in the two versions, we can guess that the "hairpins with caps,"

Figure 2

such as those over "ra-" and "-dix" in the earlier manuscript, have become, in the later manuscript, similarly shaped forms of this type:

where squares have been added to indicate the location of exact pitches. We might also hazard a guess that each "hairpin with a cap" indicates a descending pair of notes, since the form evolves into a version in which the higher pitch (a black square) comes before the lower. Likewise, we might assume that the "check mark" over "Jes-" in the earlier manuscript has evolved into a form of similar shape in the later:

And we might suppose that the check mark represents an ascending interval, since the lower part of the check appears first. If these assumptions are accurate, then it appears that the two melodies are moving in similar ways on identical syllables, suggesting that they are the same melody. Many similar comparisons would persuade us that our assumptions are indeed accurate.

By means of comparisons of this kind, and with guidance from a few medieval treatises on notation, scholars have established the meaning of these early note forms with considerable certainty. At least two important conclusions have followed. The first is that the repertory of chants recorded in the earliest manuscripts, where pitches are indefinite, is the same as that which appears over a hundred years later in manuscripts using staff lines. Clearly, then, the repertory was transmitted over at least one generation by memory. If transmission by memory across one generation is possible, then, of course, transmission across several is equally possible. The second conclusion we may draw from this early notation is that, from the very earliest manuscripts, the repertory of chants for the church year was remarkably consistent throughout Western Europe. There were local variations, to be sure, but frequently even these local variants amounted to different choices from the same basic collection of chants available for a given liturgy.

Over the centuries, as we might expect, the chant flourished in some times and places more than others, and was adapted to the needs of different monastic orders and churches. But there was no massive disruption of the repertory until the Renaissance. During the sixteenth century, under pressure from Protestants and from Humanist scholarship, the Roman Church made efforts to simplify its liturgy and remove medieval "accretions." The new liturgies, still medieval in overall design but considerably cleaner in their details, were codified by the Council of Trent (1545–63) and remained in force in the Roman Church until the Second Vatican Council (1962–65). In the spirit of the liturgical reform of the era, sixteenth- and early seventeenth-century editors of chant collections severely shortened the more elaborate chant melodies in all liturgical categories. These truncated versions remained as the standard liturgical music of the Roman Church until the early twentieth century. Early in the nineteenth century, studies of surviving ancient manuscripts began to reveal just how dramatic the Renaissance editing had been, and a movement began to restore the older forms.

This brief historical review is necessary here to demonstrate the significance of one of the most important names in chant studies in the last 150 years, the French Benedictine Abbey of St.-Pierre de Solesmes, or St. Peter of Solesmes. Rechartered in 1832, Solesmes led both the scholarly and the political struggle to restore the melodies of the Gregorian repertory to their original medieval complexity, an effort which culminated in the official adoption of the Solesmes editions for the Roman Church by Pius X in 1904.[§] Solesmes has continued to this day as a world center of chant study and the principal source of accurate, practical performing editions of the chant. (See Appendix 12, "Paraclete Press.")

AN OVERVIEW OF THE REPERTORY

The Gregorian repertory can be classified in a number of ways according to one's purpose, but two of the most important must concern us now, one musical and one liturgical. Both sets of terms are important. Musically, we can speak of three different types of chant: syllabic, neumatic, and melismatic. "Syllabic" chant matches one note to a syllable of text. Psalms, lessons, and other texts recited to a formula are syllabic, but so are hymns and sequences which are musically more complicated. Neumatic chant takes its name from "neume" which, in medieval-style chant notation, is a group of notes (usually one to five) written in one figure, such as:

A chant is said to be "neumatic" if many of the individual syllables of its text are sung either to a single neume or two or three neumes in succession, as in this line from the first Tenebrae responsory, "In monte Oliveti":

[§]For details of this history, see David Hiley's *Western Plainchant: A Handbook*.

In   mon - te   *   O - li - ve - ti   o - ra - vit   ad

Pa - trem:

Figure 3

"Melismatic" chant is characterized by the "melisma," a long series of notes sung on a single syllable. In figure 4 showing a phrase from the Alleluia "Veni Sancte Spiritus," the "melisma" is found on the syllable "-mo-" of the word "amoris" (of love):

Et   tu - i   a - mo   ris.

Figure 4

Liturgically, a distinction is made between chants for the Eucharist (Mass) and the Daily Office. Both Mass and Office include formulas for prayers, lessons, and acclamations, but the longer chants tend to belong to one or the other. The longer Mass chants can be "ordinary," referring to those texts such as the Kyrie and Creed which are sung at every eucharistic celebration, or "proper," referring to texts which are specific to the feast of the day. (Note that the terms "ordinary" and "proper" apply to the texts, not their music.) The medieval ordinary included six chants which are still found in many Anglican and Roman Catholic liturgies today: Kyrie, Gloria, Creed, Sanctus, Benedictus, and Agnus Dei. There are also six proper chants, all of which can be fit into modern liturgies but which, in most cases, have been replaced by hymns: the Introit,

(continued on page 72)

The Uses and Users of Books

Most of us today are familiar with chant notation from large pages we've seen framed on a wall, pages which have been cut from late collections, usually from the fifteenth or sixteenth century. By these late dates, memorization of the entire repertory was a thing of the past, and these large volumes were used by several singers at once, as in figure I.

Figure I

There is already something collective, something impersonal, about these pages. They're too big; who would carry or treasure such a monster book? There is no subtlety in their text or in their music. But the earliest manuscript books seem to have been very different. Those which have survived are small, almost hand-sized, and they may have been used only for reference, or by one cantor or director. And they seem even today more alive with the thoughts and moods, even the whimsy, of their creators and users. A torn page is carefully sewn with light green thread, because parchment was costly either in time to prepare the skins or in money to buy the sheets; around the edges of the stitching, a bored monk has doodled with a pen, following the stitches as you or I might trace around the wire of a spiral phone book while chatting to a friend. On another page the medieval equivalent of a "smiley face" is sketched into a capital "O" (fig. II).

In figure III, a more somber image is drawn lightly into the opening capital ("Q") of the Latin sentence, "How great is the multitude of your sweetness, Lord, which you have hidden for those who fear you" (Ps 31:19).

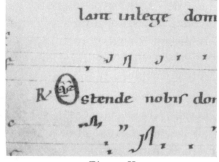

Figure II

Sometimes these signs from the past evoke an entire scene suddenly in the mind's eye. I pull down from the shelf a thirteenth-century, hand-sized volume of chants for the Night Office. The prayers, which often begin, "Orate, fratres" (pray, brothers), in this manuscript read, "Orate, sorores" (pray, sisters); this is a book used by a community of nuns. The parchment leaves are heavy and worn, the binding is made of irregular boards, roughly covered with faded red leather. The music and text are clear but not artistically done; the music has the "hobnail" look of a German scribe. This is not a "presentation" copy. It is a book that was put to hard use daily in the convent. It was not a reference copy; it was in the hands of a working musician.

Figure III

We flip through the pages, and see that what's actually in our hands is fragmentary. Not all of it has survived. We're in the middle of the book, reading words, trying to understand exactly what's in front of us. The words take shape, "Ecce dies veniunt . . . Behold, the days are coming . . ." The next word is partially covered, something soiling the page, an oval of black dirt. I reach my thumbnail under the oval to flick it to the library floor, and as I do, my mind begins to whirl; scattered bits fall into a pattern: "Ecce, dies veniunt . . . Advent . . . this is a liturgy for Advent . . . Ecce, dies . . . a familiar opening . . . a responsory for the Night Office . . . the Night Office . . . darkness . . . a medieval cloister . . . Advent . . . December . . . it is cold . . . it is 3:00 A.M. . . . the choir stall is awash in shadows. I must intone this opening phrase for my sisters; I haven't thought of it since last year . . . I should have gone over it . . . something is not quite right in what I am about to sing. What? I look down to check, but I can't quite see the page. I lean slightly in toward the manuscript in my right hand, and my candle drips on the text, to my horror . . . what am I doing? I smell the hot wax now splattered on the parchment . . . I am ruining this valuable book. The black oval. It is wax. It was put there seven hundred years ago by this nun, a cantrix who, in the dark, could not quite see what she desperately needed to see. Perhaps she was old, her eyesight not what it had been. Advent, the Year of Our Lord 1241. I pull my fingernail away from the parchment. The dark, wax oval stays where it was.

(continued from page 69)

sung as the priest and other ministers enter the church, usually replaced today by an entrance hymn; the Gradual, sung after the first lesson, where a psalm is often read or sung today; the Sequence, a late medieval form sung after the second lesson and before the Alleluia or Tract, surviving as the "sequence hymn" in Episcopal churches; the Alleluia, or, in Lent, Tract, also sung after the second lesson; the Offertory, sung as the bread and wine are brought to the altar, replaced today by a hymn or choir anthem; and the Communion, sung as the people receive communion or as the priest and servers clean the vessels after all have received.

Psalms, as we have seen, make up a large part of the Daily Office. The longer Day Hours also include several more elaborate chants. Each psalm is preceded and followed by an antiphon. The lesson is followed by a responsory, which is a simple formula for non-feast days but can be come quite complicated (a "Great Responsory") for some festal liturgies. The responsory is followed by a syllabic hymn, and that is followed by a simple formula called a "versicle and response." Each Office also includes a psalm-like section from one of the gospels, called the Gospel Canticle—the "Benedictus" at Lauds, the "Magnificat" at Vespers, and the "Nunc dimittis" at Compline.[§] Like a psalm, the Gospel Canticle is chanted to a psalm tone and preceded and followed by an antiphon. Because of the added dignity accorded a gospel text, the intonation of the psalm tone is sung, not by the cantor alone at the first verse, but by everyone at the start of each verse.

Vespers or Compline is often followed by an antiphon in honor of the Virgin Mary. Traditionally there are four of these, which are assigned to different seasons of the church year: "Alma redemptoris mater," Advent to the Presentation (February 2); "Ave regina

[§]Chant books in English customarily identify translated chants with the first word or words of the chant's original Latin text, as if these words or phrases were a kind of title. This practice holds for canticles and, in the Episcopal Book of Common Prayer, also for psalms. The Compline psalm antiphon in Appendix 10 is thus labeled "Miserere" (Have mercy), and the first psalm is labeled, "Cum invocarem" (When I called).

caelorum," the evening of the Presentation until Wednesday of Holy Week; "Regina caeli," Easter Day until the Saturday after Pentecost; and "Salve regina," from Trinity Sunday to Advent. Although these chants are called antiphons, they are sung alone, with no psalm attached.

SINGING COMPLINE

Most of the chants one encounters in books or on recordings fall into one of the categories just given. In order to give focus to our discussion of singing longer chants, we'll begin with the music for Compline, found in Appendix 10.§ The last Office before bed, Compline is short, appealing, and does not require a priest. Three leaders are required for this short service—a cantor, officiant, and someone to sing the lesson.

The chants of Compline are almost entirely syllabic except for the optional Marian antiphon at the end. The demands these chants make on the singers are exactly the same demands made by psalmody, but a brief walk through the service may help call attention to important details. The Office actually begins with "O God, make speed to save us." The preceding section labeled "The Preparation" is a call to attention and confession and, as indicated in the service, is omitted if Compline follows a Eucharist. The Eucharist is preparation enough.

The first line of the call to attention contains two pitfalls, at "a perfect end" and "Amen." An inexperienced cantor will overemphasize "-fect" and lengthen "end," both of which should be avoided. As in a psalm, the entire line should be spoken simply, in a natural rhythm. The second trap, "Amen," should be quick and natural in length here and wherever it appears. Parishes usually stretch these two syllables out beyond recognition, but this habit should be broken. The underlined portion of the phrase, "Our help

§ Compline is an excellent way to conclude a weekly rehearsal. The order given in Appendix 10 differs slightly from that in the Episcopal Book of Common Prayer in order to preserve older monastic forms which are important to our concerns here. Parishes which feel it necessary to do so may easily rearrange the liturgy to match the Prayer Book exactly.

is <u>in the Name of the Lord,</u>" presents another pitfall for the cantor. The director must insist that "in the" and "of the" be dropped to allow "Name" and "Lord" to speak naturally.

The three psalms of Compline (Ps 4 "Cum invocarem"; Ps 91 "Qui habitat"; Ps 134 "Ecce nunc") are treated as one, so there is no "Glory to the Father" or repetition of the antiphon until the end of the third psalm. The antiphon is lightly neumatic; that is, a number of syllables are sung to two or three notes. The principles and the object remain the same: to recite the antiphon so that the words sound to the inner ear clearly and naturally. The double and triple pitches should be sung quickly and evenly, so as not to obscure the flow of the sentence with excess musical sound. Even as it becomes more complicated, the music should remain transparent in the mind's ear, so that the text speaks clearly through it. The pace should be quick enough that the recitation sounds natural.

Nothing further need be said about the recitation of the psalms, but one word should be said about the lesson, which is sung by one person. Solo singing in the Gregorian style is not the norm. The most common solo role is that of the cantor, but on feast days even the cantor's part should be taken by two singers. Chant represents an effort by the community to search out the inner voice of scripture and open the singers' and listeners' minds to that voice. Listening is always the key. Any person singing alone should sing simply and naturally, with her own listening attention resting on her own voice. There should be no attempt to sing with "expression," but rather clearly and simply, always listening. Cantors and lesson singers should remember here Gregory's description quoted earlier of "holy prophets"

> . . . who hear themselves but not themselves, because they themselves are speaking, but in their speech they acknowledge with reverence the speaking of another. . . . And so they nourish ["pascunt"] others by speaking who are themselves nourished by listening to what they speak. (*G/LPR* 358–359)

The act of remaining inwardly attentive is important even though the cantor or lesson singer will not be conscious of receiving or hearing anything. The listening helps the singer remain empty of personal expression, so that something beyond personality, and probably imperceptible to the singer himself, can be heard in his voice.

Between the psalms there should be moments of silence. It is the cantor's job to gauge their length, and he should be sensitive to the quality of recitation which the choir has established and to the state of quiet in the group at that point. The silence should not be excessive, but attention should be paid to its quality. There is a larger rhythm of activity and stillness in the pacing of the liturgy itself, and it is the responsibility of the cantor to help that rhythm emerge.

"The Short Responsory," which follows "The Lesson," is also lightly neumatic. The danger point is at "com-" of "commend." The choir must not be allowed to overemphasize that syllable, which should be very quick, as it is when spoken. Each of the four notes on "spi-" of "spirit" should be touched lightly and quickly.

The hymn, "Te lucis ante terminum," should be sung like a psalm, with free recitation and careful pauses for listening between phrases. Achieving this result may require some of the detailed recitation drill described in Chapter Two. Particularly tempting in this translation of the hymn are the short words which begin phrases. The cantor has the first one, "To," at the beginning of the hymn. The temptation to stress these first words *because* they are first must be resisted. The emphasis in verse 1 must be on "you," and in verse 3 on "health." The opposite problem occurs at the beginning of verse 2. Here the choir must resist the accent pattern which the music suggests and stress "save" but drop "us." It can be done if strict attention is paid to the words. As always, the "Amen" should be light and quick, with no more sound than is necessary to articulate the word.

The hymn is followed, as is usually the case with a Gregorian hymn, by a short versicle and response, a very old and appealing form. Although it is short, the text of the versicle typically speaks from the heart of the theme of the liturgy, sometimes, as here, in poetic imagery: "Keep us, O Lord, as the apple of your eye; and hide us under the shadow of your wings."[§]

The version of Compline in Appendix 10 recommends a custom for the Lord's Prayer which may be strange to some readers. The cantor begins the prayer aloud, but then the singing stops and the choir continues the prayer silently; the prayer concludes with cantor and choir in a versicle and response pattern sung aloud. This monastic custom serves to underscore for everyone the inner quality of the service. The movement of one's attention from an exterior to an interior articulation of the prayer and back again is an almost physical reminder of the distance between the inner and outer worlds.

The high point of Compline is the Gospel Canticle, "Nunc dimittis," Latin for "Now you dismiss." The canticle is sung on a psalm tone, but, because the text is from the gospel, it receives the extra dignity of having the intonation pitches, normally sung only by the cantor on verse 1, repeated by everyone at every verse, including "Glory to the Father." Careful attention should be given to the antiphon in two places: "that awake" and "and asleep":

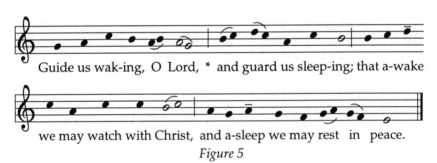

Figure 5

The first two syllables of both phrases should be dropped, but also in each case the final syllable is long and must be allowed to speak naturally. The "episema," a horizontal line placed over a note, is

---

[§]The Latin original uses "pupil" rather than "apple," a less metaphorical image but one more suggestive of vulnerability. The Latin also has "guard" instead of "keep" us.

placed over these two notes to be sure that these long syllables are not clipped short. An episema in chant notation means "lengthen this note slightly."

MELISMATIC CHANT

Once a choir has mastered free recitation, the move from syllabic to melismatic chant should not be difficult, but a conceptual adjustment is critical. The choir must internalize an approach to the musical line which is unlike what most musicians and singers are taught today, that is, the choir must learn to sing melodic phrases *without* a sense of line. Most Western singers are taught to sing "phrases" that have "shape" and "direction." The notes of a melody are to be smoothly connected, "legato" in Italian, and this "legato line" should have a certain dynamism, should "go somewhere," have a sense of movement in a certain direction. Voice and instrument teachers alike seem to collect gestures and metaphors for communicating this basic concept. Pianists are taught to use the pedal to "put the pearls on a string."

For our discussion of melismatic chant, we will use the Kyrie known as the "Marialis" (see Appendix 6). The first long melisma of the Marialis Kyrie, on the first syllable of the word "eleison," would certainly lend itself to "legato" singing; it forms the climax of a melody that begins with the beginning of the chant and seems to "move" powerfully toward rest at the end of "eleison":

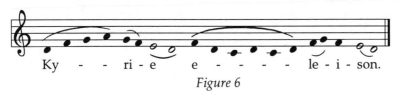

Ky - - ri - e   e - - - - le - i - son.

Figure 6

One could sing this melisma with intensifying feeling and a slight dynamic swell at the middle of the melisma, easing off at the approach to "-leison." This interpretation would arouse the emotions of both singers and listeners and could be very satisfying for both. But it is the antithesis of the spirit of the chant. The chant, we must remember, is meant to quiet emotion, not stimulate it. Rather than a "line," a chant melisma should be thought of as a succession of still moments, not coming from anywhere, not going anywhere. The choir should sound as if it could stop at any instant in the melisma and remain at that moment forever. The melisma is a kind of study in the paradox of stillness in motion. The voices move but give the effect of not moving. At any moment in the melody, the "present moment" is the only moment of consequence. If there is any feeling of movement within the singers at all, it is vertical within each singer, perfectly timeless and gentle, without force or drive, both rising and descending, as the psalmist wrote, "Let my prayer be set forth in your sight as incense, the lifting up of my hands as the evening sacrifice" (Ps 141:2); and again settling "Like the dew of Hermon that falls upon the hills of Zion" (Ps 133:4–5).

The quality which the choir must draw from the melismas must be perfectly compatible with that of balanced psalmody. During rehearsal, chanting psalms before and after chanting the Kyrie can help that quality emerge. As with the psalms, the character of the melisma must be compatible with silence, so that, during pauses between the phrases of the Kyrie, the gentle return of silent recollection can be felt. We might at this point recall St. Teresa's image of the turtle and examine it more closely:

> Don't think this recollection is acquired by the intellect striving to think about God within itself, or by the imagination imagining Him within itself. Such efforts are good and an excellent kind of meditation . . . but this isn't the prayer of recollection. . . . What I'm speaking of comes in a different way . . . one noticeably senses a gentle drawing inward, as anyone who goes through this will observe, for I don't know how to make it clearer. It seems to me that I have read where it was compared to a hedgehog curling up or a turtle drawing into its shell. (The one who wrote this example must have understood the experience well.) But these creatures draw inward whenever they want. In the case of this recollection, it doesn't come when we want it but when God wants to grant us the favor. . . . I believe that if we desire to make room for His Majesty,

He will give not only this but more, and give it to those whom He begins to call to advance further.... And this recollection is a preparation for being able to listen, as is counseled in some books, so that the soul instead of striving to engage in discourse strives to remain attentive and aware of what the Lord is working in it. (*Ter* 78–79)

The choir may find it useful to memorize this Kyrie and to sing it with eyes closed in order to listen more carefully and center the attention more fully within the body. In order to overcome the singers' ingrained inclination to sing a line, they will need to listen for every individual pitch of the melisma, and give each pitch a light, lifting touch of energy. The object is not a Baroque kind of "ha, ha, ha" articulation of each note, such as some conductors use with Bach and Handel, but a touch that is gentler, more conscious and loving, and less obvious to a listener. In order to apply these gentle, lifting touches, the singers may also need to adjust their vocal quality to give less weight to the sound. In some singers this adjustment will take place automatically in response to the exercise of "singing while listening" and in response to their sense of the recollective quality of both the psalms and the melismas. Other singers, however, may need encouragement to give up vocal habits that add excess weight to the melisma and interfere with their own listening.

The Marialis Kyrie is heavily melismatic, but there is one moment of recitation which may require attention. At the first statement of "Kyrie" after the "Christe eleison" section, the musical accent falls heavily on the second syllable of the text:

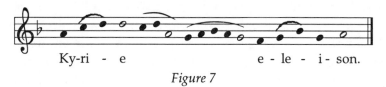

Figure 7

Without considerable effort to resist that musical accent, the choir will sing "kyRIe" at this point. With attention and effort—by slightly lengthening the first note on "KY-"—it is possible to sing "KYrie," which is the proper accent pattern for the word.

The Problem of Notation

The music we have covered to this point has been presented entirely in modern notation. However, any choir that is serious about Gregorian chant should learn to sing from what is called "square" notation, a style which developed in the twelfth century and is still standard in chant publications today. The most obvious reason for learning and using this system is solidly practical: the more complex repertory, either in published music or in manuscript reproductions, is available only in this form. A choir that declines to learn it is putting a huge burden on the director, who will have to transcribe practically everything. The same is not true of simpler chant. Simpler music for parish use is widely available in modern notation. There is no reason why a choir should not use both, whichever is conveniently available.

More importantly, any form of modern notation, even black notes without stems, carries for the modern singer some rhythmic associations. Even the plain, black "football" whispers to the singer, "one full beat," whereas the duration of such a pitch should be only as long as is necessary to articulate the syllable that goes with it. A long series of "footballs," indicating a melisma, presents to the eye a uniform succession of identical notes forming a "line" with "shape," suggesting a musical idea which, as we've seen, is very foreign to the chant. The square neume forms have none of these associations but actually have associations of an opposite character. As we saw earlier in this chapter, the neume forms originated as musical notations over text syllables, and they still bear to the eye that intimate connection between word and pitch. A single square note or "punctum" suggests no "beat" whatever but simply stands for the musical articulation of a text syllable. Likewise, a melisma is presented as a series of graphically discrete events, discouraging any concept of movement or line. Finally, because the neumes were developed specifically to notate language, they require far less physical space on the page than modern notation.[§]

[§]A table of neume forms and their equivalents in modern notation is given in Appendix 4.

A practical system for indicating exact pitches was not developed until the eleventh century, although earlier efforts to use letters to indicate pitch have survived. About the year 1025, an Italian monk, Guido of Arezzo, came up with the idea of staff lines and set the method down in his *Antiphoner*. To Guido's contemporaries, the ability to sing a melody one had never heard was nothing short of miraculous. Guido was summoned by the Pope, who had heard of this miracle, and who, according to Guido, examined the volume containing the new notation "as if it were some prodigy." In Guido's presence, the Pope immediately proceeded to try the system himself and found it worked perfectly. Guido's preface to his *Antiphoner* has survived. Here is his description of the process of using the staff lines and spaces. The letters to which Guido refers are the ancestors of our clef marks:

> The sounds, then, are so arranged that each sound, however often it may be repeated in a melody, is found always in its own row. And in order that you may better distinguish these rows, lines are drawn close together, and some rows of sounds occur on the lines themselves, others in the intervening intervals or spaces. Then the sounds on one line or in one space sound alike. And in order that you may also understand to which lines or spaces each sound belongs, certain letters of the monochord [scale] are written at the beginning of the lines or spaces and the lines are also gone over in colors, thereby indicating that in the whole antiphoner and in every melody those lines or spaces which have one and the same letter or color, however many they may be, sound alike throughout, as though all were on one line. For just as the line indicates complete identity of sounds, so the letter or color indicates complete identity of lines, and hence of sounds also. (*Guid* 118–119)

Figure 8 shows an example of this early staff. The line marking the note F is marked with the letter "f," and that marking note C is marked with its letter as well. Pinholes along the left margin were used, along with similar holes on the right which are not visible, to draw straight lines across the parchment. Another amused monk's face decorates the "Q" of "Qui regis Israel" ("you who rule Israel"), the beginning of Psalm 80.

Figure 8

Figure 8, together with the neume forms in figure 2, should clarify what is most puzzling to those using this notation for the first time, namely, the fact that the different neume shapes have no musical significance. The shapes are rather the result of convenient motions of the pen writing the neumes quickly and trying to fit the music to the syllables of the text with as little extra spacing of the text as possible. Guido, incidentally, observed in a letter to a friend that musicians after him through the ages would send prayers of gratitude to heaven for the ease with which these later singers could now learn the chant "which I and all my predecessors learned only with the greatest difficulty" (*Guid* 122).

LATIN OR ENGLISH?

The question of which language to use, English or Latin, is more complicated than the choice between notation styles and must be answered differently with respect to different types of chant. Because the recitation of psalms relies heavily on the singers' perceptions of meaning, one can say with some confidence that psalms should be recited in English as a rule, assuming an English-speaking choir. Likewise, the Latin of hymns is often poetic and oblique even for those who read the language, and so hymns also should be translated in most cases.

Shorter chants such as antiphons and short responsories, particularly when their texts are familiar, can be sung easily in Latin if the choir is experienced, open to the language, and even includes singers who read Latin. What exactly are the issues at stake? The overriding concern, of course, is that the singers know what they are singing. Any chant which is to be sung in Latin must be studied in detail. Singers should be aware of both the meaning and the grammatical function of every word. This kind of study takes time. It is also true that familiar scriptural texts in English often have the advantage of suggesting other texts the singer knows or connecting to some experience in the singer's life by means of a faint verbal echo, which can then create verbal connections which become very important for the singer. This rich world of personal verbal associations is not accessible if the text is foreign, even if the singer understands that text.

On the other hand, the contemplative tradition is a Latin tradition. To explore it, one must have at least some feel for its language. If a choir provides regular, careful exposure to Latin, some members will go further on their own, to their personal benefit. There is a wealth of historical experience surrounding this tradition which expressed itself not only in texts for the chant, but in the Latin Bible, the liturgy, the writings of the fathers, and other letters and literature. The breadth of this "rich world of verbal experience" is also a potential store of treasure for every singer who wishes to seek it out. The more one reads, sings, and gains experience in the liturgy, the stronger the associations become for certain Latin words, phrases, and images, associations which can't be transported into English.

Finally, for English speakers, singing the words of scripture in Latin represents participation in a kind of apt metaphor which the mind no doubt acknowledges at some deep level. If I am not fluent in Latin but have been coached to follow the meaning of a scriptural passage, I have the clear sense that I both know and don't know what it is I am saying. According to the fathers, this experience of uncertainty, of being in close proximity to levels of meaning which I grasp only in part, accurately represents my relationship to all scripture, whatever the language. Over the centuries, many worshipers have found a sense of "mystery" in the Latin liturgy, perhaps for this reason. In scripture more than in other texts, there are always levels of meaning lying just beyond my grasp but audible to an attentive ear. In English, by contrast, I feel that, because I know the language well, I also know exactly what it is I am saying with that language. If I say, "Abraham had become a very old man" (Gn 24:1), there's not much question in my mind that I understand what I have just said. Where scripture is concerned, however, this sense of confidence is misplaced and, the fathers would say, obscures for me the true nature of the text before me and of my relation to it. At a deep level, I am aware that the text feels flat, that something is missing, and I am right.

Our focus so far has been shorter texts which can be conveniently sung in either language. When the question of the longer, more complex chants arises, one must add two more considerations. Practically speaking, good translations are hard to find, and—if the choir sings a great deal of music—someone will have to produce translations. More to the point, the Latin of a complex chant is so carefully matched to its melody that even a good translation gives a completely different impression of the relation of text to music. The new text is presented by the music in a completely different way. The English version may "work" quite well, but it will work differently. If our aim is to produce beautiful music for a service on Sunday, the difference may not matter. But it will matter considerably if our aim is to develop a modern version of the contemplative practice of those of our spiritual ancestors who understood this discipline in such perfect detail. If we take seriously the inner coherence of this tradition, we understand that every detail reflects the whole. Granted, of course, there were careless composers in the tenth century just as there are in the twentieth. Granted, there are chants in the repertory which appear to have been created by slapping new texts rather awkwardly onto old melodies. But taking our experience of the repertory as a whole, we can be sure that the articulation of scripture by musical form works in harmony with the deepest contemplative aims of the tradition. We can further be sure that our understanding of both scripture and the tradition is guided by our experience of these melodies in ways far more complex than we are able to perceive consciously. If we are serious about the tradition, then, there can be no question but that the main body of chant should be experienced in Latin.

A word should be said about pronunciation. Scholars are virtually certain that, during the Middle Ages, Latin pronunciation in Europe and the British Isles was not uniform but varied according to local speech habits. But for the last hundred years or so, what has been accepted as "church" Latin pronunciation has been Italianate Latin and differs substantially from what has been taught as classical pronunciation. I have seen no reason to depart from the church Latin tradition, used in monasteries throughout the world. A guide to this system is included in Appendix 5.

In secular music circles there has been some confusion about two of the vowels of church Latin, the "e" and the "o." Choirs are often taught to pronounce "Christe" as "Christay," or "pleni sunt caeli" as "playnee sunt chaylee." The English "ay" is an attempt to duplicate the Italian long "e" sound, which has no real equivalent in English. The Italian long "e" is a single pure vowel, but the English "ay" is two vowels sounded in quick succession, a diphthong. The English "oh" sound, as in "donut," is likewise a diphthong. The pronunciation guide in the Appendix 5 recommends avoiding both these diphthongs by pronouncing "e" short, as in "let," and "o" as in "aw." Both will require some adjustments from many singers. The phrase "in nomine Domini" (in the name of the Lord) is a good one for practice: "een nawmeeneh dawmeenee."

NEUMATIC CHANT

Now we will examine the more complex chants in Latin and in traditional chant notation, using the names of the neumes given in Appendix 4. Of the three musical types of chant, neumatic melodies are by far the most difficult. In order to sing them well, the choir must move fluidly back and forth between free syllabic recitation and the gentle "touching" quality needed for melismas and also needed for shorter three- and four-note neumes. A choir should not take on these melodies until its psalm recitation is natural and free and its approach to melismas is confident, light, and consistent.

Most neumatic chants are specific or "proper" to one particular feast of the year and so are sung in the liturgy only on that day, once a year. For a choir just beginning to learn this style, it is helpful to repeat the same music more frequently, and for that reason Appendix 11 includes a complete liturgy for what used to be a called a "Votive Mass. "Votive" means "intention," as a "votive candle" is lighted with some particular person or purpose in mind. A Eucharist of this kind can be celebrated at any time.

The Votive Mass in Appendix 11 is a Eucharist in honor of the Holy Spirit. We will assume that the text has been carefully translated and studied, so that each singer has had a chance to understand every word. A helpful next step is to have the choir speak the text together without music, allowing them to become familiar with the text as a whole and also to begin identifying "tight phrases." Identifying "tight phrases" is a way of helping singers who do not read Latin to sing the more subtle rhythms of the language. We can illustrate the idea using English. Here is a translation of the text of the Introit for the Eucharist in Honor of the Holy Spirit[§] (omitting the psalm verse and Gloria):

> The Spirit of the Lord has filled the circuit of the worlds alleluia; and that which contains all things has knowledge of the voice alleluia alleluia alleluia.

No native speaker would pause between "The" and "spirit" or, indeed, at any point in the phrase "The Spirit of the Lord." These words are "tightly" phrased together in English. Likewise "has filled" is a tight phrase. But a pause of microscopic length might be heard between the phrase "The Spirit of the Lord" and its predicate phrase "has filled the circuit of the worlds." These two longer phrases are not tightly joined.

[§]This Introit also is used for the Day of Pentecost. The psalm verse and Gloria have been omitted here (and from all subsequent discussion of the Introit in this chapter), but the complete Introit appears in Appendix 11. The Introit text is from The Book of Wisdom (Wis 1:7).

Here is the Latin text of the Introit:

Spíritus dómini replévit orbem terrárum allelúia;
et hoc quod cóntinet ómnia, sciéntiam habet vocis
    allelúia allelúia allelúia.

In Latin, the tight phrases are "Spiritus domini" (Spirit of the Lord), "replevit orbem terrarum alleluia" (has filled the circuit of the worlds alleluia), "continet omnia" (contains all things), and "habet vocis" (has of the voice). The choir should speak these phrases separately until they fall off the tongue without the slightest hesitation. Attention should be given to the translation until each word with its grammatical function is clearly understood.

When this Introit is sung in the liturgy, the cantors sing the opening phrase, to the asterisk, then the choir joins and sings through the alleluias. The cantors then sing the first half of the psalm verse and the first half of the Gloria patri, and each time the choir joins at the asterisk. The body of the introit is then repeated, beginning with "Spiritus domini," everyone singing. The Introit ends at the double bar just before the psalm verse.

Before we look at the music, a word should be said about "alleluia." In the contemplative tradition, "alleluia" is joyful, but it is not a shout. Many translators of the psalms in recent years have returned to the Hebrew "hallelujah" to regain an exuberant quality which is not associated with the word in the Latin tradition. In the contemplative tradition, the joy of alleluia is intimately associated with the mystery of the Word speaking in the heart. Its timbre is thus more intimate and quiet. If the Word is the cluster of glowing red coals in the incense pot, the alleluia is the smoke rising from them. The movement from one to the other is seamless. For that reason, in the introit sentence translated above, as throughout the chant repertory, there should be no pause whatever between the text and the alleluia, except where a pause is needed for breath.

Square note chant notation has only three rhythmic marks: the dot, which doubles the length of the note before it, a horizontal line called an episema (which means lengthen the note or notes under it slightly),

and a third mark which looks like a jagged punctum, the quilisma (which means slightly lengthen the note just *before* it).

The note indicated by the quilisma itself is not lengthened. Both the quilisma and the episema are a challenge to choirs without a conductor, because the amount of lengthening is not fixed. There are really two challenges, to stay together and stretch the pitch by the same amount, and, even more crucial, to recover immediately after the lengthened note and return to the original pace.

Because these marks pose difficulties, it's a good idea to ignore them when the choir is first learning the chant. It is also helpful to ignore the rhythm of the words in the beginning, and practice with a steady pulse. That pulse can be slow at first, but it must be kept steady. Keeping it steady is the challenge to the attention. Progress may be less painful if the new melody is broken into short phrases. As the notes become familiar, the speed of the pace, still steady, can be increased. Once the entire chant is learned, the steady pace, now quite fast, can give way easily to the more flexible rhythm of the words themselves. Throughout, it is preferable not to use a keyboard. The leader should know the melody well and teach it by imitation if the group has trouble reading new music.

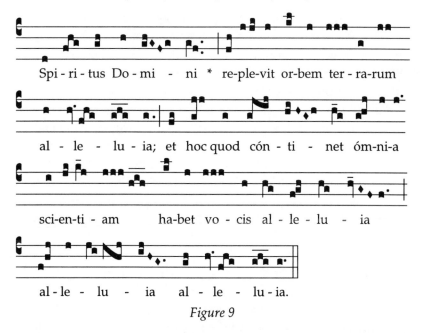

Spi - ri - tus Do - mi - ni * re-ple-vit or-bem ter - ra-rum al - le - lu - ia; et hoc quod cón - ti - net óm-ni-a sci-en-ti - am ha-bet vo - cis al - le - lu - ia al - le - lu - ia al - le - lu - ia.

Figure 9

The group is now ready to begin serious work on the Introit (see fig. 9 above). The music must be made transparent, so that the choir begins simply speaking phrases on pitches, balanced with fruitful silence between phrases. The process is similar in principle to the recitation drills described in Chapter Two, though the mechanics are different. The group is now trying to search out and eliminate even the most minute source of excess musical weight in the chant. One way to start is to return to the tight phrases which were rehearsed with text alone, and work them now with their music.

The phrase "continet omnia" contains two problems which appear in almost every neumatic chant. First, one must never under-estimate the dragging force of a single punctum. A punctum marks one pitch tied to one syllable, and so indicates a brief syllabic moment within a more complex piece. As in the psalms, these syllables, when they are short, must be dropped convincingly or the Latin word will be distorted. In "continet omnia," the short syllable is the "-i-" of "omnia." Similar short syllables elsewhere in the introit are: "-ra-" of "terrarum," the first "a-" of the first "alleluia," the "-bet" of "habet," and the "-le-" in the second of the three final alleluias. Specific attention will need to be given to all these syllables so that they are dropped to produce natural, simple recitation without excess weight of sound.

The first two syllables of "continet omnia" illustrate the second problem common to neumatic chant: distracting musical elaboration. The first syllable ("con-") is sung on three notes and the second ("-ti-") on five. This musical elaboration is a distraction for the mind, which should be thinking through "continet" to "omnia." It is crucial that singers hear the "omnia" approaching as "continet" is being sung, rather than, mentally, sing individual syllables. Another difficulty derives from the twisting character of the musical phrase. If the choir attempts to sing the five-note figure on "-ti-" with a feeling of line, of legato, the syllable inevitably will drag. Rather, as in a melisma, each note must be touched separately and lightly, at the same time without singing "tee-hee-hee-hee net." These individual syllables and the phrase "continet omnia" should be practiced separately.

When the choir has begun to find the light quality it is seeking, the episemas can be restored. Those which mark a clivis (at "-net" of "continet" and "-ti-" of "scientiam") apply to both pitches, as does an episema on a podatus:[§]

But once those pitches have been sung, the quick pace of the phrase must be immediately restored. Coming "out of" these marks cleanly will, again, require practice of these phrase details alone.

More generally, phrasing in the chant should be approached according to a logic somewhat different from that at work in other choral music. First, the meaning of the phrase must be articulated to the inner ear of the singer, not to an audience, and, second, the silence between phrases must be heard as an inseparable part of the

[§]See "clivis" and "podatus," Basic Neume Forms, Appendix 4.

phrases themselves. It should be clear by now that in the duality of action and contemplation, the contemplative moment—here, the moment of silence between phrases—is more than a period of rest. It is a moment of openness to a gentle energy for which one must prepare even though one cannot control its appearance. Its appearance gives the feel of a gift. Once the choir has had substantial experience with this phenomenon in psalmody, they should understand that a similar balance of articulation and restoring rest, or return, is at the heart of the longer chants as well. A "phrase break" is therefore not simply a place to take a breath, as it might be in a later choral work. Neither is it necessary to "stagger" the singers' breathing in order to complete a sentence of text. Phrase breaks can be taken at almost any point that makes sense to the ears of the choir, once the choir is able to feel that these breaks do not interrupt the meaning of the textual line, but rather give added life, a deeper dimension, to that meaning. As Gregory said, it is "by keeping silence [that] we learn to speak" (*G/HHP* 170). The silence is both part of the music and part of the scripture. It is as if the scripture, even when read without music, has an underlying current of silence within it, a current within which its deeper meanings are audible. The chant gives voice to that current, and to its relationship to the words themselves. Particularly when a choir is small and inexperienced, frequent phrase breaks can be a tremendous help. The regular recovery of energy at those breaks helps sustain the chant's quality, and the repeated, concrete experience of receiving that energy helps persuade the choir of the profound importance of this kind of stillness.

As the choir becomes larger and more experienced, the same principles can be applied in a different way to the problem of phrasing. The choir may decide, perhaps as an experiment, to sustain a textual phrase far longer than anyone's breath capacity. The purpose of the exercise is to challenge some singers' ingrained feeling that they *must* carry through to the end of the phrase. If that is impossible, then each singer, by careful attention to his own attitudes, must become comfortable with dropping out to breathe at absolutely any moment in the long phrase. In other words, each singer is invited to become completely free and relaxed with regard to breathing. This exercise can lead to valuable discoveries by some singers of deeply hidden emotional and mental tensions, often having to do with their own exaggerated sense of importance to the group: "If I stop singing, the whole piece will fall apart." In a strong, experienced choir, any individual should be able to drop out and reenter without disturbing the balance of the sound, and every individual must reach the place in themselves where they feel free to do so. Of course, in a small and inexperienced choir, it is often *true* that one or two voices are crucial to the group. Sometimes that situation can't be avoided, but in the singing of chant it is extremely detrimental both to those individuals and to the choir. Once the singing begins, there can be no leaders, but a perfectly ordered arrangement of voices. Over time, that harmonious order will appear if the choir understands the objective and listens faithfully.

The process of learning new music, particularly of learning new approaches to new music, is difficult. It inevitably produces tension, worry, concentration of the worst, most tension-ridden kind, and a lost sense of the larger aims of the chant. To counter these distractions, the leader must consistently, throughout the evening, stop everyone and call for a few seconds of silence. Singers can briefly close their eyes, let their "mind's eye" move to tense muscles in shoulders or face or wherever tension may be, and listen for a movement of gentle, refreshing return—Teresa's turtle coming back to itself. The leader should give frequent reminders to work with the listening attention, to return it to the sound. The group may find it helpful to stop periodically and chant a psalm, or spend a moment with the simple unison pitch exercise given in Chapter Two (see exercise 3). The difficulties of learning should be treated like the banging of chairs in Chapter Two, as distractions to be made use of. The entire rehearsal must become a contemplative exercise. In this discipline, every process, even attending to the most "technical" details, has an immediate contemplative purpose. Short readings from the fathers during the evening may help maintain a sense of context for the exercise of the moment, whatever that may be. Everything over several hours' time must contribute to the gradual gathering and harmonizing of the forces of the mind. Work with these more complex chants should not begin until the choir can return confidently to psalmody for refreshment.

The key to the longer chants, both melismatic and neumatic, is the choir's ability to move through repeated notes with a quick, precise, light quality in the sound. This quality is identifiable by its compatibility with the feel of balanced psalmody, its ease on the singers, and the simplicity with which it articulates the text. It is inseparable from active listening on everyone's part and respect for the silences between phrases. In helping a choir find it, the leader may need to teach by demonstration—sing a line and have the choir sing it immediately after; or use small groups of two or three singers who seem to have acquired the feel. It may be helpful to begin a chant with three singers and add the rest of the choir one by one, everyone listening carefully to maintain the original character of the sound.

Once the choir becomes confident in its ability to find and maintain this light energy in the longer and more difficult chants, the entire repertory lies open before it.

Chapter Four

The Subtleties of the Symbolic Mind

THE LANGUAGE OF SYMBOLS

A choir which has become secure in its recitation of psalms and longer chants, which is actively involved in the celebration of chanted liturgies, and which has begun its own reading and discussion of scripture and the fathers will find itself moving into a very different world of experience and ideas. In order to take full advantage of this world and, also, to feel comfortable in it, some adjustments in our thinking may be necessary. This chapter is designed to help with the transition.

The idea that there is more than one level to human intelligence and that the deeper levels express themselves in symbols is basic to the fathers' thinking. The text-centered monastic tradition we are exploring shows little interest, however, in explaining the structure of the mind theoretically. Its interest is practical—how to engage the deeper forces of the mind, to "become wise," to become one of those in whom the Word, Wisdom, dwells. That is our concern as well, but this "practice" which the fathers commend to us is in some ways so alien to the mind of our own times that some clearing of the way is necessary. In this chapter, then—expanding on ideas we began to consider at the beginning of Chapter Two—we will examine a few of the more surprising ways in which the symbolic mind operates in traditional writings, in scripture, and around us every day.

The Gospel of John is particularly concerned with the "Word," from its familiar opening, "In the beginning was the Word" (Jn 1:1), to its penultimate moments as Jesus prepares for his death and prays to the Father, "I have given them thy word" (Jn 17:14, RSV). Throughout, John emphasizes the difficulty that the apostles, other "disciples," and those John calls "the Jews" have in understanding a teaching which is given repeatedly in "figures" (Jn 16:25), or symbols. He seems to stress the incompatibility between the symbolic mind of Wisdom and the literal mind of the world, and he ends on what might appear to be a note of uncertainty as to the meaning of the words of Jesus concerning John himself: "The saying spread abroad among the brethren that this disciple [John] was not to die; yet Jesus did not say to him that he was not to die, but, 'If it is my will that he remain until I come, what is that to you?'" (Jn 21:23). It is as if John ends his gospel with a cautionary example of the danger of excessive concern with literal meanings, as if to give further emphasis to the symbolic meaning of the Word with which he began.

Discussions in our own day frequently give short shrift to the kind of figurative language which is central to John's gospel. If you have trouble with the Resurrection, we hear it said, think of it vaguely as "just" a symbol for rebirth. "Rebirth" is a familiar and comfortable idea. We observe it around us every day, every spring certainly. However such a statement may rate as theology, we should understand from John that the attitude behind it is not acceptable, given what it says about the use of symbolic language. A symbolic meaning is not a compromised or watered-down version of a "real" meaning. Properly used, symbolic language is not vague but is, first of all, precise, as we saw in Chapter Two. And symbolic meanings give precise expression to realities which are, if anything, of greater power and substance than what is more familiar and material. When Jesus promises that, if the temple is destroyed, he will rebuild it in three days, his words on a literal level are astonishing enough, but, on a figurative level, where he speaks of the resurrection of his body, they are unprecedented.

SYMBOLISM AND ALLEGORY

In the fathers' commentaries, what we have called "symbolism" is more often called "allegory." In literary discussions these two terms have acquired very different meanings, and the differences can cause confusion. Indeed, the theory of symbolism has become a major preoccupation of some literary critics in the twentieth century. Without venturing into these theoretical waters, we must clarify at least in broad terms what the fathers do *not* mean by these terms. To many laymen's ears today, the word "allegory" suggests a story which is told, not for its own sake, but to illustrate a moral. The term suggests a lack of realism in the story itself. A symbol, on the other hand, is generally understood to be a single word or image, as opposed to a story line, the most important meaning of which is not its literal one. The term "symbolism," in some minds, also suggests a lack of concern for realistic detail. But when the fathers say "allegory" they generally are not referring to an entire story line; they generally are referring to a series of terms or images, what modern readers would more likely understand as "symbols."

There is not any suggestion in the fathers, however, that the text is so concerned with the symbolic meaning as to ignore literal details. Not only scripture but, according to tradition, life itself, in all its complexity of detail, is symbolic of the realities of the spiritual world. Plato familiarized the ancient West with this point of view, but it is also Biblical and common in many ancient cultures. Origen, drawing on St. Paul, put it this way:

> Paul the apostle teaches us that the invisible things of God are understood by means of things that are visible, and that the things that are not seen are beheld through their relationship and likeness to things seen [Rom 1:20; 2 Cor 4:18]. He thus shows that this visible world teaches us about that which is invisible, and that this earthly scene contains certain patterns of things heavenly. (*Orig/SS* 218)

Allegorical approaches to a sacred text were common in Judaism before the Christian era, and Christian allegory begins with Jesus himself. He spoke in parables, or "figures," as we have already noted, and near the end of his ministry helped the apostles to see in the Old Testament symbolic references to his life, to see "in all the scriptures the things concerning himself" (Lk 24:27). Partly on the basis of this episode in Luke, there were traditions in the medieval church which taught that the fathers' allegorical approach to scripture had been passed to them, through the disciples, from Christ himself. A Roman Catholic papal encyclical as late as 1893 makes reference to those traditions: "For this [allegorical] method of interpretation has been received by the Church from the Apostles, and has been approved by her own practice, as the holy Liturgy attests" (*Papal* 332).

A particular text might be interpreted by such a writer as Gregory the Great in each of several allegorical senses beyond the literal—in its meaning for the inner life; as a prophecy of Christ; in its significance as a teaching about the mystical nature of the church and the "Last Things." These allegorical senses are well known to modern scholars of the medieval period. In Gregory, the mode that concerns us most directly, the interior meaning of the text, is called the "moral" sense—an odd use of that term to modern readers, for whom "morals" generally refer to guides to conduct in the outer, active world. Thus Gregory's massive commentary on the book of Job is entitled in Latin *Moralia in Job* (or *Morals on Job*), emphasizing its special concern with the inner life.

In order to enter the fathers' world, we must become comfortable with this allegorical or symbolic language. We must first of all accept at least the possibility that every word of scripture is true in an exact symbolic sense, and that symbolism is the necessary language of the inner world of the spirit. The forces that operate in that world shape our lives, and yet the language of contemporary culture gives us only the most awkward terms with which to name them. To enter that world, we must also adjust our habits of mind to accommodate multiple meanings, multiple types of meaning, the often unexpected behavior of inner forces, and different ways of "receiving" meaning. We need to examine each of these proposed adjustments in more detail.

MULTIPLE MEANINGS

Most of the images of scripture are taken by the fathers in several senses. Gregory says about "birds": "For in Holy Scripture 'birds' are sometimes given to be understood in a bad sense, and sometimes in a good sense" (G/MBJ 2: 394); or he says about water: "Waters in Holy Scripture are wont sometimes to denote the Holy Spirit, sometimes sacred knowledge, sometimes wrong knowledge, sometimes calamity, sometimes drifting peoples, sometimes the mind of those following the faith" (G/MBJ 2: 400); or he says about the sun: "Great discretion ought to be used in reading, so that in sacred expression when a certain word is used it is not always believed to signify the same thing, as the 'sun' is sometimes to be taken in a good sense, but sometimes in a bad" (G/HHP 315). There can be no test or evidence for establishing which is the "right" meaning in any given case. From the interior point of view, the "right" meaning is the one intended at that instant by the spirit for the individual. As Gregory puts it: "For the word of God is manna, and gives, in truth, that taste in the mouth of the eater, which the wish of him who partakes it rightly deserves" (G/MBJ 3: 448). But it is possible to force a symbol improperly, as Gregory explains with a vivid image from Proverbs:

> Because the Divine sentences require sometimes to be explored internally, and sometimes to be viewed externally, it is said by Solomon also, "He that strongly presseth the udder for the drawing forth [of] milk squeezeth out butter, and he that wringeth violently draweth out blood" [Prov 30:33]. For we "press the udder strongly" when we weigh with minute understanding the word of Sacred Revelation, by which way of "pressing" whilst we seek "milk," we find "butter," because whilst we seek to be fed with but a little insight, we are anointed with the abundance of interior richness. Which, nevertheless, we ought neither to do too much nor at all times, lest while milk is sought for from the udder there should follow blood. For very often persons whilst they sift the words of Sacred Revelation more than they ought, fall into a carnal apprehension. (G/MBJ 2: 514–515)

It is true that the text must be "weighed with minute understanding," but the key to the danger is in the last phrase: "a carnal apprehension." The living meaning of scripture is distorted when the natural mind "violently" forces correspondences which have no inner substance. The "ear of the heart" which alone is able to perceive the living, symbolic sense, to catch "the subtle quality of the inward utterance," opens only briefly and in conditions of stillness (*G/MBJ* 1: 279). Under ordinary conditions—when, for example, one reads a book in which these meanings are set down—it is the natural, "carnal" mind with which one reads. And indeed the author of the book, by the time he begins to write down those meanings, is writing with that same natural faculty.

So there is always a hesitancy in the fathers' presentations of symbolic meanings in writing, a hesitancy that shows up in their tone and phrasing. Gregory frequently suggests his interpretations in the form of a question: "What is denoted by the title of 'waters,' saving the hearts of the Elect?. . . Was it the aim of Holy Scripture? . . . Who is the younger son, if not? . . . What wonder is it then, if? . . ." Bernard's touch is equally light: "These are the reasons why the soul seeks the Word. No doubt there are countless others, but these occur to me at the moment. If anyone has a mind to do so, he can easily find many others in himself" (*Bern/SS* 4: 196). The multiple meanings of symbols must be discussed openly so that others may learn how this language works, but this open discussion must always proceed with tact and a light touch, with a detached spirit, never dogmatically. The commentator who must write down these ideas is always trying to catch the voice of the spirit, which "blows where it wills," or again, the voice of Wisdom, which is "subtle, free-moving, lucid, spotless, clear" and "moves more easily than motion itself" (Wis 7:22,23, NEB).

Approaching the fathers for the first time, a modern reader must accept not only multiple meanings, but multiple kinds of meaning. Considering Psalm 24, for example, we welcome the scholarship which tells us that this psalm was used in ancient Israel to accompany royal processions entering Jerusalem: "Lift up your heads, O gates" (Ps 24:7). But this historical reading need in no way contradict traditional symbolic readings which see the psalm as a prophecy of the Ascension, in which the heavenly powers rejoice and the gates of heaven are lifted up at the return of the Savior who, having ascended, will draw all things after him, since "the earth is the Lord's and all that is in it" (Ps 24:1). Neither should it contradict traditional readings which hear the psalmist speaking of the silent, interior motions of the heart, by which the mind of the heart, its outer gates and, then, its inner doors, its deeper intelligences, are opened, and "a blessing from the Lord" (Ps 24:5) is received; or a momentary, personal meaning by which the spirit tells us, perhaps, yes, what you are considering as this next step in your life you must take; this is a gate you must enter. The tradition urges us to see that all of these are the "real" meanings of scripture. And that it is in the very nature of scripture to be rich in this way. We seek "milk" and are rewarded with "butter."

INNER FORCES

These riches are discovered through contemplative study, and, when deeper levels of mind are brought into play, the results are not always what we had expected. Popular culture today tends to equate the depth of forces in the psyche with their level of violence. Deep passions are searing passions. But in the fathers' view, spiritual forces operate on a level far deeper than emotion, and they function in simplicity and silence. To the natural mind they appear almost non-existent, and it is only through experience and discipline that the natural mind acknowledges their reality. To the unprepared mind these forces within us are the blind, poor, lame, widowed, orphaned, and imprisoned. A large part of us wishes to ignore and have nothing to do with them, but, according to scripture, it is essential to our spiritual growth that they be visited and strengthened. From the inner point of view, Christ's words are literally true: "As you did it to one of the least of these my brethren, you did it to me" (Mt 25:40). The "least of these," that is, the apparently sick, impoverished, and imprisoned within us, are the divine forces themselves. To the outer world, they are the "stone which the builders rejected" and which we reject daily.

The fathers attest with a unified voice, however, that, as one learns to listen inwardly, what appeared to be insubstantial and evanescent reveals its true magnitude. Referring to the psalm passage, "I have run the way of thy commandments when thou didst enlarge my heart" (Ps 119:32, DR), St. Teresa explains that, when the "understanding" is "enlarged" as the psalm describes, the divine presence can fill the inner being. We should emphasize that the contemplative experience Teresa describes here is so powerful as to be almost visionary, but it is the *kind* of experience—the sense of gentle, inward expansion, of well-being and refreshment of the senses—in which serious contemplatives frequently share, if in less extreme form:

> To return to the verse [Ps 119:32], what I think is helpful in it for explaining this matter is the idea of expansion. It seems that since that heavenly water begins to rise from this spring I'm mentioning that is deep within us, it swells and expands our whole interior being producing ineffable blessings; nor does the soul even understand what is given to it there. It perceives a fragrance, let us say for now, as though there were in that interior depth a brazier giving off sweet-smelling perfumes. No light is seen, nor is the place seen where the brazier is; but the warmth and the fragrant fumes spread through the entire soul and even often enough, as I have said, the body shares in them. See now that you understand me; no heat is felt, nor is there the scent of any perfume, for the experience is more delicate than an experience of these things; but I use the examples only so as to explain it to you. And let persons who have not experienced these things understand that truthfully they do happen and are felt in this way, and the soul understands them in a manner clearer than is my explanation right now. This spiritual delight is not something that can be imagined, because however diligent our efforts we cannot acquire it. The very experience of it makes us realize that it is not of the same metal as we ourselves but fashioned from the purest gold of the divine wisdom. (*Ter* 75)

Teresa's description is more detailed than is typical of the tradition, but she maintains traditional reticence in that she describes the character of this kind of experience without presuming to describe a particular instance of such an experience which happened to her. The sensual character of the language, the imagery of sweetness of smell or often of taste, is also characteristic of the vocabulary of the tradition. Thirteen hundred years before Teresa, Origen used similar language: "Because He tastes so sweet and so delightful, all other flavours will seem harsh and bitter to him now; and therefore he will feed on Him alone. For he will find in Him all the sweetness that ever he desired" (*Orig/SS* 78).

The contemplative sense of "sweetness" ("dulcedo" or "suavitas" in Latin) as a sign of a deep, intimate love has almost disappeared from modern English. It survives marginally in spirituals (phrases such as "sweet Jesus") and in Shakespeare. At the end of *Hamlet*, when Hamlet has just died and Horatio speaks gently and lovingly to him ("Good night, sweet prince, and flights of angels sing thee to thy rest"), there is not the slightest hint of sentimentality in his address to his friend, but respectful love and a deep spiritual intimacy appropriate to the invocation of the songs of angels. For this moment, Shakespeare's language is drawing on connotations of "sweetness" accumulated over centuries of European monastic experience. It is remarkable that, even today, a sensitive ear hears those echoes and, having no idea of their source, still understands that the word is working in these lines with a gentle force completely separate from its more common, sentimental associations.

The reticence in Teresa's description serves two purposes. First, it reminds us of the main theme of our present discussion: that inner forces inevitably appear insubstantial in the eyes of the world, even in our own "worldly" eyes. They must therefore be described and spoken of—exposed to public and worldly scrutiny—with extreme caution. The second effect is to encourage us with the suggestion that such experiences of the Word are not limited to saints. They are offered to anyone who takes on the discipline of the contemplative life.

What Teresa does not discuss, however, is the difficulty that such experiences can cause us. These experiences of the Word are made possible by the stirring of inner forces—Teresa's "springs"—which are not normally at work in us, or, more accurately, of whose working we are not normally conscious. When our brief awareness of that stirring is past, we may feel that the experience itself has evaporated and left nothing behind. We are not accustomed to perceptions of truth which come and go in this way. We are accustomed to the idea that feelings change, but we take that as evidence of their unreliability. We are not accustomed to the idea that our ability to perceive what is most important and most deeply true also changes. The integration of these deeper forces with the natural mind is a gradual process. The natural mind, as we have seen, is reluctant to acknowledge their substance. Until that reluctance is overcome and integration has progressed considerably, we may feel ourselves at times adrift in uncertainty about the reality of our own experience—not what we expected from a spiritual discipline.

But the difficulties created in us by the elusive nature of these forces are ancient. Bernard observes: "Persons who are spiritual, or whom the Holy Spirit purposes to make spiritual, never cease to experience these alterations" (*Bern/SS* 1: 127). Peter, as we recalled earlier, loses touch with that force in himself which knows that he is a faithful disciple, understands why, and is willing to die for his faith. He denies Jesus and his best self as a result. Paul writes to the Galatians—who in days gone by "would have plucked out your eyes and given them to me"—asking, "What has become of the satisfaction you felt?" (Gal 4:15). Paul longs for this integration of disconnected minds within the Galatians in these terms: "My little children, with whom I am again in travail *until Christ be formed in you*" (Gal 4:19, emphasis mine). The children of Israel—seemingly lost in the desert and headed for a "promised land" which, after many years, begins to appear illusory to the natural mind of any "reasonable" person—flail about desperately, again and again, for any tangible support which will offer security and a sense of the normal.

For the Israelites to reach their goal—to "inherit the land which the LORD your God gives you" (Dt 16:20); to "dwell in the land"

and "be fed with its riches" (Ps 37:3, DR)—means, symbolically, to integrate these deeper forces of the mind with the natural intelligence, to become one of those in whom Wisdom dwells. In order for this to happen, the natural mind must be prepared over a long period of time. As this preparation continues, the mind becomes more closely conformed to the Word. In Bernard's imagery, the person becomes ready for marriage between the soul and the Word: "The soul which has attained this degree now ventures to think of marriage. Why should she not, when she sees that she is like him and therefore ready for marriage?" (*Bern/SS* 4: 208).

Because this integration of forces is rare and must be achieved repeatedly before it is permanent, a specific kind of memory plays a crucial role in the scriptures, in the fathers' teaching, and in the experience of the contemplative life, whatever its form. "To remember" in this sense means to open the natural mind to the depths of spiritual intelligence, to bring back to consciousness a full understanding of what the spiritual mind knows and has made conscious in the past. With that understanding comes both an emotional response and, most importantly, the will to act appropriately. Sometimes, as we saw with Peter and Jonah, this experience is healing but painful. But sometimes it brings the sense of peace, of having come home, that Teresa described above. In simpler language than Teresa's, the psalmist is "content, as with marrow and fatness, and my mouth praises you with joyful lips, when I remember you upon my bed" (Ps 63:5).§ In all cases, the movement of the mind that remembers in this way is profound. When the psalmist vows to "remember the works of the Lord, and call to mind your wonders of old time" (Ps 77:11), his desire is not simply to recall abstract events, but to be filled again with the power of the God who acts, who achieved those wonders.

The natural mind lives habitually in a state of forgetfulness. It does not remember. In this condition, familiar to all of us, spiritual realities seem far away and of little importance or interest. Often

§Gregory tells us that in scripture the "bed" can be taken to represent "the secret chambers of the heart" (*G/MBJ* 3: 201).

this forgetfulness comes over us shortly after a time of more intense spiritual consciousness, perhaps following a less extreme version of the experience of the Word which Teresa described. To use now-familiar terms, we become completely absorbed in the active life, and its contemplative dimension slips away. Or, like the Israelites (Num 14:3), we flee to the active life, back to "Egypt," to escape a brief touch of the contemplative. Inevitably, especially at the beginning, inner experience is strange and therefore unsettling. We flee to the comfort of a more familiar world.

Since this state of shifting consciousness is our natural condition, the tradition gives some attention to the forces which call us out of that condition to moments of more profound intelligence. Origen refers to a "saving wound" of love which may be struck in the worldly mind by the "chosen arrow" of the Word (*Orig/CWS* 223), as described in Isaiah: "And he hath made my mouth like a sharp sword: in the shadow of his hand he hath protected me, and hath made me as a chosen arrow: in his quiver he hath hidden me" (Is 49:2, DR). Elsewhere, Origen speaks of "particles of light" that are "shed upon the deeper mysteries" for beginners, so that they may "conceive [a] desire for higher things; for no one can even desire a thing of which he has no knowledge whatsoever" (*Orig/SS* 157). The experience Origen describes in symbols is common even today and illustrates the underlying power of spiritual desire. A brief moment of authentic inner experience, "particles of light shed upon the deeper mysteries," perhaps during childhood or adolescence or in a time of crisis, will sometimes stay with an individual for decades, resting in the back of the mind, quietly raising a question about every comfortable assumption concerning "the nature of things," until finally the individual is forced to act upon that impulse, that "still, small voice" (1 Kg 19:12), and search out its implications for his life.

Gregory, like Origen, associates a call to the spiritual life with a disturbance, or crippling, of one's ease with the material world. When Jacob struggles with the angel and injures his thigh, his injury is Origen's "wound of love," a crippling of Jacob's ability to walk easily on the earth, that is, live at ease in a strictly material world. But St. Teresa is particularly eloquent on the Lord's call to the soul immersed in the activities of life:

> Yet this Lord desires intensely that we love Him and seek His company, so much so that from time to time He calls us to draw near Him. And His voice is so sweet the poor soul dissolves at not doing immediately what He commands. Thus, as I say, hearing His voice is a greater trial than not hearing it. I don't mean that these appeals and calls are like the ones I shall speak of later on. But they come through words spoken by other good people, or through sermons, or through what is read in good books, or through the many things that are heard and by which God calls, or through illnesses and trials, or also through a truth that He teaches during the brief moments we spend in prayer; however lukewarm these moments may be, God esteems them highly. And you, Sisters, don't underestimate this first favor, nor should you become disconsolate if you don't respond at once to the Lord. His Majesty knows well how to wait many days and years, especially when He sees perseverance and good desires. This perseverance is most necessary here. (*Ter* 49)

FREEDOM OF INTERPRETATION AND LEVELS OF CONTEXT

Perhaps most troubling of all to modern minds is the traditional writers' love of fastening on single words or phrases entirely out of their literal context. But the gospels themselves are filled with such perplexities. Matthew, for example, writes that Joseph took the baby Jesus to Egypt in order to fulfill the words of the prophet: "Out of Egypt have I called my son" (Mt 2:15, RSV). Matthew is apparently quoting Hosea 11:1, but this passage in Hosea is not prophecy at all, but a recollection of God's liberating call to the people of Israel in Egypt. And in the next line of the passage, ignored by Matthew, Hosea observes that the people rejected the call: "The more I called them, the more they went from me; they kept sacrificing to the Baals, and burning incense to idols" (Hos 11:2). We are asked to believe that the first verse of the chapter is "messianic," referring to Christ, and the second is not. Can the scriptures then be twisted to mean anything anyone wishes? Even to those who are ready to accept the great messianic prophecies of Isaiah or the psalms as applying to Christ, this kind of selective, word by word prophetic reading is difficult to swallow.

And yet, according to the witness of the gospels and the traditions of the fathers, we must swallow it. What is involved here? Where are the boundaries? The tradition offers several curbs to excess, one of which we have mentioned—firm caution against speaking aloud what is heard in silence within, until that "hearing" has ripened. Another curb is found in the fathers' actual warnings, as in Gregory's caution against drawing blood from the udder, or his more literal warning from his commentary on Job that we must not "seem violently to wrest his [Job's] sayings according to the caprice of our own view" (*G/MBJ* 1: 452). As we've seen, the danger is, not listening to scripture, but imposing one's own will, allowing the intrusion of an inferior or "carnal" level of intelligence (*G/MBJ* 2: 515).

But perhaps the most powerful assumption guiding ancient interpreters and setting the boundaries of what is acceptable was a vision of the unity of the created universe, including human nature and the scriptures. As St. Maximus the Confessor put it,

> The whole world of visible and invisible things can be thought of as a man; and man, made up of body and soul, as a world . . . the spiritual world is in the material like the presence of a soul in a body; and the material world is fused with the spiritual like a body with its soul; as soul and body make one man, the two make one world. (*Max* 84)

This harmonious unity is reflected in scripture, in which the Word is present in its entirety in every small part, and speaks a single message, that of the love of God. That interpretation is true which "serves love"—as St. Augustine put it—and resonates most powerfully throughout this ordered whole.

This unified vision exists on a level above the historical context. When the Old Testament tells how God acted with Ezekiel or Job, for example, it is explaining symbolically how God always acts. An image viewed symbolically in relation to the life of prayer in one passage, likewise, will have the same symbolic meaning in other passages, because the dynamics of prayer remain the same. Medieval commentators lifted lines freely, we would say, "out of context," because their own context was larger than the literal. In that larger context, both the meaning of the text and the language and imagery that convey that meaning, are consistent. If it is a "shadow" that shelters the beloved in The Song of Songs, it is not accidental that Mary is "overshadowed" by the Holy Spirit. Just what the symbolic connections may be between those two similar images is a mystery to be revealed only by the spirit, but the fathers were secure in their confidence that it is the single Word which is present in both passages, and so the relationships are there to be revealed. This vision implies, as the fathers also make explicit, that every detail is significant to the awakened intelligence. As Origen puts it, that spiritual intelligence is able to "examine the meaning of things with more acute perception" (*Orig/SS* 79). Through the spiritual intelligence, one "gains the understanding that not even one iota or one dot in the word of God is insignificant" (*Orig/CWS* 265).

GUIDING AND ACTIVE SYMBOLS

The final guide to interpretation which we will consider is the authority of the tradition itself. During the Reformation, the question of the individual's right to read and interpret the scriptures became a major point of argument between the Catholic and Protestant sides. Within monastic tradition, however, there is little conflict between the church and the individual on this issue. First of all, it is assumed by all the fathers that the individual will know the scriptures. Most often, it is assumed he or she will read. If he is illiterate, he will memorize the sacred words. Second, it is rare that a monastic writer invokes the authority of "the church" as a threat in matters of interpretation. In practice, the authority of the church is represented by the authority of the tradition. This authority functions quietly, not as a source of restriction, but as a source of inner riches. In this case, "authority" lies in the tradition's immense appeal as a sure guide in the direction which the monk most desires to take: toward the immediate experience of the presence of God, the Word.

In order to understand more clearly the balance between guidance and individual freedom which is involved here, we might make use of two terms for symbolic interpretation, "guiding" as opposed to "active" symbols. But let me be clear: the terms themselves are not traditional. They are my own, although the ideas they represent are, I believe, at the heart of the tradition. "Guiding" symbols are the familiar, accepted interpretations of the allegorical tradition. The image of sweetness of taste, for example, is associated with the opening of the deeper, spiritual intelligence by writers throughout the tradition, from the third century to the sixteenth. Thus, a "guiding symbol" is, first of all, one that has been defined *in writing* by at least one of the fathers, but usually by several authors over the course of centuries. There are hundreds of such symbols. They form the basic vocabulary of the traditional language and refer to fundamental characteristics of human nature or the faith. A newcomer to the tradition meets them first by reading the fathers, but learns to trust their validity by private meditation and participation in the liturgy. The purpose of these symbols is to awaken the novice to the possibility of a world of meaning in the scripture that is entirely different from any form of literal meaning. As Thomas Merton put it in 1953, "What is hidden beneath the literal meaning is not merely another and more hidden *meaning*, it is also a new and totally different *reality*: It is the divine life itself" (*Bread* 166). In absorbing these meanings, the novice is being taught in broad strokes how to listen to the voice of the dove, being taught, in a sense, a certain direction in which to turn and a listening posture. The beginner learns, for example, that to enter the house of the Lord or to stand in his temple can mean to experience a change in the quality of one's outlook, an awakening of the deeper intelligence by which we begin to see "with dove's eyes." Psalm 73 is about such a change: "When I tried to understand these things, it was too hard for me; Until I entered the sanctuary of God and discerned the end of the wicked" (Ps 73:16–17). In order to absorb this symbol, to know what it means to "enter the sanctuary of God," the beginner must be aware of its meaning on a purely rational level, but must then experience the kind of change it describes in order to be persuaded of its validity.

An "active" symbol is not so public. It speaks its meaning directly to one individual in a state of readiness, to one standing "in the sanctuary of God" or "within your gates, O Jerusalem" (Ps 122:2). The result of this experience can be stated in rational terms. Afterwards one might say, for example, that I have seen in myself the "river whose streams make glad the city of God" (Ps 46:4). I have seen why there are separate "streams" which join this river; I have seen where it runs and how it connects to the divine city. I have seen why it is a source of joy. These insights I can in some fashion remember. But something has disappeared, and of that I am quite aware. And the fathers are clear on this point as well. Like the manna in the wilderness, the living knowledge of scripture can't be stored or it spoils, that is, becomes distorted into a parody of its original form. And so the fathers speak of this gentle inner process of understanding in sensory terms, as we've seen, as a "fragrance" or a "sweet taste" or the graceful leaping of the young deer of The Song of Songs. The "spoiling" of this knowledge comes as one becomes secretly proud and shares it with others, hoping to make an impression of spiritual depth. The result of this vanity, according to Gregory, is that "the strict Judge" blinds one to the scriptures, so that one "no longer sees its inward meaning" (G/MBJ 3: 345).

The temptations of vanity and their consequences are so serious that the fathers warn those who are young in the contemplative life to say nothing to anyone about what is spoken actively to them by the spirit. Like Mary, the beginner must keep "all these things" and "ponder them in her heart" (Lk 2:19). By means of this inward pondering, the soul is strengthened; it grows "in wisdom and stature" as the young Jesus did. Or, as Bernard put it, the gift of this active symbol is "pounded and refined in the heart's receptacle" (Bern/SS 1: 65) to produce a "precious ointment" of sweet taste and odor. The tradition is firm as to the need for the individual, particularly the beginner, to allow this ferment to proceed without disturbance, especially without being made public in any way.

Bernard calls attention to Psalms 65 and 104, in which he says God filled the inner and secret places of the earth before "his teeming mercies billowed over" into open places (*Bern/SS* 1: 136). He continues: "You too must learn to await this fulness before pouring out your gifts." Both Gregory (*G/MBJ* 1: 480) and Bernard (*Bern/SS* 1: 134) point to the command (Dt 15:19) which prohibits putting the first offspring of a bullock to work or shearing the firstborn of the sheep as a command intended by the spirit to raise this caution about the inner life. According to Deuteronomy, the first fruits of the herd belong to God, that is, should be reserved for the inner nourishment of one's own soul. When Jesus says the sheep will "know his voice" (Jn 10:4, RSV), "sheep" refers to the nonrational, spiritual intelligence. The bullock is the power of inner discipline which ploughs the earth of scripture even in "cold" (Prov 20:4, DR), that is, when the spirit seems to be absent. Both the sheep and the bullock must be allowed to grow, to multiply, to strengthen themselves in anyone who is young in the inner life. But there is caution in this command, also, for those who are more mature. They must be careful when the spirit reveals to them an active symbol the meaning of which appears to suggest a new direction of thought or action. This gift of personal understanding must be kept entirely private until its meaning is confirmed. In other words, this "firstborn" must be kept secret until it is followed by "brothers and sisters" that resemble it and give it substance.

In a less systematic way, Christians for centuries have absorbed the images of scripture as active symbols, and, as the fathers would say, the fragrance of that knowledge has spread through countless individual lives and, by means of poems and songs, through the church as a whole. Generations ago, an anonymous poet read with an opening intelligence Jeremiah's painful lamentation for the suffering of the land of Judah, culminating in the desperate question, "Is there no balm in Gilead? Is there no physician there?" (Jer 8:22). The force of the questions themselves—or perhaps the echo of the words of Jesus, "Those who are well have no need of a physician, but those who are sick" (Lk 5:31)—must have brought to that poet's mind the words he wrote down in answer to Jeremiah, the words of the now-familiar spiritual, "There is a balm in Gilead, to heal the sin-sick soul." In the spiritual, that healing balm becomes an image of Jesus himself. The poet has been led, as Jesus led the apostles after the resurrection, to see in "the prophets," "the things concerning himself." By means of the poem, an "active symbol" that was revealed to the poet, the "balm in Gilead" became a "guiding symbol" of healing and hope throughout the church.

FUNDAMENTAL GUIDING SYMBOLS

The guiding symbols of the monastic tradition are of special interest because they point to aspects of the inner life of which we might otherwise be unaware. The traditional understanding of human nature which we explored in Chapter One and to which we have referred again and again—the importance of the scattering of the mind preoccupied with thoughts of daily life; the larger intelligence which can be awakened when the mind is still; the power of scripture to speak to that intelligence—these fundamental aspects of the traditional understanding of human nature and the scriptures are embodied in countless scriptural images, some of which we must now explore.

On a large scale, the fathers saw the wandering of Israel in the desert following the Exodus as a symbol of the search for inner perfection. Gregory of Nyssa, a fourth-century bishop who lived in Cappadocia (now Turkey) summarized the figures this way:

When you conquer all enemies (the Egyptian, the Amalekite, the Idumaean, the Midianite), cross the water, are enlightened by the cloud, are sweetened by the wood, drink from the rock, taste of the food from above, make your ascent up the mountain through purity and sanctity . . . when you, as a sculptor, carve in your own heart the divine oracles which you receive from God, and when you destroy the golden idol . . . when you are elevated to such heights that you appear invincible to the magic of Balaam . . . when you come through all these things, and the staff of the priesthood blossoms in you, drawing no moisture at all from the earth but having its own unique power for producing fruit (that is the nut whose first taste is bitter and tough but whose inside is sweet and edible) . . . then you will draw near to the goal. (*Nyssa* 135–136)

The "goal" of course is entrance into the land promised to our ancestors, to "inherit" that "land that I will show you" (Gn 12:1) and "be fed with its riches" (Ps 37:3, DR). This "possessing of the land," as we saw earlier in this chapter, is a powerful symbol of the integration of spiritual forces within, the arrival at "home," at the inner condition for which we were created. Cassian writes:

> The beginning of our salvation is the Lord's call to "come out of your native land" and the end, the crowning perfection and purity, is when He says, "Come into the land which I shall show you." What He means is, "You cannot come to know it by yourself nor find it by your own effort, and yet to you, ignorant and uninquiring as you are, I shall reveal it." (*Cass/CWS* 92)

Of the guiding symbols that occur throughout the Old Testament, the scattering of the tribes of Israel is seen as one of the most fundamental symbols of all, defined succinctly by Richard of St. Victor:

> Let one who eagerly strives for contemplation of celestial things, who sighs for knowledge of divine things, learn to assemble the dispersed Israelites; let him endeavor to restrain the wanderings of the mind; let him be accustomed to remain in the innermost part of himself and to forget everything exterior. (*Rich* 142)

According to Richard's guiding symbol, Ezekiel's prophecy that the tribes of Israel will be gathered from the nations and given a "heart of flesh" also applies to every individual. When the wandering thoughts are gathered, then the deeper feelings, the "heart of flesh," are able to come alive also. According to the fathers, every detail of the passage has inner meanings for the awakened intelligence:

> For I will take you from the nations, and gather you from all the countries, and bring you into your own land. I will sprinkle clean water upon you, and you shall be clean from all your uncleannesses, and from all your idols I will cleanse you. A new heart I will give you, and a new spirit I will put within you; and I will take out of

your flesh the heart of stone and give you a heart of flesh. And I will put my spirit within you, and cause you to talk in my statutes and be careful to observe my ordinances. You shall dwell in the land which I gave to your fathers; and you shall be my people, and I will be your God. (Ezek 36:24–29, RSV)

Because the scattering of the mind by everyday thoughts and desires is such an important factor in the contemplative life, the tradition finds this inner condition in scriptural symbols small as well as large. Gregory interprets Egypt of the Exodus as "this world" and its plague of flies (Ex 8:20–24) as an image of the worldly mind:

But Egypt, which bears a likeness of this world, is stricken with flies. For the fly is an excessively intrusive and restless creature. Wherein what else is there represented but the intrusive solicitations of carnal desires? Whence it is said elsewhere, "Dying flies destroy the sweetness of the ointment" [Eccl 10:1]. Because superfluous thoughts, which in the mind taken up with things carnal are for ever both springing into life and dying away, destroy that sweetness, with which each individual has been inwardly anointed by the Spirit. (G/MBJ 2: 369–370)

Gregory gives a similar reading to the image of the sea in Job 28:14, "The sea says, 'It [wisdom] is not with me,'" because "minds that are devoted to this world are disturbed by the cares and anxieties of the present life, and therefore are quite unable to enjoy the repose of . . . Wisdom" (G/MBJ 2: 369).

When these agitations of the mind are still, then, as we have seen, a more profound intelligence can open. Gregory sees this process in Jesus' healing of the ruler's daughter in Matthew:

So the crowd is cast forth without, in order that the damsel may be raised up; because if the importunate throng of worldly cares be not first expelled from the inner recesses of the heart, the soul, which lies dead in the interior, cannot rise up. (G/MBJ 2: 370)

Images of sleep may have a similar meaning, as falling asleep to the world may mean awaking to the realities of the spirit. Gregory— examining the passage, "In a dream, in a vision of the night, when

sleep falleth upon men, and they sleep on their bed" (Job 33:15)—
gives this interpretation:

> In a dream the outward senses are at rest, and inward objects are
> discerned. If we wish then to contemplate things within, let us rest
> from outward engagements. The voice of God, in truth, is heard as
> if in dreams, when, with minds at ease, we rest from the bustle of
> this world, and the Divine precepts are pondered by us in the deep
> silence of the mind. (*G/MBJ* 3: 31–32)

Gregory expands on this idea in his reading of a passage from The
Song of Songs: "I sleep, but my heart waketh" (Sg 5:2). He writes,
"I am asleep to outward things, but my heart is awake within,
because, when I am insensible as it were to outward objects, I have
a keen apprehension of inward secrets" (*G/MBJ* 3: 33).

When the mind is at rest and open, the Word is able to speak its
inner meaning. Origen sees this action of the Word as the leaping
of the stag in The Song of Songs:

> If at any time some riddles or obscure sayings of the Law or the
> Prophets hem in the soul, if then she should chance to perceive Him
> to be present, and from afar should catch the sound of His voice,
> forthwith she is uplifted. And, when He has begun more and more
> to draw near to her senses and to illuminate the things that are
> obscure, then she sees Him "leaping upon the mountains and the
> hills;" that is to say, He then suggests to her interpretations of a high
> and lofty sort, so that this soul can rightly say: "Behold, He cometh
> leaping upon the mountains, skipping over the hills." (*Orig/SS*
> 209–210)

Origen sees a similar meaning in the anointing of Jesus' feet by
Mary:

> "Mary," the Scripture says, "brought a pound of ointment of
> spikenard of great price, and anointed the feet of Jesus, and wiped
> them with the hair of her head. And the whole house," it says, "was
> filled with the odour of the ointment" [Jn 12:3]. This surely shows
> that the odour of the teaching that proceeds from Christ, and the
> fragrance of the Holy Spirit have filled the whole house of the world,
> or else the whole house of the church. Or, indeed, it has filled the

whole house of the soul, who has received a share in the odour of Christ, in the first place, by offering Him the gift of her faith as the ointment of spikenard, and then receiving back the grace of the Holy Spirit and the fragrance of spiritual teaching. (*Orig/SS* 160–161)

Each of the fathers' readings is an invitation to anyone who chooses to confirm the validity of the symbol and, also, to search beyond the symbol. For example, we know from Richard that the basic symbol of the gathering of the tribes—as seen earlier in the selection from Ezekiel—may speak to me about the gathering in of the wandering forces of my own mind. But that is only a starting point. If I experience the reality of this gathering process, in chanting the psalms or in meditation, perhaps I may also experience the "clean water sprinkled" upon me, the "cleansing of idols" and the "heart of flesh." Perhaps I will discover what it means to "dwell in the land" given to my fathers. Perhaps I will open a question, "Who are my fathers?" Perhaps I will understand that to "walk in the statutes" of the Lord means something different from anything I had previously imagined.

Taking a slightly different tack, using, let us say, Gregory's reading of the sea as a figure for the turbulent mind, I search my memory, in stillness, for other images of the sea. I remember the fathers' caution that any image of scripture can have many meanings, but I bring to mind Jesus, as, "in the fourth watch of the night, he came to them, walking on the sea" (Mt 14:25); or the Red Sea, "divided in two" (Ps 136:13) for the miraculous passage of the fleeing Israelites; or the psalms, "I will bring them back from the depths of the sea" (Ps 68:22) and "he gathereth the waters of the sea together" (Ps 33:7); or Peter who, discovering that it was the risen Jesus walking on the shore, "did cast himself into the sea" (Jn 21:7). I "keep all these things," "ponder them" silently, allowing them to mix with observations of my own condition, until some perfume of incense rises from these coals.

This examination in silence of both the scriptures and myself "with more acute perception," with "minute understanding," is what fathers considered to be the real study of scripture, its study in relation to my own being. Gregory says, "We find many riches in ourselves, when in searching into the sacred writings, we receive gifts of abundant understandings" (*G/MBJ* 2: 553); or Bernard to his monks, in lines we have heard before: "Today the text we are to study is the book of our own experience. You must therefore turn your attention inwards, each one must take note of his own particular awareness of the things I am about to discuss" (*Bern/SS* 1: 16).

Symbolism and Translations of the Bible

The symbolic monastic language we have been discussing was based on the phrases and images of scripture. What Leclercq described in Chapter Two as the monks' "technical vocabulary" was a scriptural vocabulary. And since the Bible was not read in its original languages, the teachings were also tied to a particular translation of the text. For the Western church during the Middle Ages, that translation was the Latin Vulgate.[§]

Clearly, if a tradition tied to exact images and phrases in a text is to be preserved, care must be taken whenever that text is changed in any thoroughgoing way. The requirements of the tradition must be kept in mind. Translation into English is certainly a change of such a magnitude. In the sixteenth century, when the need for an English Bible began to be irresistible, the allegorical tradition had become seriously weakened even in monastic circles, and the new Protestant churches were militant in their rejection of traditional authority in the interpretation of scripture.

It was in this climate (which was not a climate in which the needs of the allegorical tradition were likely to carry much weight) that the translation of the Bible into English gained respectability. Two results of the move to an English text were the familiar King James Bible (also known as the "Authorized" version, as it was authorized by the king) and a clumsy, almost word-for-word translation of the Latin Vulgate called the Douai-Rheims Bible (commonly known as

[§]The name comes from the Latin word "vulgaris" which means "common" or "ordinary," from which we get "vulgar." Ironically, the translation received this name because, in its day, it represented a translation from Greek and Hebrew into the "common" or "shared" language of most citizens of the Roman Empire.

the Douai Bible).[§] For all its clumsiness, the Douai did maintain in English the textual basis for the traditional teachings. But the King James, now considered "traditional" by many people, was among the first of the truly modern Bibles—a deliberate attempt to break with a Latin tradition that was in disrepute.

Several examples will help illustrate the changes, from a contemplative point of view, which the King James Bible began. In the King James version, Psalm 31:19 reads: "Oh how great is thy goodness, which thou hast laid up for them that fear thee." The same verse in the Douai rendition of the Vulgate reads, "O how great is the multitude of thy sweetness, O Lord, which thou has hidden for them that fear thee." Two differences are important: "goodness/sweetness" and "laid up/hidden." The word "sweet" and its associated imagery of taste and smell are, as we have seen, at the heart of the traditional language of contemplative prayer. We become aware of God's presence in meditation, Gregory says, by a "deep inner sweetness." In the King James Bible, as in most English translations which have followed it, the sensual imagery of sweetness is almost entirely absent, replaced, as in the above psalm, with a more ethical language of "goodness." "Goodness" describes the quality of actions one performs outwardly; "sweetness" must be tasted inwardly. Or in different terms, "goodness" is a quality of action; "sweetness" is a quality of being.

Likewise, contemplative teaching gave importance to the sense of "hidden" as opposed to the more neutral verb "laid up," for two reasons. First, the tradition stresses that one must be properly prepared in order to taste this sweetness—it is unavailable to the worldly. And second, the desire and openness required for the search are required for the discovery. Part of the necessary preparation is the heightening of desire and the openness that come from the search.

The interior, traditional orientation of the Vulgate extends to many choices of word and image besides "hidden" and "sweet." In

[§]The Douai-Rheims Bible was begun by members of the English College at Douai (located in the portion of Flanders that is now France). In 1578 the College moved to Rheims, where the New Testament was published in 1582. The College eventually returned to Douai, where the the Old Testament was published in 1609.

Psalm 4, Augustine (*A/ACW* 1: 47–48) points to the verse, "By the fruit of their corn, their wine and oil, they are multiplied" as a reference to the destruction of inner unity, a quiet mind, by the "multiplying" effect of our attachments to material things ("corn," "wine," and "oil"). In the same psalm, Augustine takes the verse, "the light of thy countenance O Lord, is signed upon us"(Ps 4:6), to refer to Genesis 1:26, "Let us make man to our own image and likeness" and to Christ's contrast of the image of God with the image of Caesar on a Roman coin (Mt 22:21). That is, the image of God is signed, stamped, within us, whether we like it or not. And by the light of that image, we know, says Augustine, that joy "is to be looked for within, where the light of God's countenance is stamped upon us, for Christ has His dwelling place in a man's heart, as the Apostle has told us [Eph 3:17]." Indeed, says Augustine, "This light which shines upon the mind, not upon the eyes, constitutes mankind's whole and essential good." Later translations of Psalm 4 would not bear any of these interpretations, simply because the two words "multiply" and "signed" are missing: "Lord, lift thou up the light of thy countenance upon us. Thou hast put gladness in my heart, more than in the time that their corn and their wine increased" (Ps 4, KJV). The phrase "lift thou up" makes no reference to Genesis or Matthew or in any way suggests that the "image" of God's "countenance" is somehow imbedded in all of us. The King James version, "Lord, lift thou up the light of thy countenance upon us," is a plea to God to make his presence known, whereas the Vulgate rendering is an acknowledgment that his presence in a specific, hidden form, as his image, is always with us. The second line of the King James version says that the heart is made glad more readily by God than by an increase in material goods, but it makes no reference to the interior scattering or "multiplying" of the mind, which attachment to material goods can bring. The King James version no longer refers to an exact, psychological phenomenon which can be observed by anyone who pays careful, honest attention to the movements of his own mind.

A final comparison between the two versions will be particularly helpful in pointing up the strengths and weaknesses of each. The King James version of Psalm 23:5 concludes with eloquent simplicity and understated finality: "My cup runneth over." The Douai/Vulgate line is not so touchingly beautiful: "My chalice, which inebriateth me, how goodly is it!" For the monastic commentators, however, the image of drunkenness is important as another image of the opened, higher intelligence, a departure from the "sobriety" of the natural mind and its limitations. The simple eloquence of the King James rendering has unquestionable power, literary and spiritual. The Vulgate passage translates into awkward, Latinate English that is acceptable at best, certainly not "telling" as language. But the traditional imagery is maintained in the Douai translation of the Vulgate. If we wish to steep ourselves in this tradition, we have no choice but to turn, at least at some point in our study, to the Bible that belongs with it and, indeed, created it. This Bible also becomes essential, as we shall see in Chapter Five, when we consider excerpts of scripture used in texts for the chant.

The problem with the Vulgate is that its sources are a confused mixture. Some of it was translated from Hebrew originals by St. Jerome; some of it, including the important psalter, derives from other sources. Its Old Testament, including the psalter, was heavily influenced by a pre-Christian Greek Old Testament known as the "Septuagint." The origins of this work are also obscure, but, according to legend, the translation was made from Hebrew into Greek in Alexandria, Egypt, in the second or third century B.C.E., by a group of seventy (or seventy-two) translators who completed their work in seventy (or seventy-two) days; hence the name, "Septuagint," for seventy. The manuscript sources which they presumably used (presumably Hebrew sources) have disappeared. This translation differs substantially from Hebrew manuscripts which have survived, but many early Christian writers, including St. Augustine, believed that this translation was divinely inspired and that the translation of the Hebrew scriptures into a gentile tongue was one preparatory sign of the coming of Christ to Jews and gentiles alike.

So the Vulgate, with its roots in obscure soils, is hardly a pure text by modern critical standards. But a traditional teaching of tremendous importance, stretching over more than a thousand years, was based on the language and imagery of this Bible. And what of the King James? Early editions of this masterpiece contained a lengthy preface, "The Translators to the Reader," which provides us with a clear picture of the intentions of the translators. The preface discusses the tremendous authority of the Septuagint among early Christians, but in the end rejects that Old Testament and its Latin derivatives as "muddie," noting that the Greek sometimes "may be noted to add to the original, and sometimes to take from it."

The preface leaves no doubt that the King James translators were attempting to break with their Catholic past and establish a new beginning for a spirituality separate from that of Rome. Their antagonism to anything "Romish" is made clear. It is also true that some of the principles of scholarship set forth by the translators can be seen as a break with traditional thinking, as for example the assumption, only beginning to be questioned today, that the authority of existing written sources is to be preferred automatically to that of oral tradition.

At the same time, the translators were steeped in the old ways. Miles Coverdale, whose translation influenced the King James scholars heavily, is said to have been a passionate admirer of the monastic, allegorical tradition. And every page of the King James version speaks for the scholars' sure instinct for spiritual depth and beauty of language. They set out to create an alternative to the Roman Catholic Bible. Subsequent religious history in the English-speaking world—the passionate devotion of millions of thoughtful people to this text—can witness to their success.

And so, what of the King James? We might with some historical justification place it in perspective as a monumental text which in its time looked to both past and future. In many ways, it was filled with the spirit of the Christian millennium behind it; in other ways, as we've seen, it represented a first step in a new direction, away from traditional monastic thought and toward a modern spirituality. In practical terms, it is a Bible we can use because we love the language and because it retains more of the traditional imagery than later translations. For many readers, however, its language is more cumbersome than appealing. Newer translations such as the Revised Standard Version and its updates, the New Jerusalem and New English Bibles, all have their uses. But the Douai remains our only sure reference for traditional Vulgate wording which may in some cases be crucial, as we have seen.

Finished in the fifth century, the Vulgate was not the first Latin version of the Bible. Many of the fathers had access to what is known as the Old Latin version and to other fragmentary texts as well. The point of importance here is that they were undeterred by this multiplicity of translations. And this may be the last characteristic of the fathers' thinking we'll mention which inspires revolt in modern readers. When Gregory is aware of a translation whose phrasing would seem to disallow the interpretation he is currently expounding, he will say so, and propose a completely different reading for the second passage, feeling no obligation to reconcile the two. Again, he assumes that the text offers an infinite number of equally valid meanings. Here as elsewhere, the fathers' practice gives evidence of the radical truth of Gregory's observation: "To speak of God is to be of the most extreme quiet and freedom of mind" (*G/HHP* 182), where the accent is on "freedom."

Having examined several of the more troubling aspects of traditional, symbolic thinking, we must now turn to the chant texts themselves, created from scripture according to these same principles.

Chapter Five

Chant Texts and the Study of Scripture

THE STUDY OF SCRIPTURE

The purpose of the study of scripture from the fathers' point of view is to establish in the reader a conviction that the sacred writings come from God. The fathers assume that this essential fact will not be obvious to the unprepared mind. It must be revealed by the spirit, but the individual must be ready to hear that voice. As Guigo put it, "There is little sweetness in the study of the literal sense, unless there be a commentary, which is found in the heart, to reveal the inward sense" (*Guig* 76). In our own day, Jean Leclercq echoes his ancient predecessor and adds the essential condition:

> There is a book which the finger of God writes in the heart of each monk; no other can substitute for it. No written literature, even sacred literature, can dispense with the state of recollection essential for hearing God's word within one's self. (*Learning* 260)

The chant, as we have seen, can help guide us toward that essential "state of recollection," that is, it can help prepare the individual to receive the Word.

It is impossible to overstate either the importance or the difficulty of this preparation. The sacred quality which the tradition wishes to reveal in scripture will, as we saw in Chapter Four, evoke the most ingrained objections and resistances from the natural mind. Some of us may find this idea surprising. Who wouldn't welcome a closer relationship with God? But the ancient witnesses agree—and experience bears them out—that, in the actual encounter, we are seized with fear. And before the encounter, we are filled with suspicion and doubt. Or at least, a large part of us reacts with this negative force, a part which is in conflict with something else in us which welcomes the experience. In the Gospel of John, Jesus tells his followers that they must eat his flesh and drink his blood in order to discover the way to eternal life, and many "drew back and no longer went about with him" because of this "hard saying, who can listen to it?" (Jn 6:52–71). There is no clearer example in scripture of the mind's stubborn, even angry refusal to see beyond the literal, or of the crucial importance of doing so.

Because this preparation of the individual is both critical and difficult, the fathers understood that the text must also be prepared, if the necessary meeting between the scriptures and the inner mind is to take place. The text must be presented in ways that will evoke wonder and faith, rather than objections and resistance. Preparation of the text in specific ways, and indeed in similar ways, is evident in the fathers' commentary on scripture, in chant texts, in the medieval liturgies, and in certain parts of scripture itself.

Most obviously, the fathers interpret scripture in small pieces, sentence by sentence or even phrase by phrase. In discussing a passage from Job or Ezekiel, Gregory brings in short lines from other parts of the Old Testament, the gospels, the letters of Paul, or the psalms. Gregory's "exegesis," or interpretation of scripture, is thus "patchwork" in form, as is monastic exegesis in general. Using scriptural phrases, the interpreter creates his own pattern, his own context, based on the main passage which is being considered. The chant likewise presents scripture in small bits—the text of an antiphon may be as short as a single sentence. Even a "long" chant such as a great responsory may be only two or three sentences. When we begin to notice the importance of the simple idea that contemplative teaching is delivered in short pieces of text, we notice that even the gospels themselves are collections of short sayings, vignettes, and stories, none more than a few verses long.

The Old Testament "Wisdom literature" also—Proverbs, Ecclesiastes, The Song of Songs, Ecclesiasticus, The Book of Wisdom—all of these books are "patchwork" in character, collections of short sayings, like the chant and like the fathers' exegesis.

The patchwork quality of all these forms is related to the monks' understanding of the nature of the inner intelligence which must be reached if the primary purpose of the study of scripture is to be served. A favorite monastic metaphor for such study is "feeding," as Guigo puts it:

> I hear the words read: "Blessed are the pure in heart, for they shall see God" [Mt 5:8]. This is a short text of Scripture, but it is of great sweetness, like a grape that is put into the mouth filled with many senses to feed the soul. . . . So, wishing to have a fuller understanding of this [short verse], the soul begins to bite and chew upon this grape, as though putting it in a wine press. (*Guig* 69)

Guigo points out further that these "fragments" of scripture are like the bread of the Eucharist, the "Word made flesh" and broken for each believer:

> That portion of [scripture] which has been distributed to you is the fragment put in your mouth; but unless you reflect, often and devoutly, on what you believe, unless you will as it were break it up into small pieces with your teeth, that is, with your spiritual senses, chewing it and turning it over in your mouth, it will stick in your throat, that is, it will not go down into your understanding. . . . And yet you still cannot think at one and the same time about all that you believe, or understand at once all that you think, but only by degrees and as it were in fragments; and so your food can be properly prepared only by great labor. (*Guig* 120)

The inner mind must be fed in small pieces because, as we have seen, it is a special kind of intelligence, one able to "examine the meaning of things with more acute perception," with "minute understanding," to see that in scripture "there is no slightest detail which is without significance" (*Bern/SS* 4: 69), that "not even one iota or one dot in the word of God is insignificant [Mt 5:18]" (*Orig/CWS* 265). This is an intelligence which sees in symbols and focuses on detail, an intelligence which is compatible with the sacred text—text which contains many levels of meaning in every fragment, the whole, even, in every part.

This patchwork quality of the chant appears in two ways: first, phrases from different parts of scripture are sometimes brought together to form the text for a single chant; second, the medieval forms of the Eucharist, Matins, Lauds, and Vespers contain a number of chants which are "proper to the day," that is, used for only one particular day in the year. The texts for these proper chants will be taken from different parts of the Bible, and, when heard together as one service, will form a patchwork which illuminates the essential character of the feast of the day. Thus, the chant's patchwork character may appear both in a single text and in a collection of texts used for a single liturgy.

Wherever it occurs, this gathering of scriptural passages from widely separated parts of the Bible creates a new script, a new mini-text, with its own special focus. In both the liturgy and monastic commentary, we can identify at least five principles which are served by this gathering process. First, in the case of the liturgy for a feast, texts are selected to identify the major themes of the day. Most often, one or more of the chant texts will include a condensed narrative of the scriptural events on which the feast is based. The choice of scriptural phrases within the narrative will emphasize the most important of the actual events. Second, this process of selecting texts which present the themes of the day serves to make the individual aware of the many scattered instances in scripture where the feast is mentioned or alluded to, literally or prophetically. Often these allusions are unexpected, as we will see below when we examine the chant texts for the Ascension. In these cases, a third principle is served: emphasis on the symbolic and prophetic nature of the text. Psalm 99:2 reads, "The Lord is great in Zion; he is high above all peoples." The line is clearly praising the exalted nature of God, but, because it is an antiphon for the Ascension, the line acquires an unmistakable symbolic quality as a prophetic allusion to the Ascension of Jesus.

The fourth purpose of the textual gathering process is the personalizing of the feast for the individual. In the liturgy, this purpose is often achieved by one or more chant texts which use Biblical phrasing but give that phrasing a distinctly personal turn. For example, the Magnificat antiphon for Second Vespers of the Ascension draws on language from John, Psalm 24, and Acts in order to include the worshiper as one of those who watched the Savior depart and are fervently relying on his final promises: "O king of glory, lord of hosts [Ps 24:10], who ascended today in triumph above the heavens, do not leave us orphans [Jn 14:18], but send the promised one of the Father into us [Acts 1:4], the Spirit of Truth [Jn 15:26]."§

Finally and, perhaps, most importantly, the practice of both the liturgy and monastic commentary bear unmistakable witness to the fundamental unity of scripture. One of the most interesting examples of this witness is the construction of texts for the responsories. A responsory usually consists of two sentences of text, set to different music. The first of these, with its music, is called the "respond" and is sung by the entire choir. The second is called the "verse," sung by cantors. The verse and respond texts often come from different parts of scripture. After the cantors finish the verse, the entire choir repeats a part of the respond text, beginning at a designated place within the sentence. What makes this form interesting is that the texts make sense in all three combinations. The repeated phrase makes sense within its own sentence; the verse, though from a different part of scripture, makes sense with the respond, and the repeated portion makes sense as a follow-up to the verse. (Some responsories even appear in different manuscript sources with different verses, all of which, as a rule, fit

---

§In this chapter all translations of Latin chant texts are by the author. When chant texts contain references to scripture, these are identified within brackets. Some scriptural references are "quotations"; others are more approximate echoes. The specific translation of the scriptural reference or quotation is cited in this context only when the exact wording of that translation is critical (i.e., when the Latin Bible differs from the KJV and the RSV). Most scriptural references without citations have been taken from the RSV.

smoothly into the pattern of meaning.) As an example, here is the fourth responsory at Matins for the Ascension:

Respond: I will not leave you orphans [Jn 14:18]. I go, and I come to you [Jn 14:28]. And your heart shall be joyful [Jn 16:22].

Verse: In that day you shall know that I am in my Father, and you are in me, and I am in you [Jn 14:20]. And your heart shall be joyful.

The key idea is in the repeated phrase, "And your heart shall be joyful." And that phrase has one meaning when it appears in the first sentence (the respond) and a different and more powerful meaning when it is repeated alone after the verse. Obviously, this chant text, like hundreds of others, has been carefully constructed to allow it to read in different directions, so to speak. But despite the care of that construction, the chant delivers a clear, underlying teaching about the unity of scripture, and delivers it in an understated way, a way that appeals to the symbolic mind but could easily go unnoticed by our everyday reflections. It is delivered in the spirit of the gospels, "He who has ears to hear, let him hear" (Lk 8:8). This teaching insists that, to the mystical mind, any line of scripture "makes sense" placed next to any other line, since the message of all, the everlasting love of God, is the same.

By means of these five principles, the scripture and the liturgy together become extended "guiding symbols" which lead us to understand how sacred meaning is perceived and transmitted, how the language of wisdom and wonder is written. We know that there are kinds of knowledge and study which build faith, and there are kinds of study, even of scripture, which give us interesting information but are indifferent to faith. The fathers' teaching is clearly in the former category. In the Gospel of Luke, when the disciples ask Jesus to "increase our faith" (Lk 17:5), he replies by explaining what faith is. It must have the quality of the kingdom of God, must be "as a mustard seed" (Lk 13:19; 17:6). This kind of faith will enable the individual to perceive the spiritual meaning of material life, that is, to uproot the sycamore from the earth and make it grow in the midst of the "sea."

The fathers give a similar answer to our practical question, "How do we study the scriptures so as to increase our faith?" Seldom do any of the monastic writers say specifically, "Do this and do that." (One valuable exception is Guigo II's *The Ladder of Monks*; see Bibliography.) Rather, by the way they treat scripture in their commentaries and in the older liturgies, they point again and again to its essential character, its inner nature. They show us what scripture is. Our job is to approach it in ways which are compatible with the character which we see revealed by what they do. Listening to the words of scripture with a quiet mind is certainly one of these ways. Reciting the words of scripture in community and with gathered attention, as in the chant, must be another. The discussion which follows in this chapter assumes that it may also be valuable to observe carefully "what they do"—how the tradition has handled scripture in the chant texts of the older liturgies. But this kind of discussion is, admittedly, of only preliminary value, as illustration. At best, it may clarify the nature of these liturgies as "guiding symbols"—some of their characteristic ways of working— in order to help those who are new to their language enter more readily into the experience of scripture in the liturgy itself.

THE CONSTRUCTION OF SINGLE CHANT TEXTS

The most important of the "Day Hours" are Lauds, Vespers, and Compline. The liturgical highpoint of each of these is a Gospel Canticle, which for Vespers is the Magnificat. Consequently, the most elaborate and characteristic chant of Vespers is the antiphon which accompanies the Magnificat. On the seven days preceding Christmas Eve, these antiphons are particularly interesting. They are all sung to essentially the same melody, and all the texts are similar in form. Each opens with an address to a characteristic "Name" of the expected Savior: "O Wisdom," "O Root of Jesse," "O Emmanuel," and so on. Because of the identical form of these openings, they are called as a group the "Great O Antiphons." (The familiar Advent hymn, "O come Emmanuel" is modeled loosely on this set of antiphons.) In each antiphon, the opening "Name" of the

Savior is followed by a list of characteristics which follow from that name, then the Latin single-word plea "veni" (come), followed by a result that is expected from the advent or "coming" of that particular set of qualities.

These antiphons are among the oldest in the chant repertory (they appear in *The Hartker Antiphonal*, the oldest surviving, complete manuscript of chants for the Office), and as a group they provide, at the end of the season of Advent, a powerful summary of just exactly what this season of expectation and preparation has been preparing *for*. Several of the group are also typical of the way in which a single chant draws together phrases and images from different parts of the Bible to illustrate the meaning of the day, to direct our attention to those parts of scripture which define that meaning, to reveal the prophetic quality of scripture, and to demonstrate the unity of both its message and its imagery.

A good example of these qualities is the antiphon often assigned to December 20, "O Clavis David" (O Key of David). (Music for this antiphon is included in Appendix 9, along with a pointed text of the Magnificat.) The text, in Latin and English, is as follows, with the phrases numbered for convenient discussion:

> 1) O clavis David, 2) et sceptrum domus Israel; 3) qui aperis, et nemo claudit; claudis, et nemo aperit: 4) veni, et educ vinctum de domo carceris, sedentem in tenebris 5) et umbra mortis.

> 1) O key of David, 2) and scepter of the house of Israel, 3) you who open and no one shuts, shut and no one opens: 4) Come, and lead the prisoner out from the house of bondage, sitting in darkness 5) and in the shadow of death.

The central image, the key which opens and shuts, appears both in Isaiah and the Revelation to John. But let's look first at the secondary phrases. The image of the "scepter" echoes a Messianic prophecy from Genesis (the prophetic intention of the chant text is clearer in the Vulgate than in the Revised Standard Version): "The sceptre shall not be taken away from Juda, nor a ruler from his thigh, till he come that is to be sent, and he shall be the expectation of nations" (Gn 49:10, DR). To a mind steeped in scripture, the image of the "sceptre" is sufficient to recall the entire prophecy.

Phrase 4 uses exactly the Latin word choice of Isaiah 42: "And I have given you for a covenant of the people, for a light of the Gentiles: That you might open the eyes of the blind, and *lead the prisoner out of prison, and from the house of bondage those sitting in darkness*" (Is 42:6–7, Vulg,[§] emphasis mine)—although the antiphon text has been slightly compacted and shifted from plural to singular. But for the compiler of this text, the most crucial power of the key is over the gates of death, and, in order to add the prophecy of the Resurrection, he draws on at least three other passages that associate "sitting in darkness" with "the shadow of death." Perhaps the clearest parallel in wording is to Psalm 107 [Ps 106, Vulg[§§]]: "And he brought them out of darkness, and the shadow of death, and broke their bonds in sunder" (Ps 107:14, DR). Again, the parallel exists only in the Vulgate.[§§§]

Let us return now to the central image of the text, the key of David. In Isaiah, the key is promised to a specific ruler, Eliakim, who according to Isaiah will not be ultimately successful but will "give way":

> And I will place on his shoulder the key of the house of David; he shall open, and none shall shut; and he shall shut, and none shall open. And I will fasten him like a peg in a sure place, and he will become a throne of honor to his father's house. . . . In that day, says the Lord of hosts, the peg that was fastened in a sure place will give way; and it will be cut down and fall. (Is 22:22–23,25, RSV)

Eliakim's ultimate failure, however, does not affect the mystical power of the "key of David," mentioned here in scripture for the

---

[§]Passages in English identified as "Vulg"—for Vulgate, the Bible in Latin—are actually renderings by the author directly from the Vulgate into English in order to preserve some feature not found in the traditional English version of the Latin Bible, the Douai-Rheims. Quotations taken directly from the Douai-Rheims bear the citation "DR."

[§§]Psalm numbering throughout most of the Vulgate psalter is one behind the Hebrew numbering with which modern readers are familiar.

[§§§]The better-known parallel, thanks to Handel's *Messiah*, is Isaiah 9:2, KJV, echoed in Matthew 4:16.

first time. Isaiah's key returns in the Revelation, identified by the similar wording: "And to the angel of the church in Philadelphia write: 'The words of the holy one, the true one, who has *the key of David, who opens and no one shall shut, who shuts and no one opens'*" (Rev 3:7, RSV, emphasis mine).

The image of the key and its mystic function is echoed in Matthew 16, when Jesus gives to Peter "the keys of the kingdom of heaven, and whatever you bind on earth, shall be bound in heaven; and whatever you loose on earth shall be loosed in heaven" (Mt 19, RSV). And the image of the key is also meant to evoke related images of doors and gates. Two possibilities are these from the gospels:

> And he said to them, "Strive to enter by the narrow door; for many, I tell you, will seek to enter and will not be able. When once the householder has risen up and shut the door, you will begin to stand outside and to knock at the door, saying, 'Lord, open to us.' He will answer you, 'I do no know where you come from.'" (Lk 13:23–25, RSV)

> I am the door; if any one enters by me, he will be saved, and will go in and out and find pasture. (Jn 10:9)

We can readily see how the text has been constructed to achieve its ends, one of which is to underscore the symbolic, prophetic nature of the Old Testament phrases. But the text itself does not guide us toward any contemplative interpretation of its message. For that we must turn to Bernard, who understands the door as scripture itself. In his comments on The Song of Songs 1:4, Bernard refers to his own interpretive efforts and those of his "listeners" or readers as a process of "knocking" on this "door" of scripture:

> But it [The Song of Songs 1:4] is a door on which you are given time to knock. Those who are sincere will there encounter him whose light illumines mysteries; and he will open at once, because he invites you to knock. He it is who opens and no man shuts, the Church's Bridegroom, Jesus Christ our Lord, who is blessed for ever. (*Bern/SS* 2: 57)

Chant Texts and the Study of Scripture

THE GATHERING OF TEXTS WITHIN A SINGLE LITURGY

The patchwork construction of chant texts is sometimes evident within a single chant, as we have just seen, but is always evident within a complete liturgy, in which the patchwork is formed by a number of different chants working together. Vespers for Saturday before the Third Sunday of Advent includes four antiphons, a short lesson, a short responsory, a hymn and versicle, and an antiphon for the Magnificat. We will not consider the hymn, since—like most hymns, ancient and modern—it is a poetic composition independent of scripture. And before we consider these other texts, we need to think for a moment about Advent itself in the monastic tradition. Advent is a season of preparation. Sermons in parish churches often remind us that we are called to prepare for two very different events, the celebration of the birth of Christ at Christmas, and the Second Coming of Christ at the end of time. The second event, especially, gives the season its penitential character, since the Second Coming is to be a time of judgment.

In the monastery, however, the primary aim of the monks' contemplative work was preparation for the inward appearance of Christ as Wisdom or the Word, which could occur at any moment. Contemplative discipline is all about preparation; the monks, one could say, were specialists in this art. This year-long, inner focus on the coming of Christ adds a third, inward dimension to the monastic view of Advent. Bernard describes this experience of the Word in several places, including the following:

> It is beyond question that the vision is all the more delightful the more inward it is, and not external. It is the Word, who penetrates without sound; who is effective though not pronounced, who wins the affections without striking on the ears. His face, though without form, is the source of form, it does not dazzle the eyes of the body but gladdens the watchful heart. (*Bern/SS* 2: 129)

By now we are familiar with the form of Bernard's account. It is rich with specifics derived from his experience, but it is also too reticent to mention that experience directly. Elsewhere in these sermons, however, Bernard breaks with the usual restraints of tact and speaks in a direct, personal tone almost like that of the later fourteenth-century mystics. He is clearly uncomfortable with such a personal disclosure, but he continues, amid apologies and disclaimers. The passage is exceptional enough to quote in full:

> Now bear with my foolishness for a little [2 Cor 11:1]. I want to tell you of my own experience, as I promised. Not that it is of any importance [2 Cor 12:1]. But I make this disclosure only to help you, and if you derive any profit from it I shall be consoled for my foolishness; if not, my foolishness will be revealed. I admit that the Word has also come to me—I speak as a fool—and has come many times [2 Cor 11:17]. But although he has come to me, I have never been conscious of the moment of his coming. I perceived his presence, I remembered afterwards that he had been with me; sometimes I had a presentiment that he would come, but I was never conscious of his coming or his going [Ps 121:8]. And where he comes from when he visits my soul, and where he goes, and by what means he enters and goes out, I admit that I do not know even now; as John says: "You do not know where he comes from or where he goes" [Jn 3:8]. There is nothing strange in this, for of him was it said, "Your footsteps will not be known" [Ps 77:19]. The coming of the Word was not perceptible to my eyes, for he has no color; nor to my ears, for there was no sound; nor yet to my nostrils, for he mingles with the mind, not the air; he has not acted upon the air, but created it. His coming was not tasted by the mouth, for there was no eating or drinking, nor could he be known by the sense of touch, for he is not tangible. How then did he enter? Perhaps he did not enter because he does not come from outside? He is not one of the things which exist outside us [1 Cor 5:12]. Yet he does not come from within me, for he is good, & I know that there is no good in me [Ps 52:9]. . . . You ask then how I knew he was present, when his ways can in no way be traced? [Rom 11:33]. He is life and power [Heb 4:12], and as soon as he enters in, he awakens my slumbering soul; he stirs and soothes and pierces my heart [Sg 4:9], for before it was hard as stone [Ecclus 3:27; Ez 11:19, 36:26], and diseased. . . . So when the Bridegroom, the Word, came to me he never made known his coming by any signs. . . . Only by the movement of my heart, as I have told you, did I perceive his presence. . . . But when the Word has left me, all

134

these spiritual powers become weak and faint and begin to grow cold, as though you had removed the fire from under a boiling pot, and this is the sign of his going. (*Bern/SS* 4: 90–91, 92)

From the contemplative point of view, then, Advent is a season of preparation for the Second Coming, of preparation for the yearly festival of Christ's birth, and of attention to the ever-present possibility of the interior "birth" of Christ the Word. With these three aspects of the Advent season in mind, we may now turn our attention to the texts of Vespers for Saturday before the Third Sunday. The versicle is taken word for word from Isaiah 45:8: "Rorate caeli desuper, et nubes pluant justum. Aperiature terra et germinet salvatorem." (Drop down dew, heavens, from above, and let the clouds pour down the just. Let the earth open and bring forth a savior.) As versicles often are, it is poetic and central to the meaning of this liturgy. It is also somewhat enigmatic and symbolic in its intent. Bernard sees in these lines the central effect of the advent of Christ, the reconciliation of spirit and flesh, earth and heaven:

> In due course, while the heavens showered from above and the skies rained down the Just one, the earth opened for a Savior to spring up, and heaven and earth were reconciled. "For he is the peace between us, and has made the two into one" [Col 1:20], making peace by his blood between all things in heaven and on earth. (*Bern/SS* 2: 29)

The details of the two actions—the pouring down from heaven and the receptive opening of the earth—also suggest the now familiar balance of contemplation and action which results in the appearance of "blessing" or, here, "the Savior" (see Chapter Two).

The short lesson for this liturgy is from Philippians, and only its last phrase specifically suggests Advent: "Rejoice in the Lord always, and again I say rejoice; let your modesty be known to all people; *the Lord is near*" (Phil 4:4–5, emphasis mine). But its ties to the season are deeper. Philippians is the most eager and affectionate of all of Paul's letters. He has no reprimand for them, no threats for the faithless. But lying in prison and uncertain of his own future, he has the theme of "last things" on his mind:

For to me to live is Christ, and to die is gain. If it is to be life in the flesh, that means fruitful labor for me. Yet which I shall choose I cannot tell. I am hard pressed between the two. (Phil 1:21–23)

But it is the joy of his fellowship with the church at Philippi that turns these thoughts in a positive direction. The return of Christ is on his mind, but it is not a day of judgment he foresees; it is a day of glorious consummation of work begun in joy and continued in faith:

I thank my God in all my remembrance of you, always in every prayer of mine for you all making my prayer with joy, thankful for your partnership in the gospel from the first day until now. And I am sure that he who began a good work in you will bring it to completion at the day of Jesus Christ. (Phil 1:3–6, RSV)

He is sure that this young church will be "pure and blameless for the day of Christ, filled with the fruits of righteousness" (Phil 1:10, RSV). Unlike the Old Testament prophets' "day of the Lord," the "day of Christ" Paul evokes is filled with blessing, "the peace of God, which passes all understanding" (Phil 4:7) and evokes Paul's thoughts of "whatever is pure, whatever is lovely, whatever is gracious" (Phil 4:8).

For monks who knew the scriptures by heart, all these associations could be evoked by these two short verses of Paul's letter. And to minds accustomed to hearing on several levels at once, the last phrase, "The Lord is near," would mean not only that his Second Coming, the end of history, is near but that his presence is always at hand and that the monk's own awakening to that presence is likewise just a hair's breadth away at every moment.

The responsory to the lesson is more straightforward and less rich in overtones. It is a simple prayer that the promised salvation should arrive: "Show us you mercy, O Lord, and grant us your salvation" (Ps 85:7).

The first of the four psalm antiphons is short but compact, consisting of three distinct phrases:

1) Veniet Dominus et non tardabit, 2) ut illuminet abscondita tenebrarum, 3) et manifestabit se ad omnes gentes alleluia.

1) The Lord will come and will not tarry, 2) that he might illuminate the hidden things of darkness, 3) and reveal himself to all nations alleluia.

Phrase 1 is taken from Hebrews 10:37, whose writer is quoting Habakkuk 2:3–4. The context in Hebrews is appropriate to Advent, filled with exhortations to "hold fast the confession of our hope without wavering" to have "patience" (Vulg) in order to hold out and receive the promise, to fear judgment, and to encourage one another in the faith "all the more as you see the Day drawing near."

Phrase 3 is not found in scripture exactly. The subphrase "all nations," however, is significant. Its Latin original, "omnes gentes," is used more than a hundred and fifty times throughout the scriptures, including such crucial moments as the first promise of God to Abraham: "And by your descendants *all the nations* of the earth shall bless themselves" (Gn 22:18; 26:4, RSV, emphasis mine); Christ's commissioning of the apostles to "go therefore and make prophets of *all nations*" (Mt 28:19; Lk 24:47, emphasis mine); and the song of those who have overcome, singing the "Song of Moses and the Song of the Lamb" (Rev 15:4). To monks steeped in the Vulgate imagery, "all nations" would resonate with virtually the entire salvation story from beginning to end.

Phrase 2 is especially interesting: "That he might illuminate the hidden things of darkness." Except for a change of mood in the verb, it follows the Vulgate translation of 1 Corinthians 4:5 exactly. The Phrase 2 imagery of darkness and "hiddenness" is important in itself, as we shall see, but it also evokes the larger context of 1 Corinthians 4:5 which is central to the monk's calling. Before we turn to the exact language of phrase 2, we must consider this larger context.

At this point in 1 Corinthians, Paul addresses the fact that there are factions among the Christians in Corinth, defined by their teachers in the faith. One group follows Paul, who first brought the new gospel to Corinth, and others prefer "Apollos," who apparently came after Paul to continue the work he had begun: "According to the commission of God given to me, like a skilled master builder I laid a foundation, and another man is building upon it" (1 Cor 3:10, RSV). Paul accepts Apollos' authority, and his argument is in part unremarkable. As we would expect, he presses the point that both men are legitimate teachers and that the results are what count, not personalities. But in making this point, he uses imagery which is particularly central to monastic tradition—images of building and of agriculture, growing.

According to Paul, inner growth, the formation of the image of Christ within, depends on work done by each individual, who must construct the inner building on the foundation of Christ, a foundation which is laid by the teacher. Or again in alternative imagery, each individual must cultivate the garden which has been planted. It is in this context that we find the well-known line, "Do you not know that you are God's temple, and that God's spirit dwells in you?" (1 Cor 3:16). We realize perhaps with surprise that this "temple" within is not a given; it does not exist until it is constructed by the individual. Some will build well and some not so well, and it is at the "Day" of Christ that the quality of work will be revealed:

> Now if any one builds on the foundation with gold, silver, precious stones, wood, hay, stubble—each man's work will become manifest; for the Day will disclose it, because it will be revealed with fire, and the fire will test what sort of work each one has done. (1 Cor 3:12–13, RSV)

At the day of judgment, each Christian will suffer loss if this work has been faulty, but not a fatal loss:

> If the work which any man has built on the foundation survives [the fire], he will receive a reward. If any man's work is burned up, he will suffer loss, though he himself will be saved, but only as through fire. (1 Cor 3:14–15, RSV)

Lurking just below the surface here is the controversy over salvation by works or by faith, which ripped through the church at the Reformation. Monastic teaching avoids the controversy by taking, characteristically, an inward view that preserves the importance of both and the balance between them. Here, the "work" is itself inner. Clearly the "building" or "husbandry" that Paul speaks of is spiritual, the nurturing of the kind of deeper intelligence which has been a central theme of this book. This kind of inner "work" was the monk's most important business; it was, as we've just said, central to his calling, and so it was taken very seriously. The chanting of the liturgy was a central part of this business. The word "liturgy" itself comes from the Greek word for "work" and in the monastery the liturgy was called "opus Dei," "the work of God." Paul makes clear that there are serious consequences at judgment if this work is not done well, but the consequences are serious rather than final. Salvation does not, in the end, depend on the result, since "he will suffer loss, though he himself will be saved." Thus, for the monk hearing this Advent antiphon, two of the major themes of the season are closely linked: preparation for judgment and preparation for the appearance of the interior Word at any moment. It is only at final judgment that the quality of the monk's daily preparation through the years will be revealed.

It is here that the imagery of darkness and "hiddenness" in phrase 2 becomes important: "That he might illuminate the hidden things of darkness." In the context of Paul's letter, the quality of the individual's work of preparation is the primary "thing of darkness" that is to be "illuminated." But the power of the image has associations far beyond this particular context. For the symbolic mind, as we saw in Chapter Four, the literal meaning of a phrase is only one of several meanings, all of which may be held to be true at once. In this case, Paul's choice of language evokes the tradition's repeated emphasis on the central importance of the "mystery" of faith, the great truths "hidden in darkness." The Word is always alive. "I AM" is always present, life-giving, and ultimately unknown. Paul's language connects to several other key passages often quoted by the fathers:

> For there is not any thing secret that shall not be made manifest, nor hidden, that shall not be known and come abroad. Take heed therefore how you hear. (Lk 8:17–18, and similar lines in Lk 12:2–3, Mt 10:26, and Mk 4:22)

> And I will give thee hidden treasures, and the concealed riches of secret places, that thou mayest know that I am the Lord who call thee by thy name, the God of Israel. (Is 45:3, DR)

O how great is the multitude of thy sweetness, O Lord, which thou hast hidden for them that fear thee? (Ps 31:20, DR) [Ps 30:20, Vulg]

For I would have you know, what manner of care I have for you and for them that are at Laodicea, and whosoever have not seen my face in the flesh, that their hearts may be comforted, being instructed in charity, and unto all riches of fulness of understanding, unto the knowledge of the mystery of God the Father and of Christ Jesus, in whom are hid all the treasures of wisdom and knowledge. (Col 2:1–3, DR)

Now we see only in a riddle and in a mirror, but then we shall see face to face [1 Cor 13:12]. (*Bern/SS* 3: 103)

Origen brings two of these passages together in his interpretation of the "treasure hidden in a field" of Jesus' parable:

Now all these truths, as we have said, are concealed hidden and buried in the narratives of holy Scripture, because "the kingdom of heaven is like treasure hidden in a field, which a man found and covered up. Then in his joy he goes and sells all that he has and buys that field [Mt 13:44]." Consider very carefully whether this passage does not point out the fact that the soil and surface, so to speak, of Scripture, that is, the meaning according to the letter, is the "field" filled and flowering with plants of all kinds, while the deeper and more profound spiritual meaning is "the treasures of wisdom and knowledge" [Col 2:3], which the Holy Spirit through Isaiah calls "obscure, invisible, and hidden treasures [Is 45:3]." (*Orig/CWS* 198–199)

The "advent" or inner appearance of the mind of Christ, the opening of dove's eyes, is consistently interpreted by the monastic fathers as the momentary illumination of some aspect of these hidden mysteries of faith. Bernard describes this moment:

. . . when the conscience has been cleansed and tranquillized and there follows an immediate and unaccustomed expansion of the mind, an infusion of light that illuminates the intellect to understand Scripture and comprehend the mysteries. (*Bern/SS* 3: 102)

The second of the four psalm antiphons works very differently from the first:

Jerusalem gaude gaudio magno, quia veniet tibi Salvator alleluia.

Jerusalem, rejoice with great joy, for a Savior will come to you alleluia.

First, we must know that, for the fathers, "Jerusalem" was often a symbol of contemplative vision:

> For "Jerusalem" means the vision of peace. What then does it signify, that our Lord sits on a she ass, and guides it to Jerusalem, except that when He possesses simple minds by ruling over them, He leads them by His own sacred indwelling to the vision of peace? (*G/MBJ* 3: 689–690)

"Jerusalem," then, is that place in ourselves where "by a deep inner sweetness we may apprehend God" (*G/HHP* 234). A "daughter of Jerusalem" is in one sense the individual soul, and Jerusalem itself is the precise place in us to which the Savior is coming in simplicity, "mounted on an ass" (Mt 21:5), that one place within us which is able to receive him without reservation, with unadulterated joy.

The wording of this antiphon does not exactly match any passage of scripture, but echoes at least three:

> Shout for joy, O daughter of Jerusalem: Behold thy King will come to thee . . . riding upon an ass. (Zech 9:9, DR[§])

> Rejoice, and give praise together, O ye deserts of Jerusalem: for the Lord hath comforted his people: he hath redeemed Jerusalem. (Is 52:9, DR)

> Give praise, O daughter of Sion: shout, O Israel: be glad, and rejoice with all thy heart, O daughter of Jerusalem. (Zeph 3:14, DR)[§§]

By quoting none of these exactly, the antiphon is able to evoke all of them. And it adds one telling phrase which is found in none of the above passages, "gaudio magno" (with great joy). This phrase occurs only four times in the Latin Old Testament, in verses of no special significance, and twice in the New, once when the Wise Men see the star leading them to Bethlehem after they visit Herod—"When they saw the star, they rejoiced exceedingly with great joy"

[§]In Douai-Rheims, for Zechariah, see Zacharias.
[§§]In the Vulgate, see Sophonias 3:14.

(Mt 2:10, RSV)—and again in the very last verse of the Gospel of Luke, describing the disciples after Jesus' Ascension. Here their joy is also associated with the city: "And they returned to Jerusalem with great joy, and were continually in the temple blessing God" (Lk 24:52–3, RSV). The force of this short phrase by evocation frames the story of Jesus at its beginning and its end. The effect would not have been lost on ears which knew this one Latin text by heart and were celebrating Advent, a time of preparation for the beginning of that same story. The question we are tempted to ask today in our skepticism—wasn't this choice of words accidental?— would not have made sense to the fathers. In their world, there is no accident, only the movements of the spirit constantly making manifest the underlying, universal presence.

The third antiphon is taken entirely from Isaiah 46:12:

Dabo in Sion salutem, et in Jerusalem gloriam meam alleluia.

I will give salvation in Sion, and my glory in Jerusalem alleluia.

Sion, or Zion, is the name given in scripture to the ancient fortified hill which later became the city of Jerusalem. Scholars are not certain where the name originated, and in scripture it has many uses related to this basic one. It is also, for example, the "holy mountain" on which the "heavenly Jerusalem" will be built. Inwardly, it is the elevation of mind (the "hill") which opens the gates to the "vision of peace" within. The prophets say (Is 2; Mic 4) that in "the latter days" Jerusalem will be the center of the gathering together of the nations. The "mountain of the house of the Lord," or Zion, will be "established as the highest of the mountains" and "all nations shall flow to it" (Is 2:2, RSV).§ Because the gathering of the tribes is a persistent symbol for the inner gathering of the scattered thoughts and parts of the self, the images of the hill of Zion and the city of Jerusalem are powerful symbols of the center and the reward of contemplative effort. Inner significance is given to the walls, gates, and, especially, watch towers of the hill. A

§For "all nations" the Vulgate again uses the important phrase "omnes gentes" (see discussion of the first of four antiphons.)

"daughter of Zion" is a soul whose walls protect it from warring thoughts, but whose gates are open for the entrance of the divine king, and whose towers are vigilant. The "latter days" refers to the end of time but, inwardly, to the moment when the mind is still and the eyes of the heart open to a different perception of time.

The fourth antiphon is taken from Paul's letter to Titus:

> Juste et pie vivamus, expectantes beatam spem, et adventum Domini. (Titus 2:12–13)

> We should live justly and with blessing, sustaining a blessed hope, the coming of the Lord.

In this letter, Paul, "the greatest of contemplatives" (*Bern/SS* 3: 102–103), is almost exclusively concerned with the active life, with administrative arrangements, and with moral guidance: how Christians under Titus' care should act in public. In a few brief lines, however, he goes to the source of his advice and raises the Advent theme that all good behavior and right action derives from the presence, the coming, of the Holy Spirit (Titus 2:11–13; 3:4–6). With these references, Paul also raises one of the most basic of all questions facing those who follow a contemplative way: how to maintain a connection to the inner source while one is taken up with business in the outer world. The fathers deal with this question often, but what they have to say boils down to a single idea, the need for a constant return to "the secret recesses of the heart" (*G/MBJ* 1: 447) where the renewing spirit dwells. It is only by such a disciplined return that it is possible to "sustain a blessed hope" for the "coming of the Lord," either in historical time or in contemplation. Our clue to the monks' interest here is evident in the Latin but not in any of the English translations. We have already met (see Chapter 2) the Latin "pie," meaning "blessed" or, here, "blessedly," as a term used in the tradition specifically for the quality of grace which comes from a proper balance of the active and contemplative lives.

The antiphon's first word, "juste" (justly), also has connotations which are not captured by the major English versions: "righteously"

(KJV), or "upright" (RSV), even the literal Douai ("justly"). "Juste" and various other forms of the Latin word "justitia" are used in the Vulgate over a thousand times. The word represents a pervasive idea which involves more than legal or social fairness, although those are not excluded. The King James and Revised Standard versions most often translate these forms as "righteousness" or "righteous." But these terms have also come to have very narrow, moralistic connotations in modern ears. As Paul makes clear, the source of moral action is a state of being by which one is open to the spirit. The "just" or "righteous" person is one who is both ordered within and firmly "connected" through discipline to that source. A person in such a condition is a source of life and health to others (although few, as we have seen, are in this condition continuously). We begin to get the full sense of the character of the "righteous" or "just" person if we listen carefully to the imagery of the lines in which he is described. Consistently that imagery is of a flourishing tree, as in the psalms:

> The righteous shall flourish like a palm tree, and shall spread abroad like a cedar of Lebanon. Those who are planted in the house of the LORD shall flourish in the courts of our God; they shall still bear fruit in old age; they shall be green and succulent. (Ps 92:11–13)

And so this fourth and last of the psalm antiphons looks to the demands of the exterior world, the world of action, and calls our attention to that book in the New Testament (Titus) which is *most* concerned with that world. But even here, the antiphon reminds us, it is the inner advent of the spirit which makes this life of right action possible.

Finally, the Magnificat antiphon is composed of two verses from Isaiah:

> Ante me non est formatus Deus, et post me non erit[1]; quia mihi curvabitur omne genu, et confitebitur omnis lingua[2]. (Is 43:10;45:23)

> Before me there was no god formed, and there shall be none after me; for to me every knee shall bow, and of me every tongue shall testify.

144

Phrase 2 is taken exactly from Isaiah except for a change from plural to singular and, more importantly, the substitution of a single word: "confitebitur" (shall testify) for "jurabit" (shall swear by). Phrase 2, with "confitebitur" instead of "jurabit," is found in Romans 14:11, in which the line is quoted as a prophecy of Jesus. A similar but more elaborate statement of this prophecy is in Philippians 2:10.

TAKING THE LARGER VIEW

In the preceding pages we have seen just how compact chant texts can be. Single words or phrases evoke paragraphs, even pages, of associations. This kind of density is not peculiar to Advent Vespers. It is the norm for the ancient liturgies. But there is a different way to look at these same collections of text. We can take a larger, rather than a microscopic, view and be rewarded with a different kind of richness. As an example we will examine the liturgy for the Feast of the Ascension, and we will focus on the great responsories of Matins. First, a word about the service is necessary to clarify the functions of its many texts.

Matins, also called "Vigils" or "the Night Office," is the longest and most impressive of the eight hours. Matins for a feast such as the Ascension lasts over three hours, beginning at about two o'clock in the morning. The hour of the day, the length and intensity of the psalmody, and the quantity and intricate organization of texts make this liturgy the most compelling example of the power of the chant to create the conditions within which an individual is led deeply into the heart of sacred scripture. There are some differences in the form of Matins used in monasteries and that used in parish churches (the parish form is called the "secular" use, meaning non-monastic), and our examples will be taken from the monastic rite.

The main body of the liturgy is divided into three large sections called "nocturns." The first two are identical in form except for the type of lesson included. These nocturns open with a set of six psalms, each with an antiphon. The set concludes with a versicle and response, followed by a rather long passage of scripture, divided into four parts. After each of these parts, there is a "great" responsory, a chant of considerable complexity and length. The scripture lesson will be the major non-gospel text relevant to the day. The second nocturn is similar, except that the reading, again divided into four parts, is from one of the church fathers.

The third nocturn, called the "Gospel Nocturn," is a bit different. It begins with a single antiphon, followed by three Old Testament "canticles," or song-like passages not from the psalms. A versicle and response comes after the set of three canticles, and then the opening sentences of the day's gospel (but not the entire gospel passage) are sung. Next follows a commentary on that gospel by one of the fathers, again divided into four parts, with a great responsory after each part. After the last responsory, the entire gospel passage is sung. The last responsory is sometimes the "Te Deum," a very ancient hymn still sung in some churches today.

On the occasion of a major feast such as the Ascension, Matins is not the first liturgy celebrating the day. The feast is considered to begin on the previous evening with Vespers, so a major feast has two Vespers services, one the day before (First Vespers) and one the evening of the feast itself (Second Vespers). But as we can see from the preceding discussion, Matins is the most scripturally rich of the liturgies. The great responsories for the Ascension are particularly interesting and intricate, and they are worth quoting in full (from the *Breviarium Monasticum*). Rather than analyze a few of these texts in detail, our discussion will cover larger themes which run through all of these responsories as well as through other texts of the feast.

THE GREAT RESPONSORIES OF MATINS FOR THE ASCENSION

1.
After his passion, he appeared to them for forty days and spoke of the kingdom of God [Acts 1:3]. And, as they watched, he was lifted up, and a cloud received him from their sight [Acts 1:9].

℣. And eating together, he commanded them that they should not leave Jerusalem, but should wait for the promise of the Father [Acts

146

1:4]. And, as they watched, he was lifted up, and a cloud received him from their sight.

2.

All the beauty of the Lord is exalted above the stars; his form is among the clouds of heaven, and his name is established for ever.

℣. His going forth is from the highest heaven, and his path is to its furthest bounds [Ps 19:6]. His beauty is among the clouds of heaven, and his name is established for ever [a free paraphrase; possible sources: Ps 96:6, Ecclus 43:1, Lk 9:29, 1 Chr 17:24; Mt 24:30; Mt 26:64].

3.

Be exalted, O Lord, in your strength [Ps 21:14].

℣. Your glory has been lifted up above the heavens [Ps 8:2]. In your strength.

4.

I will not leave you orphans [Jn 14:18]. I go, and I come to you [Jn 14:28]. And your heart shall be joyful [Jn 16:22].

℣. In that day you shall know that I am in my Father, and you are in me, and I am in you [Jn 14:20]. And your heart shall be joyful.

5.

Now is the time that I must return to him who sent me, says the Lord [Jn 16:5]. Do not be sorrowful, nor let your heart be troubled [Jn 14:1]. I pray for you to the Father [Jn 14:16], that he may guard you [Ps 121:7].

℣. Unless I go away, the Comforter will not come. When I have been taken up, I will send him to you [Jn 16:7]. I pray for you to the Father, that he may guard you.

6.

Let not your heart be troubled [Jn 14:1]. I go to the Father [Jn 14:12], and when I have been taken up from you, I will send you the Spirit of Truth [Jn 16:7;15:26], and your heart will be joyful [Jn 16:22].

℣. I will pray to the Father, and he will give you another Comforter [Jn 14:16]. The Spirit of Truth, and your heart will be joyful.

7.
Christ ascending on high has led captivity captive [Eph 4:8, after Ps 68:18], and he has given gifts to humankind [Eph 4:8].

℣. God has ascended in jubilation, the Lord with the voice of the trumpet [Ps 47:5]. He has given gifts to humankind.

8.
God has ascended in jubilation, the Lord with the voice of the trumpet [Ps 47:5].

℣. Christ ascending on high has led captivity captive [Ps 68:18]. The Lord with the sound of the trumpet.

9.
I will pray to the Father, and he will give you another Comforter, that he may remain with you for ever, the Spirit of Truth [Jn 14:16–17].

℣. Indeed if I do not go away, the Comforter will not come to you; but if I go, I will send him to you [Jn 16:7]. That he may remain with you for ever, the Spirit of Truth.

10.
You take a cloud as your stairway [or, for "stairway," chariot ("ascensum")]; O Lord, you who walk upon the wings of the wind [Ps 104:3].

℣. You have been clothed with honor and comeliness, you wrap yourself with light as with a garment [Ps 104:1–2]. You walk upon the wings of the wind.

11.
Men of Galilee, why do you gaze wonderingly into heaven? In the same way that you saw him ascend into heaven, so he will come [Acts 1:11].

℣. And as they were watching him going away from them into

heaven, behold, two men stood next to them, in white garments, who said, In the same way that you saw him ascend into heaven, so he will come.

12.
Indeed if I do not go away, the Comforter will not come to you, but if I go, I will send him [Jn 16:7]. And when he has come, he will teach you all truth.

℣. He will not speak about himself, but whatever he hears, that he will speak, and he will tell you what is to come [Jn 16:13]. And when he has come, he will teach you all truth.

If we read through all of the texts of the feast, as well as these responsories, we will see that they have been "prepared" for the individual worshiper in all five of the ways discussed earlier in this chapter. The first responsory above gives us a compact summary of the events being celebrated (as do the five antiphons of Vespers and Lauds, not given here). These responsories, as do the other texts, bring out prophetic, symbolic allusions to the Ascension from many parts of the Bible. The feast is made personal in the Magnificat antiphon of Second Vespers as has been mentioned, and it is personalized in an interestingly different way in the second responsory above. These lines are both poetic and theological, especially the opening sentence: "All the beauty of the Lord is exalted above the stars; his form is among the clouds of heaven, and his name is established for ever." Here it is the meaning of the feast that is presented in warmly personal terms. And finally, there can be no mistaking the effect of these texts in bearing witness to the fact that all the scriptures speak in one voice concerning this cosmic event.

Within the responsories themselves, as throughout these Ascension liturgies, at least two major themes are emphasized: the importance of the return of the Son from the point of view of the heavenly world, and the pain which the disciples must feel at his leaving. The first antiphon of Vespers, like the Introit (entrance hymn) for the Eucharist, provides an image that combines these two themes: as the disciples, bewildered and distressed on earth, turn their gaze upwards toward a very different world, an angel asks, "Men of Galilee, why are you looking into heaven?"

The theme of rejoicing in heaven is stated most clearly in the Matins antiphons by the symbolic interpretation of Old Testament passages. As we read these lines in the context of the Ascension, we realize with a slight jolt and, perhaps, even a smile that the prophetic meaning of each one is being taken very "literally." We are seeing this event from the point of view of heaven, not earth— the Lord is "coming." We imagine heavenly trumpets blowing, the angels in jubilation, the gates opening to welcome the returning Son whose mission has been completed: "Let the heavens rejoice, and the earth exult, for the Lord is coming" (Ps 96:11,12); "God has ascended in jubilation, the Lord with the sound of the trumpet" (Ps 47:5); "Be lifted up, everlasting doors, and the king of glory will come in" (Ps 24:7). A similar line from Psalm 68 is given special prominence during the day, possibly because it is quoted by Paul (Eph 4:8) as a prophecy of the Ascension. It appears as the alleluia verse in the Eucharist and as a versicle in both Matins and Lauds: "You have gone up on high and led captivity captive" (Ps 68:8).

As a counter to the heavenly return, Jesus' words of assurance and concern for the distress of the Apostles of earth and, by extension, for us, fill the responsories: "Let not your heart be troubled. . . . I will not leave you orphans. . . . I will pray to the Father, and he will give you another Comforter, that he may re-main with you for ever. . . . and your heart shall be joyful." This is the earthly, personal side of the previous cosmic arrival theme. In order for the divine plan to be completed, human beings must suffer the grief of separation. Not only will that grief allow the plan to complete itself, but it will lead to an even greater joy for those who suffer. Lest we miss the personal connection that is being suggested between the apostles' situation and our own, we recall that the last major chant of the feast, the Magnificat antiphon at Second Vespers, makes that connection explicit, using Jesus' own words from the responsories, now shifted slightly into the point of view of those singing the text: "O King of glory, Lord of hosts, who ascended today in triumph above the heavens, do not leave us orphans, but send the promised one of the Father into us, the Spirit of Truth."

It remains for us to take note briefly of the teachings of the fathers concerning this feast. The sermons by Leo and Gregory which are actually included in the liturgy (Matins lessons) focus on the larger meanings of the feast which we have discussed already. Leo connects the cosmic and personal themes by pointing out that the apostles, and we also, learned to rejoice at Jesus' ascension because they finally understood that in Him their own human nature and ours are glorified: "In the person of our Head we are actually begun to enter into the heavenly mansions above" (*Brev* 2: 465). Gregory focuses on the importance of the events surrounding the ascension in strengthening the apostles' faith for the last charge Jesus gave them, to "preach the Gospel to every creature" (Mk 16:15; Acts 1:8). In these liturgical readings, Leo and Gregory do not comment on the inner meaning of the feast. Bernard, however, explains that the "leaving" and "coming again" of the Ascension texts refers to the coming and going of the Word in the soul. The occasion for his remarks is his commentary on the line from The Song of Songs: "Return, my beloved" (Sg 2:17, Vulg), which he interprets as the plea of a soul "which the bridegroom, the Word, is accustomed to visit often, whom friendship has made bold, who hungers for what it has once tasted" (*Bern/SS* 4: 87). Bernard first points out, however, that God is always present, and that this impression of coming and going

> ... happens as a result of [the] soul's sensitivity, and is not due to any movement of the Word. ... the Word is recalled—recalled by the longing of the soul who has once enjoyed his sweetness. Is longing not a voice? It is indeed, and a very powerful one. Then the Psalmist says, "The Lord has heard the longing of the poor." [Ps 10:17] (*Bern/SS* 4: 87)

The Word's purpose is to intensify the soul's longing, without which the Word's presence cannot be known. Bernard points out that, even during his ministry on earth, Jesus "feigned" passing his disciples by in order to lead them to discover their desire for him to stay:

For he once pretended that he was going further, not because that was his intention, but because he wanted to hear the words, 'Stay with us, for evening is coming on' [Lk 24:28–29]. And another time, when the apostles were in a boat pulling on the oars, he walked on the sea, making as though he would pass them by [Mk 6:48], not because he intended to, but to try their faith and draw out their prayers." (*Bern/SS* 4: 88)

As in his earthly life, so in his spiritual presence, says Bernard, the Lord "makes to go past, desiring to be held back, and seems to go away, wishing to be recalled."

Having discussed the dynamics of this "coming and going," Bernard then adds the tie to the Ascension texts:

Now it is clear that his comings and goings are the fluctuations in the soul of which he speaks when he says, "I go away, and come again to you" [Jn 14:28], and, "a little while and you shall not see me, and again a little while and you shall see me." [Jn 16:17] (*Bern/SS* 4: 88–89)

Bernard's inner point of view on these texts gives a very specific meaning to the plea of the Magnificat antiphon for Second Vespers, to "send the promised one of the Father into us." The antiphon carries each monk's plea for the return of the central experience of his religious life, that moment of complete inner quiet, of intensified awareness where there seems to be "in that interior depth a brazier giving off sweet-smelling perfumes" (*Ter* 75). Likewise, the intensity of the expression of Jesus' concern for the disciples' distress at his departure, which is so evident in these responsories, becomes more understandable when we see how completely the monks identified this moment in the disciples' lives with the defining experience of their own monastic vocations.

Both monastic commentary and the medieval liturgies, then, prepare biblical texts so that they may become "solid food" (1 Cor 3:2) for believers. That feeding takes place when believers begin to know with certainty, in a kind of knowing deeper than that of the natural mind, that the source of these teachings is sacred: "And it happens that as you perceive the words of sacred scripture to be of a celestial nature, so you yourself, illuminated by the grace of contemplation, are raised to the level of celestial nature" (*G/HHP* 87). This understanding is encouraged by the kind of preparation the text receives, a "gathering" of phrases which, by the very nature of the gathering process, suggests to the individual that the scriptures are symbolic, prophetic, unified, and deeply personal. One of the enduring strengths of these ancient liturgies, however, lies in the fact that these messages of scripture become "personal" by appealing to levels of intelligence in ourselves which are most deeply tied to our individuality and, yet, are universal parts of human nature. A balance is thus maintained between the personal and the objective, a balance which reflects yet again the inner harmony and consistency of the traditional teaching.

Chapter Six

Gregorian Chant in the Parish

THE DIRECTOR AND THE CANTOR

This book has argued that the faith and practice of the fathers and of the ancient chant liturgies hold tremendous promise for modern Christians. But can that promise be realized in practical terms in parish life today? That is the important question which we must address in this last chapter. It is both a practical and a philosophical question, and has yet to be answered fully.

In the operation of any chant choir, two individuals are key—the director and the cantor. The important differences between the director of chant and the director of a parish choir stem from the fact that the chant director must teach the choir to sing but must not conduct it. The chant director *must* also be a singer because, as we have seen, the chant is primarily a spiritual discipline for the singers. In order to understand the problems the choir is facing, the director must participate in that discipline. And, by reading short excerpts from the fathers (see Appendix 10) and leading occasional discussions, the director must help the group understand the inner discipline which the chant offers.

Allow me to illustrate from my personal experience. A good many years ago, I directed two chant choirs, one of men and one of women, meeting on separate nights. I quickly realized that, in our study of the longer chants, I had trouble demonstrating to the

154

women the quick, light quality which was needed in these chants, whereas, with the men, the right "feel" came easily. I soon realized where the problem lay. Both choirs began their rehearsal with about twenty minutes of psalmody. I fully participated in that exercise with the men, and, by the time we began work on the longer chants, my own mind was as quiet and collected as theirs. But while the women sang the psalms, I spent the time thinking about the upcoming evening's work, so that after twenty minutes they and I were miles apart in our readiness to proceed with more complicated music. I was, in fact, not ready for anything. The solution to this problem was not, however, to have me sing with the women and add a distracting male octave. I could fully participate by actively listening, bringing my attention always back to the psalms, as St. John Climacus and all the fathers require.

This need both to lead and fully participate as an equal is the director's most difficult challenge, particularly when the choir is inexperienced. Until the choir's understanding and skill become reliable, the director must carefully discriminate between "problems" he hears in the choir's singing which do in fact need to be addressed, and "problems" he hears which are really the voice of his own ego wishing to tinker where tinkering is unnecessary and even destructive. With a beginning choir, the director's primary task will be to lighten and simplify the group's recitation of psalms (as described in Chapter Two). In the very beginning, when the technique of free recitation is first explained, the director should select a few psalm verses with particularly tricky rhythms, both to be demonstrated by the director and to be sung by the choir. Once the choir has the idea and has made some progress toward natural, simple recitation, the director will need to remain alert for the unnatural syllable that occurs here and there, stop, point out the syllable, demonstrate what's needed, and have the choir sing the line again until it "speaks." The more expert the choir becomes, the more quickly these micro-corrections can be done, but they are essential if the choir is to continue to grow in the spontaneity and simplicity of its singing.

Like any good choir director, the leader of a chant choir must insist on perfect mastery of the pitches. With most choirs, a new chant will need to be learned phrase by phrase through simple repetition and memorization. Ideally, the director should teach these phrases by singing them, not by playing the piano or organ. A pitch pipe should be the only "instrument" the choir needs. A choir which reads the chant notation well will save the director the time and trouble of teaching phrases, but such a group may have a different problem: they may become impatient with repeating the chant because they feel they "know" it on a single reading. The director must help the choir see beyond that illusion of the ego. No choir can make full inner use of a melody until it is virtually, or even actually, memorized. A good discipline for a choir which reads well is routinely to sing liturgies without music, from memory. Some singing from memory is an excellent discipline for any choir.

In parish choirs and secular choruses a director will often work on technical problems in difficult passages, go through a score adding dynamic and other marks, and finally say to the chorus, "Okay, now let's make music." The idea of course is that, once the technical aspects of the score are mastered, then some attempt at musical expression, the interpretation of musical ideas, can begin. It is part of the chant director's job to help the choir avoid this familiar mind set. As was touched on in Chapter Three, everything which takes place during the rehearsal can contribute to the recollection of mind which is the chant's main purpose. Listening is one key. Even when learning notes, the choir can be reminded to keep the listening attention on the sound of the group and to be attentive during the silences between phrases. Singers will find that learning music is distracting in many ways: intellectually, I am trying to figure out what the notes are; emotionally, I am worried and upset that I haven't learned them already. These distractions can be valuable if the director is able to help the choir make use of them. Indeed, the director has her own special set of distractions— fixed ideas about how the chant should go, frustration with singers who aren't learning, and so on. In order to make use of all this distracting material, the director must, frequently throughout the evening, "come to herself," like the prodigal son, see that she and the choir are completely caught up in the tensions of the moment, and call a short halt. The halt may consist simply of a few seconds of recollection and quiet or a single note sung on "ah" for a minute with all eyes closed, all attention being brought back to that unison sound. The choir quickly will see that the distractions of learning are very much like the distractions of daily life in which we become so totally absorbed that we go through our days with no sense of ourselves. The short pause for recollection can be as useful an exercise during the day as during the rehearsal. Short readings from the fathers can also help the choir make the best inner use of the experiences the rehearsal provides.

Even a choir which reads chant notation well should begin learning a new chant by ignoring episemas and quilismas (see Chapter Three) and by ignoring as well the rhythm of the words. Once the preliminary study of the Latin text has been done (see Chapter Three), work on learning the melody should begin at a slow, steady pace, giving a single, equal-value pulse to each pitch. The challenge to the attention is first to maintain precise regularity in the speed of the pulse. That speed may be set as slowly as the group feels necessary, but, once a pace is set, it must be maintained, and the director must stop the group and start again at the slightest drop in speed. It is also possible to maintain a steady, "learning pace" and still sing with the lightly energetic quality which the longer chants require, once the group begins to have a feel for that quality. Again, it is the director's job to stop the group when that quality is absent and to insist on its being regained. As the notes become familiar, the pace can be speeded up until it becomes almost natural, after which the shift into the more irregular rhythms of the text itself can be made easily. Once the group is reciting the text freely, the rhythmic complications of episemas and quilismas can be added. (Dotted notes can be observed from the start, since a simple doubling of the length of a note should not cause the choir to lose its sense of pace.)

Particularly in the beginning, the director may also serve as cantor. The cantor is the singer who begins each chant, and his or her influence on the quality of the liturgy is immense. He or she should: know the eight psalm tones by heart and understand the system of psalm tone endings; understand the importance of listening and of removing the ego from his singing; be sensitive to the effects of different pitch levels on individuals in the group and on the physical space being used; and have a keen ear for the natural recitation of syllables and the light movement of melismatic passages. But above all, the cantor must have had extensive, persuasive experience of the importance of silence to the chant. Particularly in the longer Offices, it is the cantor who paces the liturgy—decides how long to wait between psalms, for example. The possibility that silence will deepen as the liturgy proceeds, and that the strength of inner attention in the choir will grow with it, is to some extent dependent on the sensitivity of the cantor to the movement of these forces of silence and attention.

In time, the director should encourage everyone in the choir (everyone who is capable and willing) to take on the role of cantor. A short Office such as Compline, which can be sung weekly at the end of each rehearsal, is a good place to train them. When a longer Office or a Eucharist is sung on a feast day, it is customary to use two cantors. One should be clearly "senior"; the senior cantor is responsible for setting pitches and pacing. The role of second cantor is excellent training for someone who is still learning the cantor's job. The roles in the Office of the lay officiant and lesson "reader" (so-called even though the lesson is sung) are less demanding than that of cantor, and most choir members should be encouraged to take them on. Singers taking on these positions may need to be coached in simple recitation, even if they recite with complete ease in the group. When we sing alone, most of us tend to revert to old habits. It is also critical that the officiant and lesson reader, like the cantor, understand how to listen and to give the text a chance to speak "in its own voice," not the voice of an individual's ego. In his *Confessions*, Augustine recalls having heard that St. Athanasius,

Bishop of Alexandria in the fourth century, "made the reader of the psalm utter it with so slight inflection of voice, that it was nearer speaking than singing" (*A/Conf* 217).

ORGANIZING A CHOIR

There are at least three ways in which Gregorian chant may be incorporated into a parish music program: as part of the repertory of the parish choir; as the sole repertory of a chant choir which meets once a week and sings for special occasions; and as the center of a program of mediation, special liturgies, and the contemplative study of scripture. Psalmody is the foundation stone of all three approaches. If the director of a parish choir will take a few minutes each week during the choir's regular rehearsal to train the group in psalm recitation until their "speaking" becomes natural and free, every aspect of the group's singing will benefit. Virtually all the teaching explained in this book can be omitted if the choir is asked simply to look for a balance that "feels right" between simple recitation and silence. Once free recitation is mastered, longer, more complicated chants can be added to the choir's repertory with greater ease, even if the director finds he must conduct them. He may wish to teach the choir the principles of light, quick movement and resistance to forward drive (as discussed in Chapter Three) without any reference whatever to the fathers' teaching. What is crucial to this approach, however, is time. The director must be patient, as these skills will come slowly and must be regularly reinforced. Once a parish choir masters these techniques, however, their strength and importance to the singers should increase steadily. Furthermore, the choir's skills are easily passed on to new members by "osmosis."

The chant can add a special quality to the choir's repertory which can help shape its identity over many years' time. As the choir becomes skilled, care must be taken, however, in the use of the chant in Sunday services. It is good to keep in mind the somber warning of Dom Joseph Pothier, one of the moving forces in the early days of the modern Solesmes revival of the chant: "An art which, like Gregorian chant, has its own special character and its own kind of beauty, once it finds itself robbed of these, no longer has character or beauty of any sort. And ceasing to be that which it is, soon ceases to be anything at all" (*Melodies* 5–6). The "special character" of the chant, this book has argued, lies in its inherently contemplative nature. This character is appropriate at those places in a Sunday service where a feeling of recollection and a deepening silence are needed. Because the chant is rooted in a special relationship between movement and stillness, it is particularly effective in procession, if the mood of the procession is to be solemn and quiet. In situations other than these, attempts to use the chant in Sunday services result more often than not in frustration for the choir and discomfort for the congregation.

A choir which sings only Gregorian chant is often called a "schola cantorum" (school of singers) or simply "schola" (school). The formation of a schola to rehearse once a week separate from the parish choir can cause friction, unless both the regular choirmaster and the rector are enthusiastic supporters. With that support, a great deal of what has been discussed in this book can be put into practice in this once-a-week format. A schola of this type can become familiar in practical terms with the fathers' teachings and their relevance to the experience of singing the chant. In time, such a group can become expert in reciting psalms and can provide its members and its parish with strong experiences of a kind of silence and recollection that many will find deeply helpful in their lives. With musically astute members, the group can also master the longer chants and, at the regular choirmaster's invitation, add both psalms and Mass chants to Sunday morning worship. If there is sufficient interest, this kind of schola can also add valuable special liturgies on weekdays for feasts the parish might not otherwise celebrate.

In forming a weekly schola, the director and the group should keep several guidelines in mind, none of them absolute. Neither voice training nor the ability to read music is important to this work. Even the most complicated chants will be sung over frequently enough that they can be learned by ear. Four qualities, however, are essential: a sincere interest in meditation and prayer; an accurate musical ear, even if it is untrained; a quick musical memory; and a mind that is open to new and different ideas.

As to numbers, six men and six women will provide a solid beginning, eight of each gender is ideal, and ten of each is too many. Alternatively, a solid choir can be formed of only one gender, six to eight of either. I would urge aspiring groups not to begin work until at least six men or six women (or six of both) are available. Whether the choir includes both genders or only one, six participants should guarantee that the group will have at least four of one gender available for any given liturgy. Where the chant is concerned, four singers represent a "critical mass." Three will experience the chant as individuals singing together, but four will begin to feel like a group. It is entirely practical for men and women to rehearse together, but, if there are at least four of each voice, plenty of opportunity should be provided for each gender to sing alone. The single octave, either of men or of women, creates a unison which reaches into the inner ear more deeply than the combined octaves of both voices singing together. In actual liturgies, there is room for all three options: men only, women only, and combined. During a chanted Eucharist, for example, it is appropriate for the ordinary (Kyrie, Gloria, Creed, Sanctus, Benedictus, Agnus Dei) to be sung by everyone. In rehearsal, the group should experiment freely with different voice arrangements, in order to learn what their effects are.

A weekly schola which flourishes will eventually discover its own limitations. The invitation to contemplative prayer and to the inner study of scripture which the chant offers cannot be fully accepted in this format. A group wishing to study the chant as an entrance to a kind of contemplative life in the world must make a larger commitment, and will find that, to make that commitment practical, all its members must live close by. One possible beginning format would be: a weekly rehearsal starting with at least fifteen minutes of psalmody and ending with Compline; Friday evening Vespers followed by a half-hour of meditation; a Sunday morning chanted

Eucharist followed or preceded by an hour of study; and at least six special liturgies during the year, which should include a Eucharist for a feast in the fall (perhaps All Souls' Day); Advent Vespers; Eucharist and procession of lights for the Presentation (February 2); Tenebrae during Holy Week; and a late spring weekend retreat to include early morning Lauds. All the special liturgies could not be undertaken in the first year, of course. A quick group, once it begins to be skilled, might add one or two new ones each year until the full cycle is familiar. Over time, more feasts could be added. This program of liturgies would require not only a substantial commitment from schola members but a tremendous amount of preparation by the director. Some of the tools the group will need are hard to find. A few useful sources are given in Appendix 12.

WHAT IS WORSHIP?

There is often tension when chant is introduced into Sunday morning parish worship, and, for that reason, many choir directors, if they try it briefly, abandon it. The tension is understandable; the chant powerfully asserts its "own special character," a character that is intensely inner and still. In parishes where the emphasis is on celebration, movement, and emotion, the chant will clash with the prevailing mood. However, the chant can be used effectively in Sunday worship if it is placed carefully, where its character is needed.

But if Sunday morning worship which includes the chant is always something of a hybrid, where would the chant be completely at home? The quick answer must be that the chant belongs in a "contemplative liturgy," but it is not at all obvious what a "contemplative liturgy" would look like. The goal of such a liturgy must be to allow the worshiping community to work together to deepen the stillness within each individual. Within that stillness, Origen's "spiritual senses" may begin to stir and show us simple facts about ourselves, about our lives, and about God's will, which we need to see but, in the rush of life, cannot see. As the Benedictine spiritual leader Henri Le Saux put it, "After such worship the

162

faithful should go on their way fully recollected within themselves" (*Prayer* 49).

But what conditions might lead to this goal? From what we have seen so far of the fathers' teaching, we can draw several tentative conclusions. First, such a liturgy must take preparation seriously. It is one thing to say, "I will now clear my mind of the thoughts of the week and turn to God," and it is quite another actually to do it. Inner forces move with different—and generally slower—rhythms than outer ones, and, as we have seen, time and inner attention are necessary for the mind, body, and feelings to become quiet. We can assume then that the pace and rhythms of a contemplative liturgy will be unlike those of everyday life, that they will make more demands on the worshipers' attention, and—most obviously—that they will take more time.

Second, we can expect such a liturgy to be repetitive, just as the inner effort of bringing the attention again and again back to its quiet focus, or the rhythmic chanting of the psalms, is repetitive. Our entire being must be brought back again and again, reminded again and again, of what it is struggling to remember, in order for that remembering, that regathering, to reach the depths.

Third, we can expect to be uncomfortable in some ways and at some times in such an environment—impatient, bored, objecting. It is the casual, ordinary mind that is being set aside in this process, and it will resist, sometimes to the point of urging us to flee the entire scene.

And finally, we can expect the texts, gestures, and movement of such a liturgy to appeal to the symbolic, as well as to the literal, mind. We need to be jolted out of our ordinary ways of thinking to a more interior point of view, in order to be reminded of an entire world of thought and experience which we have overlooked. We hear St. Paul's advice in the letter to the Ephesians, "Be angry, but do not sin; do not let the sun go down on your anger" (Eph 4:26), and we think we know what is being said. Then Cassian, discussing inner discernment, the ability to observe and recognize our own impulses, casually gives the verse an entirely new slant: "Such, then, is discernment, and not only is it called the lamp of the body but is even described as 'the sun' by the apostle when he says 'may the sun not set upon your anger'" (*Cass/CWS* 63). Here is a new idea: Paul's "sun" is my own attention, and my anger is not sinful if I am attentive to that anger, to its exact nature, as it is boiling within me. Of course, we don't expect commentary such as Cassian's from the liturgy, but we do expect to find texts used in suggestive ways and combined with movement and gestures, so as to turn the mind toward inner meanings of the text and thereby appeal to a deeper, symbolic intelligence.

Perhaps in this list of expectations we recognize, if we have had experience of it, the more elaborate entrance rite of the older eucharistic liturgies, or of Orthodox liturgies, and the extended periods of prayer, silence, and psalmody of the medieval monastic Office. Perhaps also we see in these expectations a suggestion of the great cyclical pattern of holy events represented by the church year, which is itself a kind of large, year-long liturgy of many parts, in which every hour of every day, every day of the week, every season of the year, has its special place in this pattern—a pattern the foundation of which is God's action in scriptural events and in the natural world; a time frame that belongs to God. The rhythms of this circling year are in part mysterious, in part familiar from scripture: "In the beginning, God created the heavens and the earth, and the earth was without form, and void . . . and evening and morning were the first day . . . a time to be born and a time to die, a time to weep, and a time to laugh . . . but God has put eternity into man's mind . . . in the beginning was the Word, and the Word was with God, and the Word was God."

Ancient monastic life was an attempt to order a community's entire existence entirely according to this great cyclical pattern of sacred history and cosmic rhythms. Our own everyday lives are quite different and are organized around secular schedules and demands. In one of its most profound insights into our spiritual nature, the church understood centuries ago that the whole being of the individual cannot be brought near to God unless the secular pattern is periodically, often joltingly, intruded upon and upset. It is sometimes said that God may send into a life what appear to be suffering and calamity for this very reason—to turn the individual aside from the routine and force that individual to reexamine his or her life. On a smaller scale, but in a similar way, the church urges us at various times throughout the year to break our routine—be at church on a weekday evening, or at midnight, or in the early morning; or change diet; or for a short time take up special prayers and observances which turn out to be a "bother," an inconvenience —in order to turn the depths of our being toward God's time and the holy events which are both the record of his action and the life-source of our own. In these periodic demands to turn aside from the ordinary, in our objections and discomfort and perhaps in our discovery of something new within that discomfort, we recognize again a contemplative theme.

And finally, in a contemplative liturgy, we find the scriptural texts of the chant playing their characteristic roll—telling us again and again in short, suggestive phrases what our presence here today is all about. These phrases are the same on this day, this feast, every single year of our lives—"To you, O Lord, I lift up my soul" at the beginning of Advent; "This is the day which the Lord has made," at Easter; "The Lord has gone up with a shout" on Ascension Day; and at every Eucharist of the year, "Lift up your hearts. We lift them to the Lord." These texts are clear suggestions, laid out in plain view but never calling attention to themselves, inviting me to see that the lines of scripture I am hearing and singing have mysteriously hidden meanings which are speaking immediately to my condition, to every aspect of my being, right here, right this moment, even to my physical movements. As I go to receive communion I pray with the psalmist, "I will go to the altar of God, to the God of my joy and gladness" (Ps 43:4), and as I receive, "I will receive the cup of salvation, and call upon the Name of the Lord" (Ps 116:13); "My feet are standing without your gates, O Jerusalem" (Ps 122:2).

And so we can expect that a contemplative Eucharist will take time, will move in rhythms more natural to the inner world, in cycles, in seemingly repetitive forms, taking more time than the active mind at first thinks necessary; will make demands on our attention, requiring effort from us; will make us uncomfortable at times, and arouse resentment, resistance in our "outer" parts; and, finally, in its texts, patterns of movement, and physical surroundings, will suggest symbols of everything both within us and beyond us of which an awakened attention might become fleetingly aware.

These qualities remain accessible to modern Christians to a remarkable degree in the older forms of the monastic Office—Lauds, Vespers, Compline, and Tenebrae.§ These liturgies, faithfully celebrated, will give sympathetic parishioners an authentic taste of contemplative worship. On the other hand, they are not holy relics. They can be expected to grow and change to express the contemplative life more perfectly for contemporary communities. But they must change in order to evoke contemplative experience more deeply, not suppress it by conforming to the expectations of worldly minds. The element of "offense" to the world of the everyday is at the heart of these liturgies and must never be blunted. As Fr. Le Saux, the Benedictine quoted earlier, put it many years ago, legitimate contemporary needs must first "be assimilated interiorly in prayer," so that their liturgical expressions "may not be simply the repetition of popular slogans, but may be a vehicle for truly personal prayer which springs from the contemplation of those same values [as those of the early monks] as they are grounded in the mystery of God himself" (*Prayer* 49).

The Eucharist is more problematic. Even with the chant, medieval monastic Mass rites, translated into English, communicate little more than heaviness and dust even to sympathetic modern communities. Appendix 8 contains an experimental adaptation of a Eucharist for the Holy Spirit which may serve as a starting point. It attempts to simplify the language of the older rite, let in a bit of light and air, while at the same time retaining and highlighting the

§Forms for the last three of these are included in the appendices: Vespers: Appendix 8; Compline: Appendix 10; Tenebrae: Appendix 9.

ancient symbolic patterns of language and movement. Fr. Le Saux suggests a somewhat different approach: for modern contemplative communities, "times of silence for all should be still further extended" and "the use of words could be reduced to the essential minimum" (*Prayer* 49). The crucial point is that guidance for change should come from the promptings of the inner mind, not from an impulse to compromise with the expectations of popular culture.

CONTEMPLATIVE LIFE IN THE MODERN WORLD

A chant choir which commits itself to these liturgies and to a serious study of the contemplative life, a choir organized to meet several times each week as suggested above, is stepping into the unknown. There is no question that when the chant is celebrated with disciplined listening attention, it will provide an entrance into the contemplative world, a first taste of the "strange sweetness" of Augustine, which he found hard to distinguish from the life to come (*A/Conf* 228). But in our secular world, the road to the "full measure" of that experience, "shaken together and running over" (Lk 6:38), is waiting to be discovered. To some extent we know that, as Gregory and so many others have insisted, we must "walk in the way of our spiritual ancestors." But what is the full character of a discipline which may lead modern, active Christians to that "purity of heart" by which Cassian says the mind is able to "gaze on the mysteries of scripture" (*Cass/SL* 245)? We know that this purity requires and makes possible, in times of prayer, complete stillness of mind, body, and emotion. But what else is required of our lives?

A hundred years after Cassian's death, his teachings were organized into a rule of living for monks by St. Benedict. Benedict's rule remains the standard for European monasticism to this day. Both writers have been praised through the centuries for their moderation and realism. They unequivocally rejected extremes of fasting and deprivation that many around them claimed led to "true purity." Cassian, particularly, tells colorful stories of good monks driven mad by excessive zeal, such as the poor man who became convinced that, by sacrificing his son, he "might equal the merit of Abraham the patriarch." His son was saved only by the fact that, "noticing that [his father] was sharpening a knife in an unusual manner and that he was getting chains ready as a preliminary to sacrifice, [he] guessed the crime to be committed and ran away in terror" (*Cass/CWS* 66).

The genius of both Cassian and Benedict lay in the fact that they made it possible for generations of serious Christians to live the contemplative life within the conditions available to them in their own times. In our time, it is not likely that groups of active Christians will begin to live on two small loaves of dried bread a day, the norm for Egyptian hermits. Neither are we likely to reject family, friends, and material goods, or remain celibate from husbands and wives, or "show contempt for ourselves" (*Cass/CWS* 105), or regard our bodies as a "corporeal burden" and an "inhibiting grossness" (*Cass/CWS* 50). Even the critical question of obedience, so central to the tradition, is problematic in modern, active life. According to Cassian, beginners in the spiritual life must submit every impulse "to the scrutiny of our elders. . . . One trusts one's own judgment in nothing [and] yields to their authority in everything." In short, "We will most easily come to a precise knowledge of true discernment if we follow the paths of our elders, if we do nothing novel, and if we do not presume to decide anything on the basis of our own private judgment" (*Cass/CWS* 69–70). But in our own contemporary desert, there are no elders who have passed this way before us, to whom we might submit our impulses and plans.

Perhaps we can begin to define a contemplative direction in the modern world by reviewing what guides the tradition does provide. We begin with fundamentals, the goal. Bernard put it clearly: "We seek for the things that no eye has seen and no ear has heard, things beyond the mind of man [1 Cor 2:9]. To search after these things, whatever they may be, is a source of pleasure and relish and delight" (*Bern/SS* 1: 72). But how do we pursue a search of this kind? Again we turn to Cassian. At the beginning of his quest in the Egyptian desert, he is asked by one of the hermits, "What is the end and the objective which inspires you to endure all these trials so gladly?" Cassian replies, "The kingdom of God." The monk answers that it is a noble objective, but asks essentially the question we are now asking, "What direction should we take which, if closely followed, will bring us to our objective? This, above all, is something of which you ought to be aware." The monk's answer to this question makes clear the underlying rationale for every aspect of his way of life. The objective is "purity of heart," and "we must follow completely anything that can bring us to this objective, to this purity of heart, and anything which pulls us away from it must be avoided as being dangerous and damaging. After all, it is for the sake of this that we undertake all that we do and all that we endure." In what immediately follows, Cassian gives an example of particular relevance to our own situation. Even those who give up "gold and silver" and "splendid estates" to come to the desert in search of this purity of heart, often are found to "guard a book so jealously that they can barely endure to have someone else read it or touch it." They have given up "everything" for Christ, except what is most important—"their old heart-longings for things that do not matter, things for whose sake they grow angry" (*Cass/CWS* 41).

The key to a contemplative way in the world, then, is not rejection of possessions, but rejection or—to use Cassian's term—"renunciation" of our attachment to possessions. We must practice this renunciation in moments of active living. We must be able to see ourselves in daily life being wracked by our attachment to "things that do not matter." (We will return shortly to this theme of the active life.) But we must also practice renunciation in our prayer. In individual meditation or in chanting the psalms, we place ourselves for a limited time in exactly the position of complete renunciation which the tradition values so highly. For these brief periods, as Cassian put it, "We hold family, country, honors, riches, the delight of this world and indeed all pleasures in low esteem, and we do so always so as to hold on to purity of heart. With this as our continuous aim, all our acts and thoughts are fully turned toward its achievement" (*Cass/CWS* 40). Here, for a short time, for the sake of this purity, this stillness, we give up everything and place ourselves with the fathers in the desert. Our reward, as we have seen in earlier chapters, is small at first, a gentle easing of body and mind, but it is of a quality all its own, a quality entirely distinct from that of the everyday world, one which appears quietly out of the barrenness we have entered: "The Lord changed deserts into pools of water and dry land into water-spring. He settled the hungry there, and they founded a city to dwell in" (Ps 107:35–36).

But in active life—on the job or in traffic or at home with the kids—how are we to recognize our own passions for what they are? If we are "growing angry over things that do not matter," who is to let us know it? If a new impulse of attention appears in us, how are we to recognize it? We know that our authentic inner impulses are of a character completely different from the materials of ordinary life, and that they appear within us as the smallest, almost imperceptible movements, shifts, and changes. The best of them is the stirring of the Word which "is very near you; it is in your mouth and in your heart, so that you can do it" (Dt 30:14) or

> a grain of mustard seed, which, when sown upon the ground, is the smallest of all the seeds on earth; yet when it is sown it grows up and becomes the greatest of all shrubs, and puts forth large branches, so that the birds of the air can make nests in its shade. (Mk 4:31–32)

We must learn to recognize and understand these elusive forces.

Tradition calls this learning process the acquisition of "discernment." In order to acquire discernment, Cassian says, we have "need of a teacher." But for direction in this new way, there is for us today no teacher, no elder who has gone before us. Here again, Cassian suggests an alternative which may fit the conditions within which we find ourselves. The aged monk, Hero, who lived for fifty years in holy abstinence in the desert, was seized by the illusion that angels would protect him due to the "merits of his own virtue," and in the middle of the night he threw himself down a well. His mistake lay in that fact that "he preferred to be guided by his own ideas." The alternative which could have saved him, and which is available to us as well, was "to bow to the advice and conferences of his brethren" (*Cass/CWS* 64–65). Clearly then, where all are equally beginners, the "advice of the brethren," the exchange with others of our experiences in this effort, is of crucial importance.

But discernment has, according to tradition, a moral dimension as well as an instructional one. We must also, according to Cassian, lay before our spiritual elders those thoughts, desires, and guilty feelings of which we are most ashamed. Cassian's reasoning here sounds very contemporary in its psychology: "An evil thought sheds its danger when it is brought out into the open . . . its dangerous promptings hold sway in us [only] as long as these are concealed in the heart" (*Cass/CWS* 68). "You need to talk about it," we say today, and Cassian would agree. This advice suggests that, if confession is available in our church, we should consider it.

In a monastery, today as in ancient times, obedience in its external form consists of unquestioning deference to the instructions of the abbot. Among contemplative groups in the modern world, there will be no abbot. Here the external form of obedience may consist, as we have just seen, in respectful deference to the counsel of the contemplative community. But like the renunciation of possessions, obedience also has an important inner dimension. No one enters a serious study of the contemplative life without a call from the spirit, and that call must be obeyed. The call may take many forms—a nameless urge for something different, depression, the excitement of discovery—but it must be obeyed. Often, obedience is not cheap. Today, when reliable inner disciplines are not readily available, such a call may bring months or years of fruitless searching, blind alleys, frustration, and difficulty. Cassian points out that this call from God is in two parts: a command followed by a promise, as in God's call to Abraham, "Go from your country and your kindred and your father's house to the land that I will show you" (Gn 12:1). Cassian observes that "Abraham by coming out was exercising obedience," but the second half of the command, "'that I will show you.' . . . has to do with the grace of God, who gave a command—and a promise." And what is this land which is promised? It is "a land gained in this life when all passion is ousted and the heart is pure, a land which neither the virtue nor the effort of a toiling man will open up but which the Lord Himself promised to reveal" (*Cass/CWS* 92–93). For some, a response to this call to seek out the contemplative life may be their first experience with interior listening of this kind. This interior listening is an activity that the contemplative life will encourage and support. In stillness of heart and mind, guided by discernment and sustained by patience, we find that the will of God for every aspect of our lives becomes more clearly evident. We find that, through listening and obedience, we discover a new approach to ordering our lives, as scripture says: "He set love in order within me" (Sg 2:4, Vulg).

If groups working today are to be blessed by this tradition, then, following Jacob's example, we must both wrestle with it and make demands of it. In these last few pages, we have considered only a few of the demands which must be made of the tradition and of ourselves. Of the tradition there are others, some simply practical but some lying at the very heart of the traditional teaching. The clearly feminine nature of the Spirit of Wisdom, mentioned in Chapter One, must be acknowledged and incorporated. With that acknowledgment must come a new emphasis on the creative, nurturing, and sustaining power of that force which "moves more easily than motion itself" and "pervades and permeates all things because she is so pure" (Wis 7:24–25). The traditional, uncompromising rejection of the body and everything material, the idea that we must come to "despise, in heart and mind, all that is done in this world" (*Cass/CWS* 92) cannot be allowed to stand in this form. This shortsighted teaching has led to almost total silence in monastic writing on the many ways by which the spirit lives in and through the body, supported and not weighed down by it. It has led to a similarly crippling silence within the tradition on the spiritual importance of both the natural world and the world of secular culture and work. But fidelity to the tradition demands that changes be more substantial than intellectual quibbling. This kind of change must involve more than rewording a few prayers to make them more palatable. The tradition is emphatic in its insistence on the authority of inner experience and action. A different attitude toward the body must produce a different and more profoundly spiritual experience of the body. Time, prayer, silence, and discernment by serious communities are the prerequisites for meaningful change.

But as this book has tried to show, our "elders" have left us at least two powerful tools with which to create a new kind of future for the contemplative life: a rich tradition of their writings, and an art form, the chant, by which the elusive realities they are trying to describe can be made real. Most encouraging of all, we have the historical record of the tradition itself, its proven ability generation after generation in deserts, in the countryside, in cities, in every conceivable environment, to lead men and women to "the prime good of contemplation, that is, the gaze turned in the direction of the things of God" (*Cass/CWS* 43).

Bibliography

Amadeus of Lausanne. "Homily IV." *Magnificat: Homilies in Praise of the Blessed Virgin Mary by Bernard of Clairvaux and Amadeus of Lausanne.* Introduction by Chrysogonus Waddell. 18 of Cistercian Fathers Series. Kalamazoo, Michigan: Cistercian Publications, 1979.

Antiphonale Monasticum Pro Diurnis Horis: Juxta Vota RR. DD. Abbatum Congregationum Confoederatarum. Paris: Desclée, 1938.

Athanasius. "The Letter to Marcellinus." *Athanasius.* Ed. Robert C. Gregg. The Classics of Western Spirituality. New York: Paulist Press, 1980.

Augustine, Saint. *The Confessions of Saint Augustine.* Trans. E.B. Pusey. Mount Vernon, n.s.: Peter Pauper Press, n.d.

———. *Expositions on the Book of Psalms.* Trans. Anon. A Library of Fathers of the Holy Catholic Church. Vol. 6. Oxford: John Henry Parker, 1857.

———. *On the Psalms.* Trans. Scholastica Hebgin and Felicitas Corrigan. Ancient Christian Writers: The Works of the Fathers in Translation. Eds. Johannes Quasten and Walter J. Burghardt. Vol. 1. New York: Newman Press, 1960.

Benedict, Saint. *RB 1980: The Rule of St. Benedict in Latin and English with Notes.* Ed. Timothy Fry. Collegeville, Minnesota: The Liturgical Press, 1981.

Bernard of Clairvaux. *On the Song of Songs*. Trans. various. Cistercian Fathers Series. 4 vols. Kalamazoo, Michigan: Cisercian Publications, 1971–80.

The Book of Common Prayer (New York: The Church Hymnal Corporation, 1979).

Cassian, John. *The Conferences*. A Select Library of Nicene and Post-Nicene Fathers of the Christian Church, Second Series. Vol. 11. Grand Rapids, Michigan: Wm. B. Eerdman, 1982. 291–545.

———. *John Cassian: Conferences*. Trans. Colm Lubheid. The Classics of Western Spirituality. Ed. John Farina. New York: Paulist Press, 1985.

———. *The Twelve Books on the Institutes of the Coenobia*. A Select Library of Nicene and Post-Nicene Fathers of the Christian Church, Second Series. Vol. 11. Grand Rapids, Michigan: Wm. B. Eerdman, 1982. 161–290.

Climacus, John. *The Ladder of Divine Ascent*. Ed. Kallistos Ware. Trans. Colm Luibheid and Norman Russell. The Classics of Western Spirituality. Ed. Richard J. Payne. New York: Paulist Press, 1982.

Evagrius Ponticus. "The Praktikos." *The Praktikos & Chapters on Prayer*. Third Printing, 1981. Ed. John Eudes Bamberger. Kalamazoo, Michigan: Cistercian Publications, 1972. 4 of Cistercian Studies Series.

Graduale Sacrosanctae Romanae Ecclesiae de Tempore et de Sanctis. Sarthe, France: Abbey St.-Pierre de Solesmes, 1974.

Gregory of Nyssa, Saint. *The Life of Moses*. Trans. Abraham J. Malherbe and Everett Ferguson. The Classics of Western Spirituality. Ed. Richard J. Payne. New York: Paulist Press, 1978.

Gregory the Great, Saint. *Expositiones: In Canticum Canticorum; In Librum Primum Regum*. Ed. Patricius Verbraken. Corpus Christianorum, Series Latina. 144. Turnhout, Belgium: Brepols, 1963.

———. *Homiliae in Hiezechihelem Prophetam*. Ed. Marcus Adriaen. Corpus Christianorum, Series Latina. 142. Turnhout, Belgium: Brepols, 1971.

———. *Morals on the Book of Job*. Trans. Anon. A Library of Fathers of the Holy Catholic Church. 4 Vols. Oxford: John Henry Parker, 1844–50.

Guido of Arezzo, see Strunk, Oliver.

Guigo II. *The Ladder of Monks and Twelve Meditations*. Trans. Edmund Colledge and James Walsh. Cistercian Studies Series. 48. Kalamazoo, Michigan: Cistercian Publications, 1981.

Hesychius of Jerusalem. "Hesychius of Jerusalem." *Writings from the* Philokalia *on Prayer of the Heart*. Tenth impression, 1979. Ed. E. Kadloubovsky and G. E. H. Palmer. London: Faber and Faber, 1951. 420.

Hiley, David. *Western Plainchant: A Handbook*. Oxford: Clarendon Press, 1995.

Ihm, Clauria Carlen, ed. *The Papal Encyclicals, 1878–1903*. McGrath: n.p., 1981.

Leclercq, Jean. *The Love of Learning and the Desire for God: A Study of Monastic Culture*. Trans. Catharine Misrahi. New York: Fordham UP, 1982.

Le Saux, Henri. *Prayer*. Philadelphia, PA: Westminster Press, 1967.

The Liber Usualis with Introduction and Rubrics in English. Eds. Benedictines of Solesmes. Tournai: Desclée & Co., 1934.

Litton, James, ed. *The Plainsong Psalter*. New York: Church Publishing Incorporated, 1988.

Maximus the Confessor, Saint. *The Church, the Liturgy and the Soul of Man: The* Mystagogia *of St. Maximus the Confessor*. Trans. Stead, Julian. Still River, Massachusetts: St. Bede's Publications, 1982.

Merton, Thomas. *Bread in the Wilderness*. Collegeville, Minnesota: The Liturgical Press, 1986.

Officium Majoris Hebdomadae et Octavae Paschae Cum Cantu. Paris: Desclée & Co., 1925.

Origen. *Origen*. Trans. Rowan A. Greer. The Classics of Western Spirituality. Ed. Richard J. Payne. New York: Paulist Press, 1979.
———. *The Song of Songs: Commentary and Homilies*. Trans. R.P. Lawson. Ancient Christian Writers. Vol. 26. New York: Newman Press, 1956.

Papal Encyclicals, The. See Ihm, Clauria Carlen

Plainsong Psalter, The. See Litton, John.

Pothier, Joseph. *Les mélodies grégoriennes.* Tournai: Desclée, 1880.

Richard of St. Victor. *The Twelve Patriarchs; The Mystical Ark; Book Three of The Trinity.* Trans. Grover A. Zinn. The Classics of Western Spirituality. Ed. Richard J. Payne. New York: Paulist Press, 1979.

The Roman Breviary. Trans. John, Marquess of Butte. 4 vols. London: William Blackwood and Sons, 1908.

Strunk, Oliver, ed. *Source Readings in Music History.* New York: W.W. Norton, 1950.

Taft, Robert. *The Liturgy of the Hours East and West: The Origins of the Divine Office and Its Meaning for Today.* Collegeville, Minnesota: The Liturgical Press, 1986.

Teresa of Avila, Saint. *The Interior Castle.* Trans. Kieran Kavanaugh and Otilio Rodriguez. The Classics of Western Spirituality. Ed. Richard J. Payne. New York: Paulist Press, 1979.

Wagner, Peter. *Introduction to the Gregorian Melodies: A Handbook of Plainsong.* Trans. Agnes Orme and E.G.P. Wyatt. Reprint introduction by Richard L. Crocker. London: The Plainsong & Mediaeval Music Society, 1901.

Werner, Eric. *The Sacred Bridge: The Interdependence of Liturgy and Music in Synagogue and Church During the First Millennium.* Hoboken, New Jersey: KTAV Publishing House, 1985.

Appendix 1

Monastic Writers on the Inner Life

OUR SITUATION IN EVERYDAY LIFE

We do many earthly things every day, and after these we return to prayer. The mind is fired to compunction, but images of those things we have done are turned over in the mind, and hamper the intention of compunction in prayer, and what we did willingly outwardly, inwardly we allow still to be entertained, so that certain fantasies of thought spread through the mind by means of the fleshly imagination, so that the mind does not collect itself closely into a unity in prayer. This is the voice of the flesh.

–Gregory the Great, 6th century (*G/HHP* 108)

And when we have been feeling that the aim of our heart was directed towards what we purposed, insensibly the mind returns to its previous wandering thoughts . . . and is taken up with daily distractions and incessantly drawn away by numberless things that take it captive, [and we are finally] overcome and in despair driven to this opinion, that it is from no fault of our own but from a fault of our nature that these wanderings of the mind are found in mankind.

–John Cassian, 5th century (*Cass/SL* 362)

The soul [in its 'everyday' state] has not in fact put off its original [divine] form, but it has put on one foreign to it. This latter is an addition; the former has not been lost.

–Bernard of Clairvaux, 12th century (*Bern/SS* 4: 172)

THE INNER STRUGGLE AGAINST OUR EVERYDAY, "NATURAL" SITUATION

Let one who eagerly strives for contemplation of celestial things, who sighs for knowledge of divine things, learn to assemble the dispersed Israelites—let him endeavor to restrain the wanderings of the mind.

 —Richard of St. Victor, 12th century (*Rich* 142)

Fight always with your thoughts and call them back when they wander away. . . . Do not lose heart when your thoughts are stolen away. Just remain calm, and constantly call your mind back.

 —John Climacus, 7th century (*Clim* 112)

Unless the mind is kept in its stationary place by stringent discipline in self-keeping, it is always sliding back into worse. . . . When one strives after better things, one has, as it were, to strain against the force of the stream. . . . Unless there is an ardent striving of the heart, the water of the world is not overcome, that water by which the soul is ever being borne down to the lowest place.

 —Gregory the Great, 6th century (*G/MBJ* 2: 43)

We read in the Gospel how the Word [Jesus] says, "Agree with your adversary quickly, while you are in the way with him, so that he does not hand you over to the judge, and the judge to the executioner." [Mt 5:25] [Agreeing with your adversary] will be impossible unless you disagree with yourself and become your own adversary, and fight against yourself without respite in a continual and hard struggle, and renounce your inveterate habits and inborn inclinations. But this is a hard thing. If you attempt it in your own strength, it will be as though you were trying to stop the raging of a torrent, or to make the Jordan run backwards. What can you do then? You must seek the Word, to agree with him, by his operation. Flee to him who is your adversary, that through him you may no longer be his adversary, but that he who threatens you may caress you and may transform you by his outpoured grace more effectually than by his outraged anger.

 —Bernard of Clairvaux, 12th century (*Bern/SS* 4: 196)

LISTENING AS A DISCIPLINE FOR THE MIND

We merit the beatific vision by our constancy in listening. . . . Since the sense of [inner] sight is not yet ready, let us rouse up our hearing, let us exercise it and take in the truth. . . . The hearing, if it be loving, alert and faithful, will restore the [inner] sight.

–Bernard of Clairvaux, 12th century (*Bern/SS* 2: 92, 94)

PSALMODY AS A DISCIPLINE FOR THE WANDERING MIND

Rising up from the prayers, the monks begin the psalmody. And now, divided into two sections, they chant alternately with one another, thus reinforcing the study of the scriptural passages, and at the same time producing for themselves attentiveness and an undistracted heart.

–Basil the Great, 4th century (*Hours* 39)

The harmonious reading of the psalms is a figure and type of such undisturbed and calm equanimity of our thoughts. . . . For thus beautifully singing praises, [the singer] brings rhythm to his soul and leads it, so to speak, from disproportion to proportion . . . and gaining its composure by the singing of the phrases, it becomes forgetful of the passions and, while rejoicing, sees in accordance with the mind of Christ.

–Athanasius, 4th century (*Athan* 124, 126)

By means of the voice of psalmody, directed by the attention of the heart, a way to the heart is prepared for almighty God, so that he may pour into an attentive mind either the mysteries of prophecy or the grace of compunction.

–Gregory the Great, 6th century (*G/HHP* 12)

THE INTELLIGENCE OF A QUIET MIND AND SACRED SCRIPTURE

When the mind is at rest from outward employments, the weight of the divine precepts is more fully discerned. It is then that the mind penetrates, in a more lively manner, the words of God, when it refuses to admit within, the tumult of worldly cares. . . . For the crowd of earthly thoughts, when it clamors around, closes the ear of the mind.

—Gregory the Great, 6th century (*G/MBJ* 3: 32)

Unless the minds of readers are perfected to a high level, the divine scriptures, as if on the lowest plane, lie uncomprehended. [But if you lift your mind] in contemplation, then what you first thought was spoken in the scriptures according to the ways of the earth, appears not of the earth. And it happens that as you perceive the words of sacred scripture to be of a celestial nature, so you yourself, illuminated by the grace of contemplation, are raised to the level of celestial nature.

–Gregory the Great, 6th century (*G/HHP* 87)

[In a quiet state one may feel] an unaccustomed expansion of the mind, an infusion of light that illuminates the intellect to understand scripture and comprehend the mysteries.

–Bernard of Clairvaux, 12th century (*Bern/SS* 3: 102)

The first and principle thing for the soul that strives to ascend to the height of knowledge must be the effort to know itself."

–Richard of St. Victor, 12th century (*Rich* 133)

SPEAKING UNDER THE DISCIPLINE OF SILENCE

To speak of God is to be of the most extreme quiet and freedom of mind. For the tongue is well directed in speech when the inner mind has been quieted in secure tranquility.

–Gregory the Great, 6th century (*G/HHP* 182)

The censure of silence is a kind of nourishment of the word. . . . We ought not to learn silence by speaking, but rather by keeping silence we must learn to speak.

–Gregory the Great, 6th century (*G/HHP* 170)

SPEAKING UNDER THE DISCIPLINE OF LISTENING

Because it is Christ and his Spirit who speak through holy prophets, the more clearly these prophets hear this speaking, the closer kin they are to Him whose seat or resting place they are worthy of being. The more completely they are able to be refreshed with the nourishment of the Word, the more they have within themselves a

small room or cell for refreshment. For indeed they are friends of
the bridegroom, and they stand and rejoice with joy because of the
voice of the bridegroom [Jn 3:29]. Therefore, when holy prophets
speak divine things, they also hear; and because they have under-
gone a definite experience, when the Spirit speaks in them, they
hear themselves but not themselves, because they themselves are
speaking, but in their speech they acknowledge with reverence the
speaking of another. Therefore, in that which they both hear and
speak, they refresh others and at the same time are refreshed. They
refresh their hearers when they make the Word known in its own
voice; they themselves are refreshed when that Word, which they
make known, is made known to them by divine revelation. . . . And
so those prophets feed others by speaking, who are themselves fed
by listening to that which they speak.

–Gregory the Great, 6th century (*G/LPR* 358–359)

THE ACTIVE AND CONTEMPLATIVE LIVES

The lives of holy prophets are double, obviously active and
contemplative, but the active comes before the contemplative
because a person is directed from good works toward contemplation. But the contemplative is greater in merit than the active,
because the active labors in the manner of our ordinary efforts, but
the contemplative indeed savors now, by means of a deep inner
taste, the rest to come. . . . And however good the active work might
be, the contemplative nevertheless is better, because the first dies
with this mortal life, but the second truly grows more complete in
the life of immortality. . . . For even though by action we accom-
plish something good, nevertheless by contemplation we awake to
the desire for heaven. Hence also with Moses the active life is called
service, but the contemplative is called freedom.

–Gregory the Great, 6th century (*G/HHP* 37)

That mind is blessed indeed, which, the higher it is taken in divine
contemplation, the more devotedly it exerts itself in holy work.

–Gregory the Great, 6th century (*G/LPR* 95)

Appendix 2

The Eight Psalm Tones Annotated

PSALM TONE 1

The Tone

In the example below, the cantor begins Psalm 142 using the first notes of the tone, called the "intonation." The underlined words in the psalm tell the cantor where to leave the reciting note, which is an A in tone 1 and is indicated here with a lozenge. The choir joins at verse 2 ("I pour . . . ") and omits the intonation:

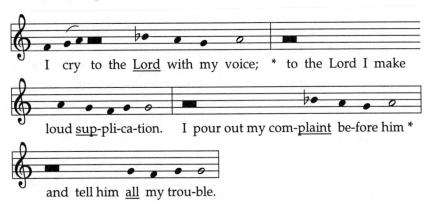

I cry to the <u>Lord</u> with my voice; * to the Lord I make

loud <u>sup</u>-pli-ca-tion. I pour out my com-<u>plaint</u> be-fore him *

and tell him <u>all</u> my trou-ble.

The Flex

If the first half of the psalm verse contains two clauses, the first half may be broken with a flex. The flex is indicated by a cross in the text. The flex never is used in the second half of the tone, and it never is used on the first verse of the psalm by the cantor. After the flex, singing resumes on the reciting note:

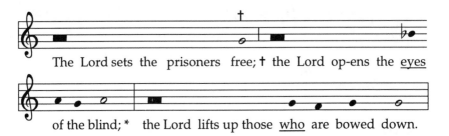

The Lord sets the prisoners free; † the Lord op-ens the <u>eyes</u>

of the blind; * the Lord lifts up those <u>who</u> are bowed down.

If the last word of the first clause contains more than one syllable, the change of pitch at the flex comes just *after* the accented syllable:

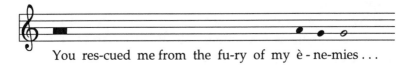

You res-cued me from the fu-ry of my è-ne-mies . . .

Extra Syllable Positions

As explained in Chapter Two, some tones may require added notes to accommodate all the syllables of the verse at the mediation or ending. At the mediation of tone 1, these added syllables may be placed in any or all of three positions, in order to achieve natural recitation of the line. These positions are indicated by the optional black notes in parentheses below:

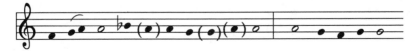

Added syllables are never placed on the B♭. One or more syllables may be added at each optional note. The syllables are distributed in the three positions according to the natural accent pattern of the sentence. Ties (‿) may be used to indicate syllables which should be sung on the same note. Where syllables are not tied, it is assumed that each new syllable moves to the next note of the tone. Here are a few examples:

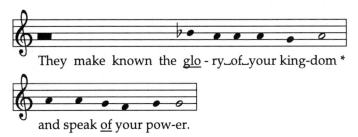

They make known the glo - ry‿of‿your king-dom *

and speak of your pow-er.

In this case added syllables are sung on the A until the second accent of the phrase is reached, the first syllable of "kíngdom." In the next verse, syllables are added in two of the three positions. "Words" is accented, and it is allowed to rest on the A alone to avoid placing emphasis on "his":

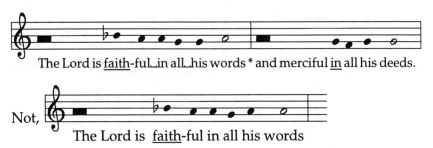

The Lord is faith-ful‿in all‿his words * and merciful in all his deeds.

Not, The Lord is faith-ful in all his words

By the same logic we might be tempted to sing "his deeds" in the second half on the notes "F–G" instead of "G–G" in order to give emphasis to the accented word "deeds." But here the two G's are part of the structure of the tone, and we do not have the option of changing the first one.

In this final example, an extra syllable is required at the third position:

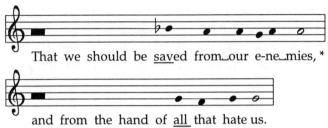

That we should be sa<u>v</u>ed from our e-ne mies, *

and from the hand of <u>all</u> that hate us.

Here the accent is on the first syllable of "énemies," and so that syllable is left alone on the G and the final two syllables are placed on the A. Otherwise, the ear would hear an unnatural stress on the last syllable of "eneMIES."

Alternate Endings

The ending of any psalm tone is determined by the antiphon which goes with the psalm. An ending is chosen which will provide a smooth transition from the end of the psalm back to the beginning of the antiphon. Tone 1 has many possible endings. Three common ones are:

PSALM TONE 2
The Tone

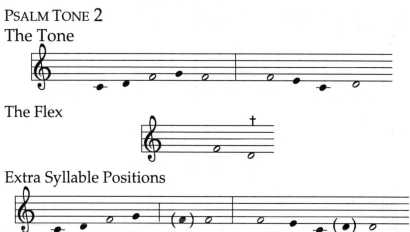

The Flex

Extra Syllable Positions

Extra syllables are never added on the G of the mediation. As indicated by the vertical half bar, the mediation ends after the G if the half-verse ends in an accented word or syllable. Here are examples of both added syllables and the truncated mediation:

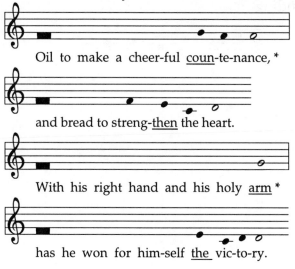

Oil to make a cheer-ful <u>coun</u>-te-nance, *

and bread to streng-<u>then</u> the heart.

With his right hand and his holy <u>arm</u> *

has he won for him-self <u>the</u> vic-to-ry.

Alternate Ending

PSALM TONE 3 (MONASTIC FORM)

The Tone

The Flex

Extra Syllable Positions

Extra syllables are never sung on the D of the mediation.

Alternate Ending

PSALM TONE 4

The Tone

The Flex

Extra Syllable Positions

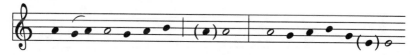

As in tone 2, the mediation may be truncated if the first half-verse ends in an accented word or syllable. Here are examples of added syllables and the truncated mediation:

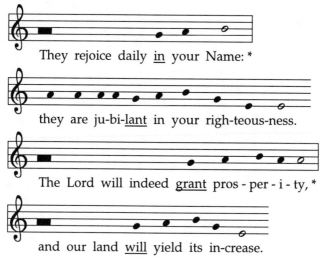

They rejoice daily <u>in</u> your Name: *

they are ju-bi-<u>lant</u> in your righ-teous-ness.

The Lord will indeed <u>grant</u> pros - per - i - ty, *

and our land <u>will</u> yield its in-crease.

Alternate Ending

PSALM TONE 5

The Tone

The Flex

Extra Syllable Positions

As in tone 2 and as indicated by the vertical line, the mediation may be truncated. Please see tone 2 for an example.

Alternate Endings
None

PSALM TONE 6

The Tone

The Flex

Extra Syllable Positions

Alternate Endings
None

PSALM TONE 7
The Tone

The Flex

Extra Syllable Positions

Extra syllables are never added on the F of the mediation. The three positions at the mediation are used as in tone 1. Please refer to the annotations for that tone.

Alternate Endings

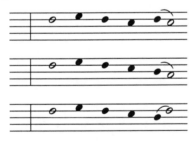

PSALM TONE 8
The Tone

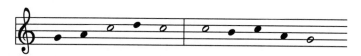

The Flex

Extra Syllable Positions

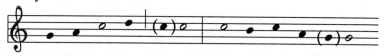

Extra syllables are never placed on the D of the mediation. As in tone 2 and as indicated by the vertical line, the mediation may be truncated. Please see tone 2 for an example.

Alternate Endings

Appendix 3

What Is a "Mode"?

1. Most simply, a mode is a musical scale. In the medieval system there are four pairs, or eight modes. There are only two modes commonly used in later Western music, the major and minor. Chants in different modes have roughly the same kind of difference in sound as between songs in major keys and songs in minor keys. Each mode has its characteristic sound or "feel." Each mode also has short melodic patterns, often as the beginnings and ends of phrases, which are common in many chants of that mode.

2. There are four modal scales in the medieval system, one for each pair of modes. The four scales can be heard by playing the white keys of the piano beginning on D, E, F, then G. One can sing the scale for modes one and two by beginning on "re" and singing up the scale to "re" an octave higher. To sing the scale for modes 3/4, begin on "mi," for modes 5/6 begin on "fa," and for modes 7/8 begin on "sol." You will discover that the essential differences among these scales lie where the half-steps fall (the steps between mi-fa and ti-do). Practicing these scales—always beginning on the same pitch, though on a different syllable according to the mode—will give singers a good feel for the qualities of these scales.

3. Each of the eight modes has a psalm tone associated with it. That tone is used for the recitation of psalms or canticles following an antiphon in that mode.

4. How do you tell what mode a chant is in?

a. Look at the last note of the chant. If it is a D, you have either mode 1 or mode 2; E indicates 3 or 4; F indicates 5 or 6; G, 7 or 8.
b. Look back from the final (i.e., from the last note of the chant) at the range of the chant. If the notes are all above the final (or perhaps all above except for an occasional one-note drop below the final), then the chant is probably in one of the odd-numbered modes, that is, the first of the two possible modes that end on that final. If the chant ranges well above and below the final, it is probably in the second, even-numbered mode of the two which end on that final.
c. The medieval modal system was devised in theory after many of the chants were composed. The system is very useful, but don't be surprised to find melodies which don't fit into any class very well.
d. It is customary today to refer to the modes by number. Each chant in the *Graduale Romanum* and the *Antiphonale Monasticum* has its mode indicated by a Roman numeral at the beginning of the chant. For many years, however, the modes were referred to by Greek names. The odd-numbered modes, those whose ranges are above the final, were called the "authentic" modes and given the names Dorian (D), Phrygian (E), Lydian (F), and Mixolydian (G). The even-numbered modes on these same pitches, those with ranges above and below the final, were called "plagal" modes and were given names derived from their authentic partners: Hypo-dorian, Hypo-phrygian, Hypo-lydian, and Hypo-mixolydian.

Appendix 4

Chant Notation Guide

Chant publications today always use a four-line staff. "Clef signs" are simply stylized letters placed on the line to which they refer. For example, the following C indicates that the top line of the staff is the note C, or "doh" on the scale of "doh, re, mi":

The C clef sometimes appears on other lines than the top one. In these cases, "doh" moves to the line indicated by the clef:

An F clef is also used. The line it marks is the note F or "fa" on the scale.

The clef may move within a single chant, in order to keep the melody on the staff and avoid leger lines. In all cases pitches are relative. The entire chant should be placed in a range comfortable for singers. Reciting notes are often marked on C, but this indication especially should be taken as relative. An actual C pitch is almost certain to be too high. A range between $F^\sharp$ and $A^\flat$ is more manageable for most choirs.

Only one accidental, "$B^\flat$," is common in chant notation. It is usually added as an accidental, although occasionally (see the "Alma redemptoris," Vespers liturgy, Appendix 8) it is placed with the clef sign in each staff and holds good for the entire staff. When used as an accidental, it usually holds good until the end of the word in which it occurs or to the next bar line, even a half or quarter bar.

BASIC NEUME FORMS
A Single Pitch

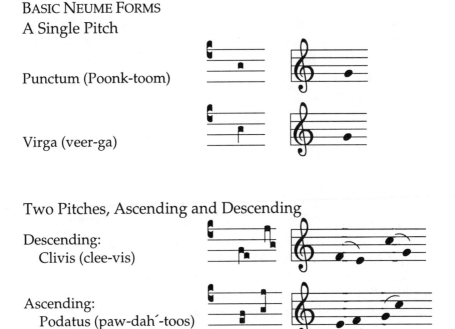

Punctum (Poonk-toom)

Virga (veer-ga)

Two Pitches, Ascending and Descending

Descending:
 Clivis (clee-vis)

Ascending:
 Podatus (paw-dah´-toos)

Three Pitches

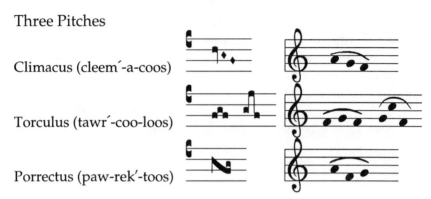

Climacus (cleem´-a-coos)

Torculus (tawr´-coo-loos)

Porrectus (paw-rek´-toos)

Rhythmic Signs

The differing shapes of the neumes above have no rhythmic significance. As most often performed today, each of the above pitches receives one rhythmic "pulse." The earliest manuscripts (although they do not indicate exact pitches) do contain rhythmic signs. Only three of these are in common use today, the dot, the episema, and the quilisma.

The "dot" doubles length of the note preceding it:

The "episema" ("eh-pi-see´-ma") lengthens the note under it slightly, but does not double it. Over (or under) the first note of a podatus or clivis, the episema lengthens *both* pitches of the neume. Over the virga of a climacus, it applies only to the virga. If it is meant to apply to all three notes of a torculus, it will be long enough to cover all three. Over a porrectus, it applies only to the part of the neume it actually covers. There is no equivalent marking in modern notation, but the following examples show what the episema looks like.

Punctum   Podatus   Clivis   Climacus   Torculus   Porrectus

The "quilisma" ("qui-lis'-ma") is always on a rising pitch and appears as a jagged note. It is most often interpreted by lengthening the note *before* it slightly. The quilisma pitch itself is sung at normal speed.

Appendix 5

A Guide to the Pronunciation of "Church" Latin

"Church" Latin pronunciation is based on Italian. In an attempt to imitate the Italian pronunciation of the "e" vowel in a Latin word like "pleni," many American choirs have been taught to sing "playnee." The sound "ay" in English, however, is a diphthong, composed of two sounds, and the Italian equivalent is not. The broad Italian "e" is a single, pure vowel which only roughly resembles the English "ay." The diphthong can be avoided if American choirs are asked to sing the Latin "e" short but pure, as in "met." The "o" diphthong of "so" can likewise be avoided if choirs are asked to sing the Latin "o" as "aw." A good practice phrase is "in nomine Domini" (in the name of the Lord)—"een nawmeeneh dawmeenee"

VOWELS
   A as in father
   E as in met
   I as in sweet
   O as the aw in awkward
   U as in soon
   AE and OE as in met (saeculum)

A Guide to the Pronunciation of "Church" Latin

CONSONANTS

C as K (cum = koom) except before e, ae, oe, i, when it sounds
like ch in chin (caeli =chehlee)

CC before a, ae, oe, i as ch in chin (ecce = ehcheh)

CH always as K

SC before e, ae, oe, i as sh in shelf (ascendit = ahshendeet)

G as in get, except before e, ae, oe, i, then as in genuine

GN as NY (agnus = ahnyoos)

H is mute except in the words nihil and mihi.

J as Y

S as in season, not as a z

Ti as in tzee (gratia = grahtzeeah)

TH as T

X as KS (examine = ehksahmeeneh); but before e, ae, oe, i X =
KSH (ekshehlsees)

Appendix 6

The "Marialis" Ordinary with Simple Gloria

e - le - i - son. Ky - ri - e

e - le - i - son. Ky - - - ri - e e-

le - i - son *Cantor:* Ky- ri - e

All: e - - - - - - - - - -

le - i - son.

Cantor: Glo-ri - a in ex-cel-sis De-o ; *All:* Et in ter-ra pax

ho-mi-ni-bus; bo-nae vo-lun-ta-tis. Lau-da-mus te. Be-ne -

di- ci-mus te. A - dor - ra-mus te. Glo-ri - fi - ca-mus te.

Gra-ti - as a - gi-mus ti - bi; prop-ter mag-nam glo-ri-am tu-am.

Do-mi-ne De-us, Rex cae-les-tis, De-us Pa-ter om-ni-po-tens.

Do-mi-ne Fi - li un - i - ge - ni - te, Je - su Chri-ste. Do-mi-ne

De-us, Ag-nus De-i; Fi - li -us Pa-tris; Qui to - lis pec-ca-ta

mun-di; mi-se-re-re no-bis. Qui tol - lis pec-ca - ta mun-di;

su - sci - pe de-pre - ca - ti - o - nem nos-tram. Qui se-des ad

dex-te-ram Pa-tris; mi-se - re - re no-bis. Quo-ni-am tu so - lus

Sanc-tus. Tu so-lus Do-mi-nus. Tu so - lus Al - tis - si-mus;

Je - su Chri - ste. Cum Sanc-to Spi-ri- tu; in glo - ri - a

De - i Pa - - tris. A - - - - men.

We be-lieve in one God, the Fa-ther, the Al-might-y,

ma-ker of hea-ven and earth, of all that is, seen and

un - seen. We be-lieve in one Lord, Je-sus Christ, the on - ly

Son of God, e - ter-nal-ly be-got-ten of the Fa-ther, God

from God, Light from Light, true God from true God,

be - got-ten, not made, of one Be-ing with the Fa-ther.

Through him all things were made. For us and for our

sal - va - tion he came down from hea-ven: by the pow-er

of the Ho-ly Spi-rit he be-came in-car-nate from the Vir-gin

Ma-ry, and was made man. For our sake he was cru-ci-fied

un-der Pon-tius Pi-late: he suf-fered death and was bur-ied.

On the third day he rose a-gain in ac-cord-ance with the Scrip-

tures; he a-scend-ed in - to hea-ven and is seat-ed at the

right hand of the Fa-ther. He will come a-gain in glo - ry

to judge the liv-ing and the dead, and his king-dom will have

no end. We be-lieve in the Ho-ly Spi - rit, the Lord, the

Giv-er of life, who pro-ceeds from the Fa-ther and the Son.

With the Fa-ther and the Son he is wor-shiped and glo -

ri - fied. He has spo-ken through the Pro-phets. We be-lieve

in one ho-ly cath-o-lic and a-po-sto-lic Church. We ac-

know-ledge one bap - tism for the for-give-ness of sins.

We look for the re-sur-rec-tion of the dead, and the life of the

Appendix 7

"O clavis David" (O Key of David) and Magnificat

Mode 2

O cla-vis Da - vid, * et scep-trum do - mus Is - ra - el,   qui

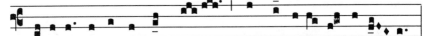

á-pe-ris, et ne-mo clau - dit,   clau-dis, et ne - mo á-pe - rit,

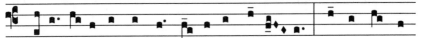

Ve-ni, et e-duc vin-ctum de do-mo cár-ce - ris,   se-dén-tem in

te - ne - bris   et um-bra mor-tis.

Or the antiphon may be sung in English:

O Key of Da - vid, * and scep-ter of the house of Is-ra-el, you o - pen and no one shuts, you shut and no one o - - pens, Come and bring the pri-son-er out of the pri - - son and them sit-ting in dark - ness and the sha - dow of death.

The Magnificat

Tone 2

The intonation is repeated on each verse.

Cantor: My soul doth magnify the <u>Lord</u>, *
 and my spirit hath rejoiced in God <u>my</u> Savior.

All: For he hath re<u>gar</u>ded *
 the lowliness of his <u>hand</u>maiden.

For behold from <u>hence</u>forth *
 all generations shall call <u>me</u> blessèd.

For he that is mighty hath mag<u>ni</u>fied me, *
 and holy <u>is</u> his Name.

And his mercy is on them that <u>fear</u> him *
 throughout all gen<u>er</u>ations.

He hath showed strength with his <u>arm</u>; *
 he hath scattered the proud in the imagination <u>of</u> their hearts.

He hath put down the mighty from their <u>seat</u>, *
 and hath exalted the hum<u>ble</u> and meek.

He hath filled the hungry with <u>good</u> things, *
 and the rich he hath sent emp<u>ty</u> away.

He remembering his mercy hath holpen his servant <u>Is</u>rael, *
 as he promised to our forefathers; Abraham and his seed <u>for</u> ever.

Glory to the Father and to the Son and to the Holy <u>Spi</u>rit: *
 as it was in the beginning is now; and will be for <u>ev</u>er. Amen.

The antiphon "O clavis David" is repeated.

Appendix 8

First Vespers for the Third Sunday of Advent

WHY VESPERS?

"Daily Evening Prayer" in the Episcopal Church's Book of Common Prayer was created in the sixteenth century, primarily from late medieval forms of Vespers (sung in the early evening) and Compline (sung just before retiring). Evening Prayer has many advantages over Vespers for routine parish use, but as a contemplative liturgy it has three serious limitations.

First, the length of the psalmody of Evening Prayer has been reduced from that of Vespers. A community which understands the role of the psalms in gathering and quieting the mind will find the lengthier Vespers psalmody invaluable, particularly as singers come into the church filled with the distractions of a full day in the secular world.

Second, the antiphons of Vespers, short passages of scripture which tie the service to a specific day of the church year, are not included with Evening Prayer. A community which is seeking to understand the contemplative approach to scripture—an approach which offers the inner mind short excerpts, in many contexts, suggesting many varied symbolic meanings for the individual, the day, and the season—will find the antiphons a nourishing addition. If the community begins to expand its Vespers repertory to include additional feasts, singers will begin to discover in the ancient collection of Office antiphons a rich scriptural "commentary" on the Christian life and the seasons of the church year. This commentary is particularly valuable in that it was selected and assembled by minds far more sensitive than our own to the underlying symbolic unities of scripture, the liturgy, and human nature. Similarly, the short lesson or "chapter" of Vespers is typically a single verse, appealing more to the inner, symbolic mind than to the discursive intelligence.

Finally, Vespers includes only one gospel canticle, the "Magnificat." The second canticle most often associated with Evening Prayer, the "Nunc dimittis," is reserved for the Office of Compline. The effect is to allow each Office to move toward a very specific but very different gospel focus. The "Magnificat" ("My soul doth magnify the Lord . . . ") offers praise for the blessings of the day and for the return to recollection and quiet at the end of the day. The "Nunc dimittis," sung much later, looks forward to the night's rest ("Lord, now lettest thou thy servant depart in peace . . .").

The liturgy below also includes a final antiphon and prayer to the Virgin Mary. There are traditionally four "antiphons" to the Virgin provided for the year. The appointed antiphon is sung at the end of Compline, or at the end of Vespers if Compline is not to be sung. The Virgin was particularly important to monastics in the Middle Ages, as is obvious from the number of European churches named for her. One reason may be her role as an image of the perfect contemplative. Earlier statues of the Virgin and Child show her in this role very strikingly: she sits without expression, seeming to stare into the far distance, with the Child sitting upright on her lap. Frequently the Child carries a book or a globe. These early statues are the outward representation of an inner condition, as described very clearly by the twelfth-century monk Amadeus of Lausanne: "Filled therefore with the knowledge of God as the waters of the sea when they overflow, she is carried outside herself and with heart raised on high she stands still in deepest contemplation" (*Amad* 95).

First Vespers for the Third Sunday of Advent

ENTRANCE PROCESSION
Rorate caeli desuper   Mode 1

Cantor: Ro - ra - te cae-li de - su-per, et nu-bes plu-ant ju - stum.

[Drop down ye heavens from above, and let the skies pour down righteousness.]

The above refrain is repeated in full by the Choir before the Cantor begins the verses.

Cantor: Ne i-ras-cá - ris Do - mi-ne, ne ultra memíneris in-i-qui -

tà - tis; ec-ce civitas sancti facta est desérta; Sion de-sért - a

fa - cta est; Je - rú - sa-lem de - so-la - ta est;

domus sanctificatiónis tuae et glo-ri - ae tu - ae,

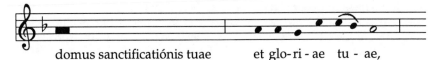

u - bi lau-da - vé - runt te pa - tres no - stri.

Refrain [Choir]: Rorate caeli desuper . . .

Refrain [Choir]: Rorate caeli desuper . . .

[*Verse 1:* Do not be angry, O Lord, or further be mindful of our sins. Behold, Zion, the Holy City has been made waste, Jerusalem has been made desolate, the home of your holiness and your glory, where our fathers praised you.

Verse 2: Comfort ye, comfort ye, my people. Your salvation shall speedily come to you. Why are you consumed with grief, and why do you renew your sorrow? Do not be afraid; I will save you. For I am the Lord your God, the Holy One of Israel, your Redeemer.]

The following prayers are said kneeling. The Officiant speaks only the words in capital letters aloud. All finish the prayers in silence.

OPEN THOU, O LORD, MY MOUTH to bless thy holy Name; cleanse also my heart from all vain, evil, and wandering thoughts; enkindle my affections; that I may say this Office worthily, with attention and devotion, and so be meet to be heard in the presence of thy divine Majesty. Through Jesus Christ our Lord. Amen.

O LORD, in union with that divine intention wherewith thou thyself on earth didst render thy praises to God, I desire to offer this my Office of prayer unto thee.

HAIL MARY, full of grace, the Lord is with thee. Blessed art thou among women, and blessed is the fruit of thy womb, Jesus. Holy Mary, Mother of God, pray for us sinners, now and at the hour of our death. Amen.

OUR FATHER, who art in heaven, *or*	OUR FATHER IN HEAVEN,
hallowed be thy Name,	hallowed be your Name,
thy kingdom come,	your kingdom come,
thy will be done,	your will be done,
on earth as it is in heaven.	on earth as in heaven.
Give us this day our daily bread.	Give us today our daily bread.
And forgive us our trespasses,	Forgive us our sins
as we forgive those	as we forgive those
who trespass against us.	who sin against us.
And lead us not into temptation,	Save us from the time of trial,
but deliver us from evil. Amen.	and deliver us from evil. Amen.

All stand.

Cantor: O God, make speed to save us.

All: O Lord, make haste to help us.

Glory to the Father and to the Son and to the Holy Spi-rit,

as it was in the beginning is now; and will be for ever. A-men.

Al - le - lu - ia.

All sit.

The Psalms

Pause at semicolons. Punctuation in the psalms has been adjusted for easier singing.

ANTIPHON *Veniet Dominus*   Mode 1

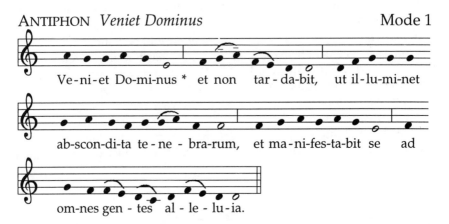

Ve-ni-et Do-mi-nus * et non tar-da-bit, ut il-lu-mi-net

ab-scon-di-ta te-ne-bra-rum, et ma-ni-fes-ta-bit se ad

om-nes gen-tes al-le-lu-ia.

[The Lord will come and will not tarry; he will bring to light the hidden things of darkness and show himself to all people alleluia. —Habak 2:3; Heb 10:37; 1 Cor 4:5]

PSALM 145:10–22 *Confiteantur tibi, Domine*

10 All your works praise you, O LORD, *
      and your faithful servants bless you.

11 They make known the glory of your kingdom *
      and speak of your power;

12 That the peoples may know of your power *
      and the glorious splendor of your kingdom.

218

13 Your kingdom is an ever<u>last</u>ing kingdom; *
    your dominion endures through<u>out</u> all ages.

14 The LORD is <u>faith</u>ful in all his words *
    and merciful <u>in</u> all his deeds.

15 The LORD upholds <u>all</u> those who fall; *
    he lifts up those <u>who</u> are bowed down.

16 The eyes of all <u>wait</u> up on <u>you</u>, O LORD, *
    and you give them their food <u>in</u> due season.

17 You <u>o</u>pen wide your hand *
    and satisfy the needs of every <u>liv</u>ing creature.

18 The LORD is <u>right</u>eous in all his ways *
    and loving <u>in</u> all his works.

19 The LORD is near to those who <u>call</u> upon him, *
    to all who call up<u>on</u> him faithfully.

20 He fulfills the desire of <u>those</u> who fear him; *
    he hears their <u>cry</u> and helps them.

21 The LORD preserves all <u>those</u> who love him, *
    but he destroys <u>all</u> the wicked.

22 My mouth shall speak the <u>praise</u> of the LORD; *
    let all flesh bless his holy Name for ev<u>er</u> and ever.

    Glory to the Father and to the Son and to the <u>Ho</u>ly Spirit; *
    as it was in the beginning is now; and will be for <u>ev</u>er. Amen.

Ve-ni-et Do-mi-nus * et non tar - da-bit, ut il-lu-mi-net
ab-scon-di-ta te - ne - bra-rum, et ma-ni-fes-ta-bit se ad
om-nes gen - tes al - le - lu-ia.

A period of silence is observed.

ANTIPHON *Jerusalem gaude*   Mode 7 (transposed)

Je-ru-sa-lem gau-de * gau-di-o ma-gno, qui - a

ve - ni - et ti-bi Sal - va - tor al - le - lu - ia.

[Rejoice, Jerusalem, with great joy, for a Savior will come to you alleluia.—cf. Is 52]

PSALM 146 *Lauda, anima mea*

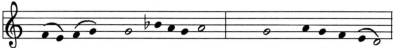

1 Hallelujah!
   Praise the <u>LORD</u> O my soul! *
      I will praise the LORD as long as I live;
      I will sing praises to my God while I <u>have</u> my being.

2 Put not your trust in rulers; nor in <u>any</u> child_of earth, *
      for there is <u>no</u> help in them.

3 When they breathe their last they <u>return</u> to earth, *
      and in that day <u>their</u> thoughts perish.

4 Happy are they who have the God of <u>Jacob</u> for_their help! *
      whose hope is in <u>the</u> LORD their God;

5 Who made heaven and earth; the seas and <u>all</u> that_is in them; *
      who keeps his <u>promise</u> for_ever;

6 Who gives justice to those <u>who</u> are oppressed, *
      and food to <u>those</u> who hunger.

7 The LORD sets the prisoners free; †
   the LORD opens the <u>eyes</u> of the blind; *
      the LORD lifts up those <u>who</u> are bowed down;

8 The LORD loves the righteous; †
 the LORD <u>cares</u> for the stranger; *
  he sustains the orphan and widow; but frustrates the <u>way</u> of the
  wicked.

9 The LORD shall <u>reign</u> for ever, *
 your God O Zion throughout all generations. <u>Hal</u>lelujah!

 Glory to the Father and to the Son and to the <u>Ho</u>ly Spirit; *
  as it was in the beginning is now; and will be for <u>ev</u>er. Amen.

Je-ru-sa-lem gau-de * gau-di-o ma-gno, qui - a

ve - ni - et ti-bi Sal - va - tor al - le - lu - ia.

A period of silence is observed.

ANTIPHON *Dabo in Sion* Mode 8

Da - bo in Si - on sa - lu - tem, * et in Je - ru -

sa - lem glo-ri-am me-am al - le - lu - ia.

[I will give salvation in Zion, and my glory in Jerusalem alleluia. —Is 46:12]

PSALM 147 *Laudate Dominum*

1 Hallelujah! How good it is to sing praises to our God! *
   how pleasant it is to honor him with praise!

2 The LORD rebuilds Jerusalem; *
   he gathers the exiles of Israel.

3 He heals the brokenhearted *
   and binds up their wounds.

4 He counts the number of the stars *
   and calls them all by their names.

5 Great is our LORD and mighty in power; *
   there is no limit to his wisdom.

6 The LORD lifts up the lowly, *
   but casts the wicked to the ground.

7 Sing to the LORD with thanksgiving; *
   make music to our God upon the harp.

8 He covers the heavens with clouds *
   and prepares rain for the earth;

9 He makes grass to grow upon the mountains *
   and green plants to serve mankind.

10 He provides food for flocks and herds *
   and for the young ravens when they cry.

11 He is not impressed by the might of a horse; *
   he has no pleasure in the strength of a man;

12 But the LORD has pleasure in those who fear him, *
   in those who await his gracious favor.

   Glory to the Father and to the Son and to the Holy Spirit; *
   as it was in the beginning is now; and will be for ever.   Amen.

Da - bo in Si - on sa - lu - tem, * et in Je - ru -

sa - lem glo-ri-am me-am al - le - lu - ia.

A period of silence is observed.

ANTIPHON *Juste et pie* Mode 2

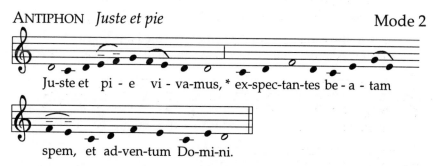

Ju-ste et pi - e vi - va-mus, * ex-spec-tan-tes be - a - tam

spem, et ad-ven-tum Do-mi-ni.

[We should live justly and with blessing, sustaining a blessed hope, the coming of the Lord. —Titus 2:13]

PSALM 147:13–21 *Lauda, Jerusalem*

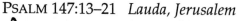

13 Worship the LORD, O Jerusalem; *
    praise your God, O Zion;

14 For he has strengthened the bars of your gates; *
    he has blessed your children within you.

15 He has established peace on your borders; *
    he satisfies you with the finest wheat.

16 He sends out his command to the earth, *
    and his word runs very swiftly.

17 He gives snow like <u>wool</u>; *
   he scatters hoarfrost <u>like</u> ashes.

18 He scatters his hail like <u>bread</u> crumbs; *
   who can stand a<u>gainst</u> his cold?

19 He sends forth his word and <u>melts</u> them; *
   he blows with his wind, and the <u>wa</u>ters flow.

20 He declares his word to <u>Ja</u>cob, *
   his statutes and his judgments <u>to</u> Israel.

21 He has not done so to any other <u>na</u>tion; *
   to them he has not revealed his judgments. Halle<u>lu</u>jah!

   Glory to the Father and to the Son and to the Holy <u>Spi</u>rit; *
   as it was in the beginning is now; and will be for e<u>ver</u>. Amen.

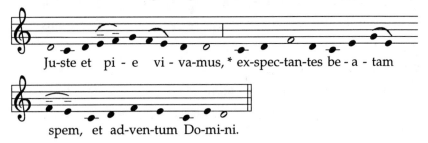

Ju-ste et pi - e vi - va-mus, * ex-spec-tan-tes be - a - tam

spem, et ad-ven-tum Do-mi-ni.

A period of silence is observed, somewhat longer than after previous psalms.

THE LITTLE CHAPTER   (Lesson—Phil 4:4–5)

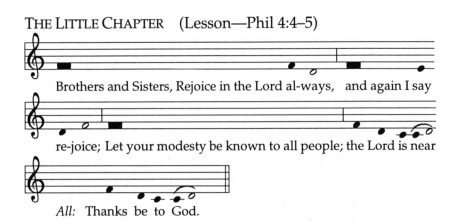

Brothers and Sisters, Rejoice in the Lord al-ways, and again I say

re-joice; Let your modesty be known to all people; the Lord is near

All: Thanks be to God.

THE SHORT RESPONSORY

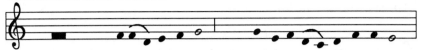

Cantor: Os-ten-de no-bis Do-mi-ne * *All:* Mi-se-ri - cor-di-am tu-am.

All repeat the entire above line together.

℣. *Cantor:* Et sa - lu - ta - re tu -um da no - bis.

All: Mi-se - ri-cor - di - am tu-am.

Cantor: Glo-ri-a Pa - tri, et Fi-li - o,   et Spi-ri - tu - i Sanc-to.

All repeat the entire first line together, "Ostende nobis. . . tuam."

THE HYMN *Conditor alme siderum* Mode 4

The Cantor begins; all join at the asterisk.

Cre - a - tor	of	the	stars	of	night;	*
When	this	old	world drew	on	toward	night.
At	your great	name,	O	Je - sus,	now
To	God the	Fa - ther,	God	the	Son,

Your peo - ple's ev - er - last - ing light;
you came but not in splen - dor bright,
all knees must bend all hearts must bow,
and God the Spi - rit Three in One,

O Christ, Re - deem - er of us all,
not as a mon - arch but the child
all things on earth with one ac - cord,
praise, hon - or, might, and glo - ry be

we pray you, hear us when we call.
of Mar - ry, blame - less moth - er mild.
like those in heav'n shall call you Lord.
from age to age e - ter - nal - ly.

A - men

226

VERSICLE AND RESPONSE

The Verse is sung by the Cantor.

℣. Drop down ye heavens from above; and let the skies pour down

right-eous-ness

℟. *All:* And let the earth open; and bring forth a Sa - vior.

THE MAGNIFICAT

Antiphon *Ante me*   Mode 1

An-te me * non est for - ma - tus De-us,   et post

me non e - rit;   qui-a mi-hi cur - va-bi - tur

om - ne ge - nu, et   con-fi - te-bi - tur   om - nis

lin-gua.

[Before me there was no god formed, and there shall be none after me; for to me every knee shall bow, and of me every tongue shall testify. —Is 43:10;45:23]

All stand. The intonation is repeated with each verse.

My soul doth <u>mag</u>nify‿the Lord, *
    and my spirit hath rejoiced in <u>God</u> my Savior.

For he <u>hath</u> regarded *
    the lowliness of <u>his</u> handmaiden.

For be<u>hold</u> from henceforth *
    all generations shall <u>call</u> me blessèd.

For he that is mighty hath <u>mag</u>nified me, *
    and ho<u>ly</u> is his Name.

And his mercy is on <u>them</u> that fear him *
    throughout all <u>gen</u>erations.

He hath showed <u>strength</u> with his arm; *
    he hath scattered the proud in the imagi<u>na</u>tion of their hearts.

He hath put down the <u>mighty</u> from‿their <u>seat</u>, *
    and hath exalted the <u>hum</u>ble and meek.

He hath filled the <u>hun</u>gry with‿good things, *
    and the rich he hath sent <u>emp</u>ty away.

He remembering his mercy; hath holpen his <u>ser</u>vant Isra‿el, *
    as he promised to our forefathers;
    Abraham and his <u>seed</u> forever.

Glory to the Father and to the Son and to the <u>Holy</u> Spirit, *
    as it was in the beginning is now; and will be for<u>ev</u>er. Amen.

An-te me * non est for - ma - tus De-us,   et post

me non e - rit;   qui-a mi-hi cur - va - bi - tur

om - ne ge - nu, et con-fi - te-bi - tur om - nis

lin-gua.

The PRAYERS

Officiant: Ky-ri-e e-le-i-son. *All:* Chri-ste e-le-i-son.

Ky-ri-e e-le-i-son.

All face the altar. The Lord's Prayer is sung on one note.

Our Father. . . . and deliver us from evil. Amen.

~or~

Our Father in heaven,
   hallowed be your Name,
   your kingdom come,
   your will be done,
     on earth as in heaven.
Give us today our daily bread.

Forgive us our sins
   as we forgive those
    who sin against us.
Save us from the time of trial,
   and deliver us from evil. Amen.

Officiant: The Lord be with you. *All:* And with your spi - rit.

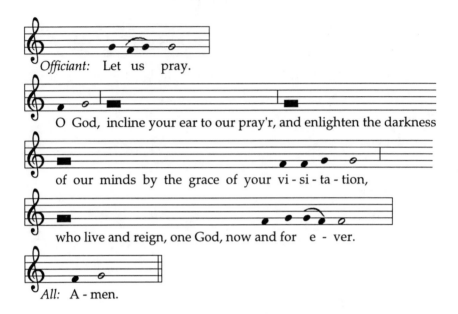

Officiant: Let us pray.

O God, incline your ear to our pray'r, and enlighten the darkness

of our minds by the grace of your vi - si - ta - tion,

who live and reign, one God, now and for e - ver.

All: A - men.

THE DISMISSAL

Officiant: The Lord be with you. *All:* And with your spi - rit.

Officiant: Be - ne - di - ca - mus Do - mi - no.

All: De - - - o gra-ti - - as.

Officiant (sung on one note): May the souls of the faithful departed
through the mercy of God rest in peace.
All: Amen.

If Mass or Compline is to follow, Vespers ends here. If not, Our Father *is now said silently, followed by:*

Officiant *(sung on one note):* The Lord grant us His peace.
All: And life everlasting. Amen.

One of the following antiphons to the Virgin, with its collect, may be sung.

Cantor: A-ve Ma-ri-a, gra-ti-a ple - na All: Do - mi-nus te-cum.

The above line is repeated in full, everyone singing.

Cantor: Be-ne - di - cta tu in mu-li-e - ri-bus, et be-ne -

dic-tus fru-ctus ven-tris tu - i. All: Do - mi-nus te-cum.

The first line is repeated in full, everyone singing, "Ave Maria. . . . tecum."

Or the following may be sung in place of "Ave Maria."

Al - - - - ma * Re-demp-to - ris Ma - ter,

quae per - vi - a cae - li Por - ta ma - nes, Et stel - la

ma - ris, suc-cur-re ca - den - ti. Sur-ge - re qui

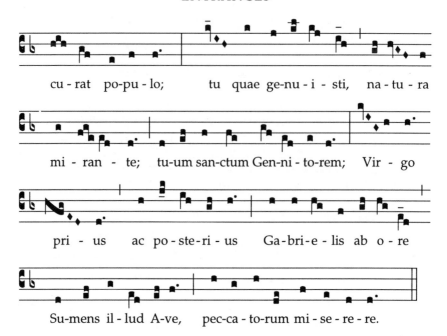

cu - rat po-pu - lo; tu quae ge-nu - i - sti, na - tu - ra

mi - ran - te; tu-um san-ctum Gen-ni - to-rem; Vir - go

pri - us ac po-ste-ri - us Ga-bri-e - lis ab o - re

Su-mens il - lud A-ve, pec-ca - to-rum mi - se - re - re.

After either of the above antiphons is sung:

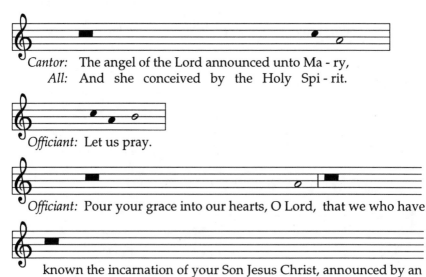

Cantor: The angel of the Lord announced unto Ma - ry,
All: And she conceived by the Holy Spi - rit.

Officiant: Let us pray.

Officiant: Pour your grace into our hearts, O Lord, that we who have

known the incarnation of your Son Jesus Christ, announced by an

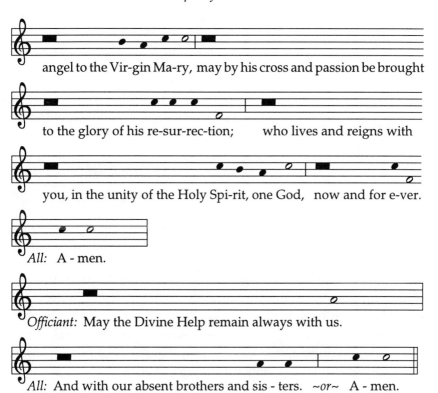

angel to the Vir-gin Ma-ry, may by his cross and passion be brought

to the glory of his re-sur-rec-tion;   who lives and reigns with

you, in the unity of the Holy Spi-rit, one God,   now and for e-ver.

All: A - men.

Officiant: May the Divine Help remain always with us.

All: And with our absent brothers and sis - ters. ~or~ A - men.

All leave the church in silence.

Appendix 9

Tenebrae for Wednesday Evening of Holy Week

WHY TENEBRAE?

"Tenebrae," which means "shadows," consists of two liturgies—Matins, sung in the monastery at about 2:00 A.M., and Lauds, sung after Matins and just before sunrise. According to custom, during Holy Week these liturgies have been sung in parish churches the evening before their appointed days, so that Wednesday Tenebrae is actually Matins and Lauds for Maundy Thursday.

For a community exploring the contemplative uses of the chant, Tenebrae is of tremendous importance. Nowhere else, not in any other liturgy available for parish use, is the sustained power of the psalms more clearly evident. Nowhere else can the symbolic force of the antiphons (mentioned in the Appendix 8 preface, "Why Vespers?") be more powerfully felt. This is not, however, a liturgy for inexperienced choirs. As the psalmody proceeds during the three hours the liturgy requires, the group's unison must grow stronger and stronger, and the energy of recitation must become steadily lighter, more gentle. The depths of silence around the phrases must open. Considerable experience with chanting the psalms is necessary if this kind of experience is to be possible.

Even an experienced choir will find the nine Latin responsories a challenge. They are given here, but the following service also includes simpler, alternative four-part settings of the responsories with English texts. The heart of the service is in the psalmody. The harmonized responsories will allow a choir to experience this uniquely powerful chanted liturgy while it is still mastering the more difficult, longer melodies. If necessary, the responsories can be spoken. If the Latin responsories are to be sung, some explanation of their form may be needed. The opening word or phrase to the asterisk is sung by one or two cantors. The choir joins and sings the rest of the "respond," that is, until the "verse," marked "℣." The cantors sing the verse. After the verse, the choir sings from a point within the responsory text marked with a second asterisk to the end of the respond. In the last responsory of the nocturn only, the entire choir then repeats the respond from beginning to end. Both of these repeats (of a portion of the respond beginning with the asterisk and of the entire respond when that is required) are indicated in the chant notation by the opening word and musical phrase printed at the end of the verse. These "cue" phrases mean that the choir is to sing from that point in the chant to the end of the respond (just before the verse).

The psalms in the following liturgy are from the Book of Common Prayer. Lesson texts are from the Revised Standard Version of the Bible, with small adjustments for easier singing. Many of the antiphon texts are in older, Elizabethan-style translations, which have been retained here because of their excellent adaption to the melodies, which were sung originally in Latin. The syntax of Elizabethan English was heavily influenced by Latin cadences, since Latin was the language of learning in England in the sixteenth century. For this reason, older English translations of chant texts sometimes adapt themselves to the "Latin" shape of the melodies more readily than do modern ones.

Tenebrae can be just as important for the parish as for the choir. Except for the Tenebrae candles and enough light for the singers, the church will be dark for the entire service. Indeed, choir lighting should be arranged so that the church is as dark as possible. These conditions underscore the contemplative nature and purpose of the service. What is usually considered "active" participation by the congregation will not be possible. The choir's offering to the congregation is one of stillness and recollected attention. Parishioners should be encouraged to come and pray, or simply sit, for as long or as short a time as anyone wishes. Silent coming and going throughout the liturgy will add to the quality of the evening, not detract from it. With its offering of recollection and prayer, Wednesday Tenebrae is an especially prayerful way to prepare for the final three days of Holy Week.

An Outline of *Tenebrae*

The Preparation
Four Prayers and the Creed

Matins
Nocturn 1
1. Three psalms, with an antiphon before and after each psalm
2. Versicle and Response and the Lord's Prayer
3. Three Lessons, each followed by a Responsory
Nocturn 2
Same as Nocturn 1
Nocturn 3
Same as Nocturn 1

Lauds
1. Five psalms, each with an antiphon before and after ("The Song of Moses," a canticle from Exodus, is considered a psalm.)
2. Versicle and Response
3. Gospel Canticle with its antiphon ("The Song of Zechariah," Lk 1:68–79)

Antiphon
"Christus factus est," The Lord's Prayer, Psalm 51, final Collect, a loud knock symbolizing the earthquake at Christ's death, return of the Tenebrae candle.

Wednesday Tenebrae

When the service begins, fifteen candles are burning on a Tenebrae hearse at the front of the church. Six altar candles also are burning. After each psalm of Matins and Lauds, one Tenebrae candle is put out. After each pair of verses in the Benedictus at Lauds, one altar candle is put out. After the Benedictus, the single burning Tenebrae candle is moved out of sight of everyone. It is returned to view after the symbolic knock from the Choir.

The following prayers are said silently, kneeling. The Officiant says the first words of all five prayers aloud.

OPEN THOU, O LORD, MY MOUTH to bless thy holy Name; cleanse also my heart from all vain, evil and wandering thoughts; enkindle my affections; that I may say this Office worthily, with attention and devotion, and so be meet to be heard in the presence of thy divine majesty. Through Jesus Christ our Lord.

O LORD, in union with that divine intention wherewith thou thyself on earth didst offer thy praises to God, I desire to offer this my Office of prayer unto thee.

All stand.

OUR FATHER . . .

HAIL MARY, full of grace, the Lord is with thee. Blessed art thou among women, and blessed is the fruit of thy womb, Jesus. Holy Mary, Mother of God, pray for us sinners, now and at the hour of our death. Amen.

I BELIEVE IN GOD, the Father almighty, maker of heaven and earth; and in Jesus Christ his only Son our Lord, who was conceived by the Holy Ghost, born of the Virgin Mary, suffered under Pontius Pilate, was crucified, dead, and buried. He descended into hell. The third day he rose again from the dead. He ascended into heaven, and sitteth on the right hand of God the Father almighty. From thence he shall come to judge the quick and the dead. I believe in the Holy Ghost, the holy catholic Church, the communion of saints, the forgiveness of sins, the resurrection of the body, and the life everlasting. Amen.

Matins—Nocturn I

ANTIPHON 1 *Zelus domus*   Mode 8

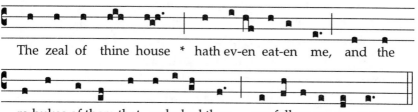

The zeal of thine house * hath ev-en eat-en me, and the
re-bukes of them that re-buked thee are fall-en up-on me.

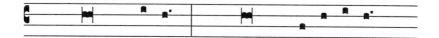

PSALM 69 *Salvum me fac*

1 Save me, O <u>God</u>, *
     for the waters have risen <u>up</u> to my neck.

2 I am sinking in deep <u>mire</u>, *
     and there is no firm <u>ground</u> for my feet.

3 I have come into deep <u>waters</u>, *
     and the torrent <u>washes</u> over me.

4 I have grown weary with my <u>cry</u>ing; †
     my throat is in<u>flamed</u>; *
         my eyes have failed from <u>look</u>ing for my God.

5 Those who hate me without a cause are more
             than the hairs of my <u>head</u>; †
     my lying foes who would destroy me are <u>mighty</u>. *
         Must I then give back what <u>I</u> never stole?

6 O God, you know my <u>foolish</u>ness, *
     and my faults are not <u>hidden</u> from you.

7 Let not those who hope in you be put to shame through me,
             Lord G<small>OD</small> of <u>hosts</u>; *
     let not those who seek you be disgraced because of me,
             O <u>God</u> of Israel.

8 Surely, for your sake have I suffered re<u>proach</u>, *
    and shame has <u>cov</u>ered my face.

9 I have become a stranger to my own <u>kin</u>dred, *
    an alien to my <u>moth</u>er's children.

10 Zeal for your house has eaten me <u>up</u>; *
    the scorn of those who scorn you has <u>fallen</u> upon me.

11 I humbled myself with <u>fast</u>ing, *
    but that was turned <u>to</u> my reproach.

12 I put on sack-cloth <u>al</u>so, *
    and became a by<u>word</u> among them.

13 Those who sit at the gate murmur a<u>gainst</u> me, *
    and the drunkards make <u>songs</u> about me.

14 But as for me, this is my <u>pray'r</u> to you, *
    at the time you <u>have</u> set, O LORD:

15 "In your great mercy, O <u>God</u>, *
    answer me with your <u>un</u>failing help.

16 Save me from the mire; do not let me <u>sink</u>; *
    let me be rescued from those who hate me and
        out of <u>the</u> deep waters.

17 Let not the torrent of waters wash over me,
    neither let the deep swallow me <u>up</u>; *
        do not let the Pit shut its <u>mouth</u> upon me.

18 Answer me, O LORD, for your love is <u>kind</u>; *
    in your great com<u>pas</u>sion, turn to me."

19 "Hide not your face from your <u>serv</u>ant; *
    be swift and answer me, for I <u>am</u> in distress.

20 Draw near to me and re<u>deem</u> me; *
    because of my ene<u>mies</u> deliver me.

21 You know my reproach, my shame, and my dis<u>hon</u>or; *
    my adversaries are <u>all</u> in your sight."

22 Reproach has broken my heart, and it cannot be <u>healed</u>; *
    I looked for sympathy, but there was none,
        for comforters, but I <u>could</u> find no one.

23 They gave me <u>gall</u> to eat, *
    and when I was thirsty, they gave me vin<u>e</u>gar to drink.

24 Let the table before them be a <u>trap</u> *
     and their sa<u>cred</u> feasts a snare.

25 Let their eyes be darkened, that they may not <u>see</u>, *
     and give them continual trem<u>bling</u> in their loins.

26 Pour out your indignation up<u>on</u> them, *
     and let the fierceness of your anger <u>ov</u>ertake them.

27 Let their camp be <u>desolate</u>, *
     and let there be none to <u>dwell</u> in their tents.

28 For they persecute him whom you have <u>stricken</u> *
     and add to the pain of those <u>whom</u> you have pierced.

29 Lay to their charge guilt upon <u>guilt</u>, *
     and let them not receive your <u>vind</u>ication.

30 Let them be wiped out of the book of the <u>living</u> *
     and not be written a<u>mong</u> the righteous.

31 As for me, I am afflicted and in <u>pain</u>; *
     your help, O God, will lift <u>me</u> up on high.

32 I will praise the Name of God in <u>song</u>; *
     I will proclaim his greatness <u>with</u> thanksgiving.

33 This will please the Lord more than an offering of <u>oxen</u>, *
     more than bullocks <u>with</u> horns and hoofs.

34 The afflicted shall see and be <u>glad</u>; *
     you who seek God, <u>your</u> heart shall live.

35 For the Lord listens to the <u>needy</u>, *
     and his prisoners he <u>does</u> not despise.

36 Let the heavens and the earth <u>praise</u> him, *
     the seas and <u>all</u> that moves in them;

37 For God will save Zion and rebuild the cities of <u>Ju</u>dah; *
     they shall live there and have it <u>in</u> possession.

38 The children of his servants will in<u>herit</u> it, *
     and those who love his Name <u>will</u> dwell therein.

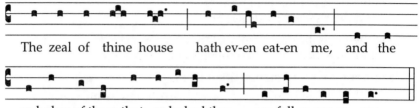

The zeal of thine house hath ev-en eat-en me, and the

re-bukes of them that re-buked thee are fall-en up-on me.

A period of silence is observed.

ANTIPHON 2 *Avertantur retrorsum* Mode 8

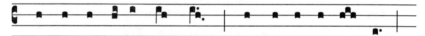

Let them be turned back-ward * and put to con - fu - sion,

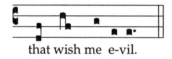

that wish me e-vil.

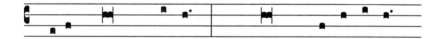

PSALM 70 *Deus, in adjutorium*

1 Be pleased, O God, to de<u>li</u>ver me; *
   O LORD, make <u>haste</u> to help me.

2 Let those who seek my life be ashamed and altogether dis<u>mayed</u>; *
   let those who take pleasure in my misfortune
        draw back <u>and</u> be disgraced.

3 Let those who say to me "Aha!" and gloat over me turn <u>back</u>, *
   because <u>they</u> are ashamed.

4 Let all who seek you rejoice and be <u>glad</u> in you; *
   let those who love your salvation say for ever, "<u>Great</u> is the LORD!"

5 But as for me, I am poor and <u>need</u>y; *
   come to me speed<u>i</u>ly, O God.

6 You are my helper and my de<u>li</u>verer; *
O Lord, <u>do</u> not tarry.

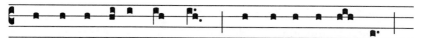

Let them be turned back-ward   and put to con - fu - sion,

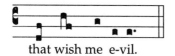

that wish me e-vil.

A period of silence is observed.

Antiphon 3 *Deus meus*   Mode 8

De-li-ver me * O my God, out of the hand of the un-god-ly.

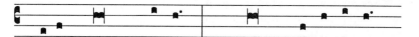

Psalm 71 *In te, Domine, speravi*

1 In you, O Lord, have I taken <u>ref</u>uge; *
let me ne<u>ver</u> be ashamed.

2 In your righteousness, deliver me and set me <u>free</u>; *
incline your ear to <u>me</u> and save me.

3 Be my strong rock, a castle to keep me <u>safe</u>; *
you are my crag <u>and</u> my stronghold.

4 Deliver me, my God, from the hand of the <u>wick</u>ed, *
from the clutches of the evildoer and <u>the</u> oppressor.

5 For you are my hope, O Lord <u>God</u>, *
my confidence <u>since</u> I was young.

6 I have been sustained by you ever since I was <u>born</u>; †
from my mother's womb you have been my <u>strength</u>; *
my praise shall be <u>al</u>ways of you.

7 I have become a portent to <u>ma</u>ny; *
    but you are my re<u>fuge</u> and my strength.

8 Let my mouth be full of your <u>praise</u> *
    and your glory <u>all</u> the day long.

9 Do not cast me off in my old <u>age</u>; *
    forsake me not <u>when</u> my strength fails.

10 For my enemies are talking a<u>gainst</u> me, *
    and those who lie in wait for
        my life take coun<u>sel</u> together.

11 They say, "God has forsa<u>ken</u> him; †
    go after him and <u>seize</u> him; *
    because there is <u>none</u> who will save."

12 O God, be not <u>far</u> from me; *
    come quickly to help <u>me</u>, O my God.

13 Let those who set themselves against me be
        put to shame and be dis<u>graced</u>; *
    let those who seek to do me evil be
        covered with <u>scorn</u> and reproach.

14 But I shall always wait in <u>patience</u>, *
    and shall praise <u>you</u> more and more.

15 My mouth shall recount your mighty
        acts and saving deeds all day <u>long</u>; *
    though I cannot know the <u>number</u> of them.

16 I will begin with the mighty works of the Lord <u>GOD</u>; *
    I will recall your righteous<u>ness</u>, yours alone.

17 O God, you have taught me since I was <u>young</u>, *
    and to this day I tell of your <u>wonderful</u> works.

18 And now that I am old and gray-headed,
        O God, do not for<u>sake</u> me, *
    till I make known your strength to this generation
        and your power to all <u>who</u> are to come.

19 Your righteousness, O God, reaches to the <u>heavens</u>; *
    you have done great things; who is <u>like</u> you, O God?

20 You have showed me great troubles and ad<u>ver</u>sities, *
    but you will restore my life and bring me up again
        from the deep pla<u>ces</u> of the earth.

21 You strengthen me more and <u>more</u>; *
     you en<u>fold</u> and comfort me,

22 Therefore I will praise you upon the lyre
          for your faithfulness, O my <u>God</u>; *
     I will sing to you with the harp, O Holy <u>One</u> of Israel.

23 My lips will sing with joy when I <u>play</u> to you, *
     and so will my soul, which <u>you</u> have redeemed.

24 My tongue will proclaim your righteousness all day <u>long</u>, *
     for they are ashamed and disgraced who sought <u>to</u> do me harm.

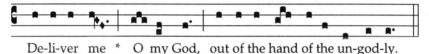

De-li-ver me * O my God, out of the hand of the un-god-ly.

℣. Let them be turned backward and put to con-fu-sion.

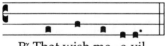

℞. That wish me e-vil.

The Lord's Prayer is said silently, standing. The M.C. may accompany the reader to the lectern. All then sit for the lesson.

LESSON 1 Lamentations 1:1–5

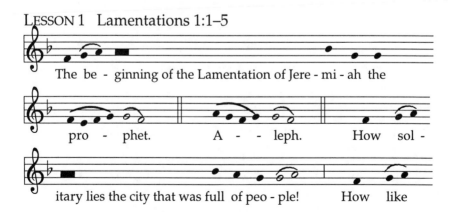

The be - ginning of the Lamentation of Jere - mi - ah the

pro - phet.   A - - leph.   How sol -

itary lies the city that was full of peo - ple!   How like

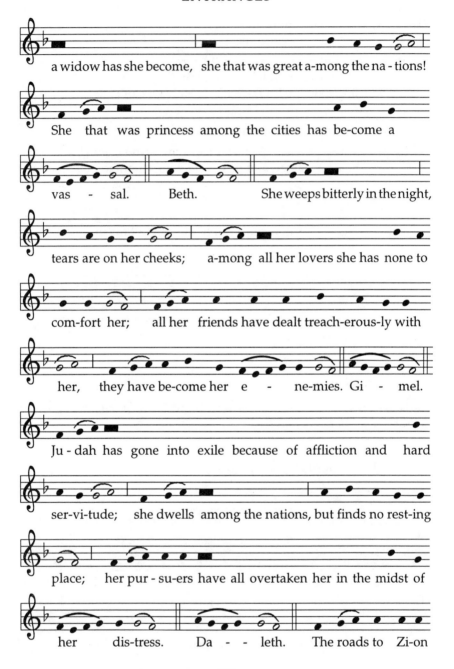

a widow has she become, she that was great a-mong the na - tions!

She that was princess among the cities has be-come a

vas - sal. Beth. She weeps bitterly in the night,

tears are on her cheeks; a-mong all her lovers she has none to

com-fort her; all her friends have dealt treach-er-ous-ly with

her, they have be-come her e - ne-mies. Gi - mel.

Ju - dah has gone into exile because of affliction and hard

ser-vi-tude; she dwells among the nations, but finds no rest-ing

place; her pur - su-ers have all overtaken her in the midst of

her dis-tress. Da - - leth. The roads to Zi-on

Tenebrae

mourn, for none come to the ap-point-ed feasts; all her

gates are desolate, her priests groan; her maidens have been

dragged a-way, and she her-self suf-fers bit - ter - ly

He. Her foes have become the head, her e - ne - mies

pros-per be-cause the Lord has made her suffer for the

multitude of her trans-gres-sions; her chil - dren have gone

a-way, cap-tives be-fore the e - - ne - my. Je - ru -

sa-lem, Je - ru - sa - lem, re - turn to the

Lord your God.

RESPONSORY 1 *In monte Oliveti*   Mode 8

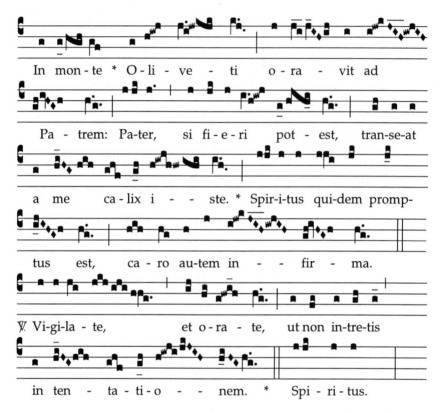

In mon-te * O-li-ve-ti o-ra-vit ad Pa-trem: Pa-ter, si fi-e-ri pot-est, tran-se-at a me ca-lix i - - ste. * Spir-i-tus qui-dem promp-tus est, ca-ro au-tem in - - fir - ma.

℣. Vi-gi-la - te, et o-ra - te, ut non in-tre-tis in ten - ta - ti-o - - nem. * Spi - ri - tus.

[Upon the Mount of Olives I prayed to the Father: Father, if it be possible, cause this cup to pass from me; the spirit truly is willing, but the flesh is weak. Thy will be done. ℣. Nevertheless, not as I will, but as thou wilt. ℟. Thy will be done.]

An alternative form of Responsory 1:

RESPONSORY 1 *In monte Oliveti*   Anglican chant

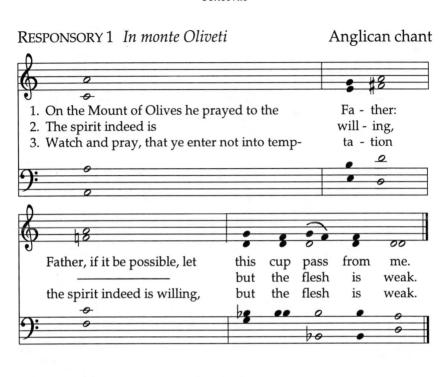

1. On the Mount of Olives he prayed to the   Fa - ther:
2. The spirit indeed is   will - ing,
3. Watch and pray, that ye enter not into temp-   ta - tion

Father, if it be possible, let   this cup pass from me.
        but the flesh is weak.
the spirit indeed is willing,   but the flesh is weak.

LESSON 2   Lamentations 1:6–9

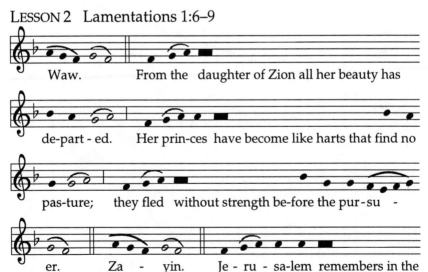

Waw.   From the daughter of Zion all her beauty has

de-part - ed.   Her prin-ces have become like harts that find no

pas-ture;   they fled without strength be-fore the pur-su -

er.   Za - yin.   Je - ru - sa-lem remembers in the

days of her affliction and bitterness   all the precious things that

were hers from days of old.   When her people fell into the

hand of the enemy,   and there was none to help her;   the

e - ne-my gloated over her,   mocking at her down - fall.

Heth.   Je - ru - sa-lem has sinned grievously;

therefore has she be - come fil - thy;   all who hon-ored her

de-spise her,   for they have seen her na-ked-ness;   yea, she

her-self groans, and turns her face   a - way.   Teth.

Her un - clean-ness was in her skirts;   she took no thought of

her doom;   there-fore her fall is terrible, she has no com-for-ter.

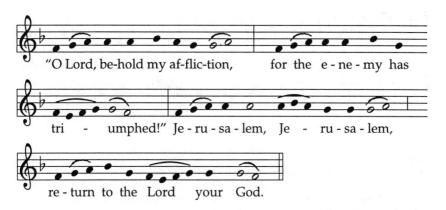

"O Lord, be-hold my af-flic-tion, for the e - ne - my has tri - umphed!" Je - ru - sa - lem, Je - ru - sa - lem, re - turn to the Lord your God.

RESPONSORY 2 *Tristis est* Mode 8

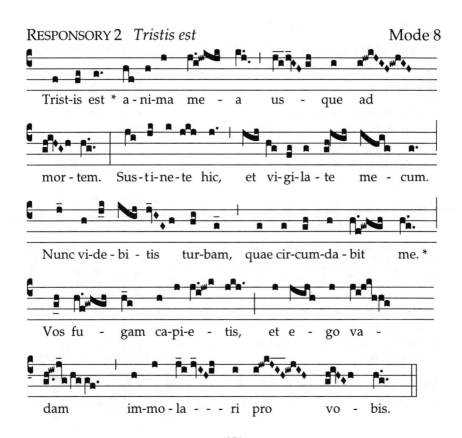

Trist-is est * a - ni-ma me - a us - que ad mor - tem. Sus-ti-ne-te hic, et vi-gi-la - te me - cum.

Nunc vi-de - bi - tis tur-bam, quae cir-cum-da - bit me. *

Vos fu - gam ca-pi-e - tis, et e - go va - dam im-mo-la - - - ri pro vo - bis.

251

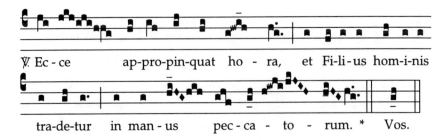

℣. Ec - ce ap-pro-pin-quat ho - ra, et Fi-li-us hom-i-nis

tra-de-tur in man - us pec - ca - to - rum. * Vos.

[My soul is exceeding sorrowful, even unto death; tarry ye here, and watch with me; now shall ye behold a multitude, which will throng about me; ye will flee, and forsake me, and I shall go hence to be offered for you. ℣. Behold, the hour is at hand, and the Son of man is betrayed into the hands of sinners. ℟. Ye will flee, and forsake me, and I shall go hence to be offered for you.]

An alternative form of Responsory 2

RESPONSORY 2 *Tristis est anima* Anglican chant

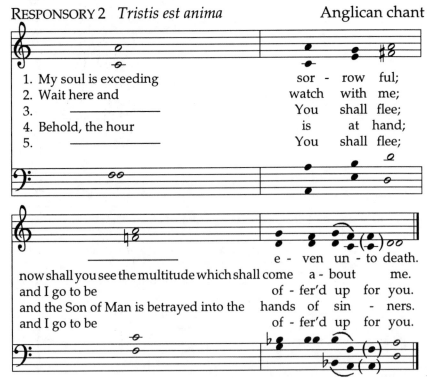

1. My soul is exceeding   sor - row ful;
2. Wait here and   watch with me;
3. _____   You   shall flee;
4. Behold, the hour   is   at hand;
5. _____   You   shall flee;

_____   e - ven un - to death.
now shall you see the multitude which shall come a - bout   me.
and I go to be   of - fer'd up for you.
and the Son of Man is betrayed into the hands of sin - ners.
and I go to be   of - fer'd up for you.

LESSON 3 Lamentations 1:10–14

Yodh. The e - ne-my has stretched out his hands over all her pre-cious things; yea, she has seen the nations invade her sanctuary, whom you had forbidden to enter your con - gre-ga - - tion. Kaph. All her peo-ple groan and search for bread; they trade their treasures for food to re-vive their strength. "Look, O Lord, and be - hold, for I am des - pised." La - medh. "Is it noth-ing to you, all you who pass by? Look and see if there is any sorrow like my sorrow which was brought up-on me, which

the Lord inflicted on the day of his fierce an - ger.

Mem. "From on high he sent fire; into my bones he

made it de-scend; he spread a net for my feet; he turned me

back; he has left me desolate and faint all the day long.

Nun. My trans - gres-sions were bound into a yoke;

by his hand they were fas-tened to-geth - er; they were set up-on

my neck; he caused my strength to fail; the Lord gave me

into the hands of those whom I can-not with - stand.

Je - ru - sa-lem, Je - ru - sa - lem, re - turn to the

Lord your God.

RESPONSORY 3 *Ecce vidimus*   Mode 5

Ec - ce * vi-di-mus e - um   non ha-ben-tem

spe - ci - em, ne - que de - - - co - rem. _ As - pe - ctus

e - jus in e - - - o   non est.   Hic

pec-ca - ta nos-tra por - ta - - - vit,   et pro no-bis

do - let. Ip-se au - tem vul-ner-a - tus est

prop-ter in - i-qui-ta-tes no - stras. * Cu-jus   li-vo - re

sa - na - - - ti su - mus ℣. Ve-re   lan -

guor-es nos-tros ip-se tu - lit,   et do-lor-es nos-tros

i - pse por - ta - - - vit. Cu - jus. ℟. Ec - ce.

[Behold, we have seen him, and he has no form nor comeliness. His bearing is not in him. He has borne our sins and offenses, and he grieves for us. But he was

255

wounded for our iniquities, and with his stripes we are healed. ℣. Surely he has borne our sicknesses, and carried our sorrows. ℟. And with his stripes we are healed.]

An alternative form of Responsory 3

RESPONSORY 3 *Ecce vidimus*   Anglican chant

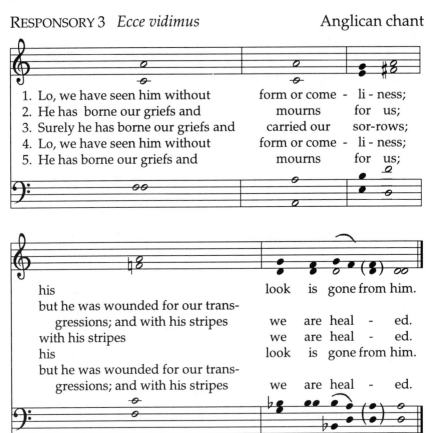

1. Lo, we have seen him without   form or come - li - ness;
2. He has borne our griefs and   mourns   for us;
3. Surely he has borne our griefs and   carried our   sor-rows;
4. Lo, we have seen him without   form or come - li - ness;
5. He has borne our griefs and   mourns   for us;

his   look   is   gone from him.
but he was wounded for our trans-
    gressions; and with his stripes   we   are   heal - ed.
with his stripes   we   are   heal - ed.
his   look   is   gone from him.
but he was wounded for our trans-
    gressions; and with his stripes   we   are   heal - ed.

A period of silence is observed.

256

Matins—Nocturn II

ANTIPHON 1 *Liberavit*   Mode 7

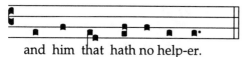

He shall de - li - ver the poor * when he cri-eth; the nee-dy al-so,

and him that hath no help-er.

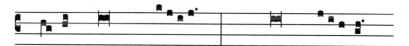

PSALM 72 *Deus, judicium*

1 Give the King your justice, O God, *
   and your righteousness to the King's Son;

2 That he may rule your people righteous-ly *
   and the poor with justice;

3 That the mountains may bring prosperi-ty-to-the people, *
   and the little hills bring righteousness.

4 He shall defend the needy among the people; *
   he shall rescue the poor and crush the-oppressor.

5 He shall live as long as the sun and moon-endure, *
   from one generation to another.

6 He shall come down like rain upon the mown field, *
   like showers that water the earth.

7 In his time shall the righteous flourish; *
   there shall be abundance of peace till the moon shall be no more.

8 He shall rule from sea-to sea, *
   and from the River to the ends of the earth.

9 His foes shall bow down before him, *
   and his ene-mies lick-the dust.

10 The kings of Tarshish and of the isles shall-pay tribute, *
    and the kings of Arabia and Saba of-fer gifts.

11 All kings shall bow <u>down</u> before him, *
 and all the nations <u>do</u> him service.

12 For he shall deliver the poor who cries <u>out</u> in distress, *
 and the oppressed who <u>has</u> no helper.

13 He shall have pity on the <u>low</u>ly and poor; *
 he shall preserve the <u>lives</u> of⌣the needy.

14 He shall redeem their lives from op<u>pression</u>⌣and vio⌣<u>lence</u>, *
 and dear shall their blood <u>be</u> in his sight.

15 Long may he <u>live</u>! †
 and may there be given to him <u>gold</u> from⌣Arabia; *
  may prayer be made for him always,
   and may they bless him <u>all</u> the day long.

16 May there be abundance of grain on the earth,
 growing thick even <u>on</u> the hilltops; *
  may its fruit flourish like Lebanon,
   and its grain like <u>grass</u> upon⌣the earth.

17 May his Name remain for ever
 and be established as long as <u>the</u> sun endures; *
  may all the nations bless themselves in him and <u>call</u> him blessed.

18 Blessed be the Lord GOD, the <u>God</u> of Isra⌣el, *
 who alone <u>does</u> wondrous deeds!

19 And blessed be his glorious <u>Name</u> for ever! *
 and may all the earth be filled with his glory. <u>A</u>men. Amen.

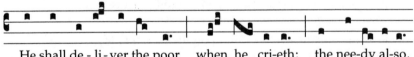

He shall de - li - ver the poor when he cri-eth; the nee-dy al-so,

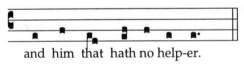

and him that hath no help-er.

A period of silence is observed.

258

ANTIPHON 2 *Cogitaverunt impii* Mode 8

The un - god - ly * have thought and spo-ken wick-ed-ness;

they have spo-ken i - ni - qui-ty on high.

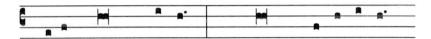

PSALM 73 *Quam bonus Israel*

1 Truly, God is good to <u>Is</u>rael, *
   to those who <u>are</u> pure in heart.

2 But as for me, my feet had nearly <u>slipped</u>; *
   I had almost <u>tripped</u> and fallen;

3 Because I envied the <u>proud</u> *
   and saw the prosperity <u>of</u> the wicked:

4 For they suffer no <u>pain</u>, *
   and their bodies <u>are</u> sleek and sound;

5 In the misfortunes of others they have no <u>share</u>; *
   they are not afflicted <u>as</u> others are;

6 Therefore they wear their pride like a <u>neck</u>lace *
   and wrap their violence about <u>them</u> like a cloak.

7 Their iniquity comes from gross <u>minds</u>, *
   and their hearts overflow <u>with</u> wicked thoughts.

8 They scoff and speak ma<u>li</u>ciously; *
   out of their haughtiness they <u>plan</u> oppression.

9 They set their mouths against the <u>heav</u>ens, *
   and their evil speech <u>runs</u> through the world.

10 And so the people <u>turn</u> to them *
   and find <u>in</u> them no fault.

11 They say, "How should God <u>know</u>? *
   is there knowledge <u>in</u> the Most High?"

12 So then, these are the <u>wick</u>ed; *
   always at ease, they <u>in</u>crease their wealth.

13 In vain have I kept my heart <u>clean</u>, *
   and washed my <u>hands</u> in innocence.

14 I have been afflicted all day <u>long</u>, *
   and punished <u>every</u> morning.

15 Had I gone on speaking this <u>way</u>, *
   I should have betrayed the generation <u>of</u> your children.

16 When I tried to understand these <u>things</u>, *
   it <u>was</u> too hard for me;

17 Until I entered the sanctuary of <u>God</u> *
   and discerned the end <u>of</u> the wicked.

18 Surely, you set them in slippery <u>pla</u>ces; *
   you cast them <u>down</u> in ruin.

19 Oh, how suddenly do they come to de<u>struc</u>tion, *
   come to an end, and pe<u>rish</u> from terror!

20 Like a dream when one awakens, O <u>Lord</u>, *
   when you arise you will make their <u>i</u>mage vanish.

21 When my mind became em<u>bit</u>tered, *
   I was sorely wound<u>ed</u> in my heart.

22 I was stupid and had no under<u>stand</u>ing; *
   I was like a brute beast <u>in</u> your presence.

23 Yet I am always <u>with</u> you; *
   you hold me <u>by</u> my right hand.

24 You will guide me by your <u>coun</u>sel, *
   and afterwards receive <u>me</u> with glory.

25 Whom have I in heaven but <u>you</u>? *
   and having you I desire no<u>thing</u> upon earth.

26 Though my flesh and my heart should waste a<u>way</u>, *
   God is the strength of my heart and my por<u>tion</u> for ever.

27 Truly, those who forsake you will <u>pe</u>rish; *
   you destroy all who <u>are</u> unfaithful.

28 But it is good for me to be near <u>God</u>; *
    I have made the Lord <u>GOD</u> my refuge.

29 I will speak of all your <u>works</u> *
    in the gates of the cit<u>y</u> of Zion.

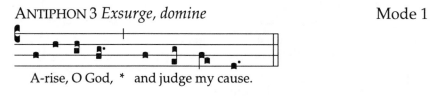

The un - god - ly have thought and spo-ken wick-ed-ness;

they have spo-ken i - ni - qui-ty on high.

A period of silence is observed.

ANTIPHON 3 *Exsurge, domine*   Mode 1

A-rise, O God, * and judge my cause.

PSALM 74 *Ut quid, Deus?*

1 O God, why have you <u>utter</u>ly cast us off? *
    why is your wrath so hot against the sheep <u>of</u> your pasture?

2 Remember your congregation that you <u>pur</u>chased long ago, *
    the tribe you redeemed to be your inheritance,
        and Mount <u>Zi</u>on where you dwell.

3 Turn your steps toward the <u>end</u>less ruins; *
    the enemy has laid waste everything in your <u>sanc</u>tuary.

4 Your adversaries <u>roar</u>ed in your ho<u>ly</u> place; *
    they set up their banners as tok<u>ens</u> of victory.

5 They were like men coming up with axes to <u>a</u> grove of trees; *
    they broke down all your carved work with hatch<u>ets</u>
        and hammers.

6 They set fire to your holy place; *
    they defiled the dwelling-place of your Name
        and razed it to the ground.

7 They said to themselves, "Let us destroy them altogether." *
    They burned down all the meeting-places of God in the land.

8 There are no signs for us to see; †
    there is no prophet left; *
    there is not one among us who knows how long.

9 How long, O God, will the adversary scoff? *
    will the enemy blaspheme your Name for ever?

10 Why do you draw back your hand? *
    why is your right hand hidden in your bosom?

11 Yet God is my King from ancient times, *
    victorious in the midst of the earth.

12 You divided the sea by your might *
    and shattered the heads of the dragons upon the waters;

13 You crushed the heads of Leviathan *
    and gave him to the people of the desert for food.

14 You split open spring and torrent; *
    you dried up ever-flowing rivers.

15 Yours is the day, yours also the night; *
    you established the moon and the sun.

16 You fixed all the boundaries of the earth; *
    you made both summer and winter.

17 Remember, O LORD, how the enemy scoffed, *
    how a foolish people despised your Name.

18 Do not hand over the life of your dove to wild beasts; *
    never forget the lives of your poor.

19 Look upon your covenant; *
    the dark places of the earth are haunts of violence.

20 Let not the oppressed turn away ashamed; *
    let the poor and needy praise your Name.

21 Arise, O God, maintain your cause; *
    remember how fools revile you all day long.

22 Forget not the clamor of your adversaries, *
    the unending tumult of those who rise up against you.

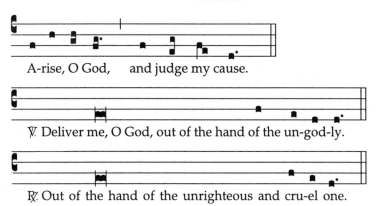

A-rise, O God,   and judge my cause.

℣. Deliver me, O God, out of the hand of the un-god-ly.

℟. Out of the hand of the unrighteous and cru-el one.

The Lord's Prayer is said silently, standing. The M.C. may accompany the reader to the lectern. All then sit for the lesson.

LESSON 4   From Saint Augustine's Treatise on the Psalms

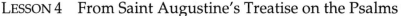

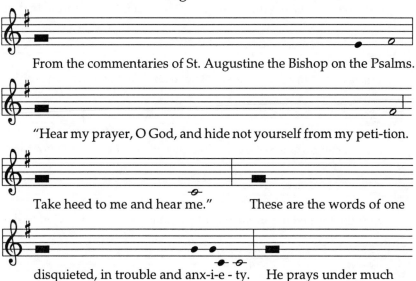

From the commentaries of St. Augustine the Bishop on the Psalms.

"Hear my prayer, O God, and hide not yourself from my peti-tion.

Take heed to me and hear me."   These are the words of one

disquieted, in trouble and anx-i-e - ty.   He prays under much

suffering, desiring to be released from e-vil.   Let us now see

under what evil he lies;   and when he begins to speak, let us place

ourselves by him;   that sharing his tribulation we may also join

in his prayer.   "I mourn," says the psalmist, "in my trial, and am

trou-bled."   When does he mourn? When is he trou-bled?

He says, "in my trial. "He speaks of the wicked whom he en-dures

and this endurance of the wicked he calls his trial.   Do not think

that the wicked are in the world for no reason, or that God makes

no use of them.   Every wicked person lives that he may be

corrected in him-self,   or that by him the righteous may be tried."

RESPONSORY 4 *Amicus meus* — Mode 8

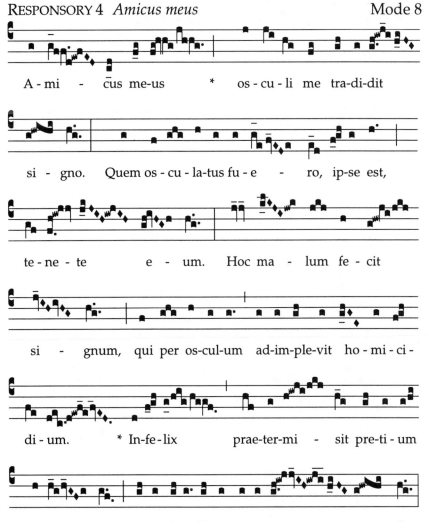

A - mi - cus me-us   *   os - cu - li me tra-di-dit

si - gno. Quem os - cu - la-tus fu - e - ro, ip-se est,

te - ne - te   e - um. Hoc ma - lum fe - cit

si - gnum, qui per os-cul-um ad-im-ple-vit ho - mi - ci -

di - um.   * In-fe-lix   prae-ter-mi - sit pre-ti-um

san-gui - nis, et in fi-ne la-que-o se su - - - spen - dit.

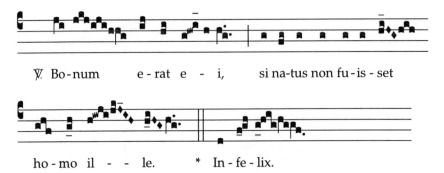

℣. Bo-num   e - rat e - i,   si na-tus non fu - is - set

ho - mo il - - le.   * In - fe - lix.

[My friend has betrayed me with the sign of a kiss: He whom I kiss is the one—seize him. This evil sign he gave, who with a kiss committed murder. Unhappy man, he threw down the price of blood, and in the end hanged himself. ℣. It were better for that man if he had not been born. Unhappy man, he threw down the price of blood, and in the end hanged himself.]

An alternative form of Responsory 4:

RESPONSORY 4   *Amicus meus*   Anglican chant

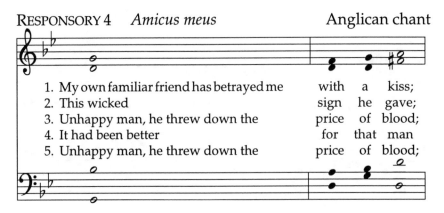

1. My own familiar friend has betrayed me   with   a   kiss;
2. This wicked   sign   he   gave;
3. Unhappy man, he threw down the   price   of   blood;
4. It had been better   for   that   man
5. Unhappy man, he threw down the   price   of   blood;

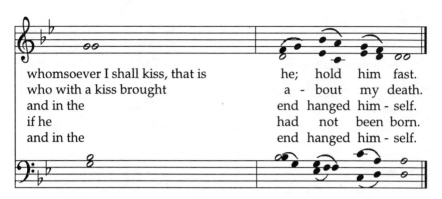

whomsoever I shall kiss, that is   he;   hold   him   fast.
who with a kiss brought   a - bout   my   death.
and in the   end   hanged   him - self.
if he   had   not   been born.
and in the   end   hanged   him - self.

LESSON 5   Saint Augustine on the Psalms, continued

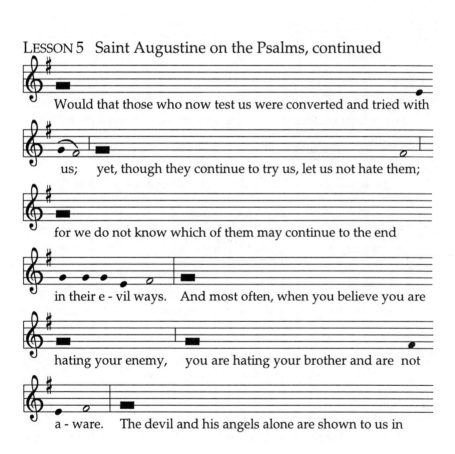

Would that those who now test us were converted and tried with

us;   yet, though they continue to try us, let us not hate them;

for we do not know which of them may continue to the end

in their e - vil ways.   And most often, when you believe you are

hating your enemy,   you are hating your brother and are not

a - ware.   The devil and his angels alone are shown to us in

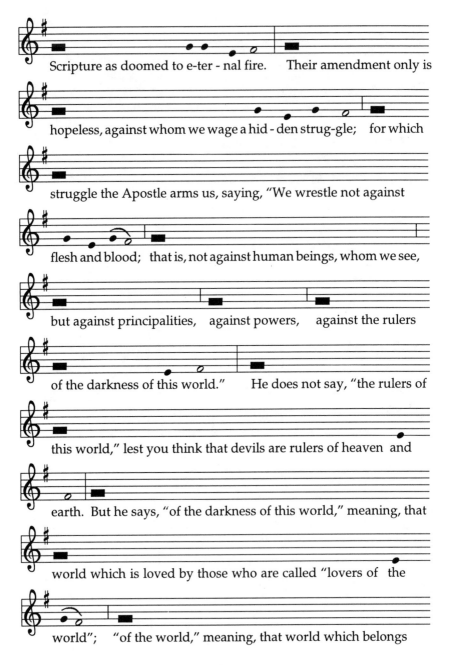

Scripture as doomed to e-ter-nal fire.   Their amendment only is

hopeless, against whom we wage a hid-den strug-gle;   for which

struggle the Apostle arms us, saying, "We wrestle not against

flesh and blood; that is, not against human beings, whom we see,

but against principalities,   against powers,   against the rulers

of the darkness of this world."   He does not say, "the rulers of

this world," lest you think that devils are rulers of heaven and

earth. But he says, "of the darkness of this world," meaning, that

world which is loved by those who are called "lovers of the

world";   "of the world," meaning, that world which belongs

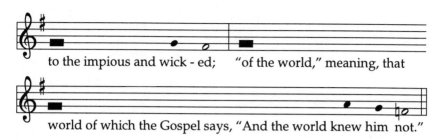

to the impious and wick - ed; "of the world," meaning, that

world of which the Gospel says, "And the world knew him not."

RESPONSORY 5 *Judas mercator* Mode 2

Ju - das * mer-ca-tor pes-si-mus os-cu-lo pe - ti - it

Do-mi - num. Il - le ut a - gnus in - no - cens

non ne - ga - vit Ju - dae o - scu - lum * De-na-ri-o - rum

nu-me - - ro Chris - tum Ju-dae-is tra-di - dit.

℣. Me - li - us il - li e - rat, si na - tus non fu -

is - set. * De - na - ri - o-rum.

[Judas, most evil merchant, sought to betray the Lord with a kiss; he, like an innocent lamb, did not refuse the kiss of Judas; for thirty pieces of silver he betrayed Christ to the Jews. ℣. It were better for that man if he had never been born. ℟. For thirty pieces of silver he betrayed Christ to the Jews.]

An alternative form of Responsory 5:

RESPONSORY 5 *Judas mercator pesssimus*   Anglican chant

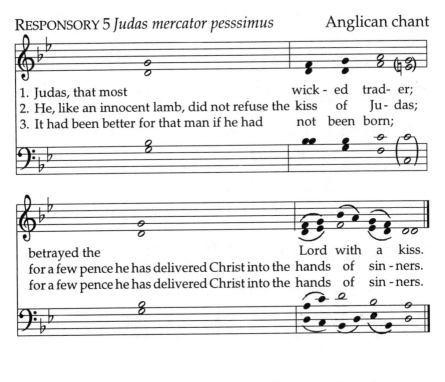

1. Judas, that most   wick - ed trad- er;
2. He, like an innocent lamb, did not refuse the kiss of Ju- das;
3. It had been better for that man if he had not been born;

betrayed the   Lord with a kiss.
for a few pence he has delivered Christ into the hands of sin - ners.
for a few pence he has delivered Christ into the hands of sin - ners.

LESSON 6   Saint Augustine on the Psalms, continued

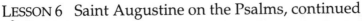

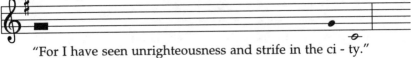

"For I have seen unrighteousness and strife in the ci - ty."

In these words of the psalm, see the glory of the Cross it - self.

Now on the brow of kings is placed that Cross, which enemies did

de-ride.   This result has shown the measure of its pow-er:

It has subdued the world, not with steel but with wood.   The wood

of the Cross seemed a worthy object of scorn to his enemies,

and standing before that wood they wagged their heads,

say-ing,   "If you are the Son of God, come down from the Cross."

He stretched forth his hands to a rebellious and unbelieving

peo - ple.   If one who lives by faith is con-sid-er-ed right-eous,

then one is unrighteous who does not have faith; Therefore when

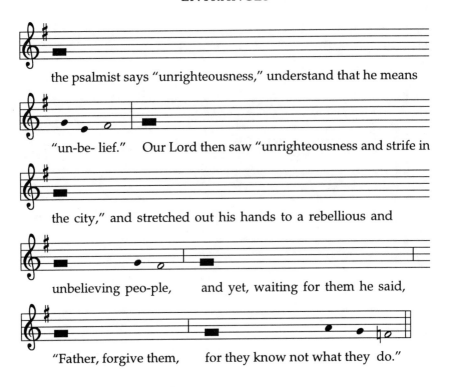

the psalmist says "unrighteousness," understand that he means

"un-be- lief." Our Lord then saw "unrighteousness and strife in

the city," and stretched out his hands to a rebellious and

unbelieving peo-ple, and yet, waiting for them he said,

"Father, forgive them, for they know not what they do."

RESPONSORY 6 *Unus discipulis*   Mode 8

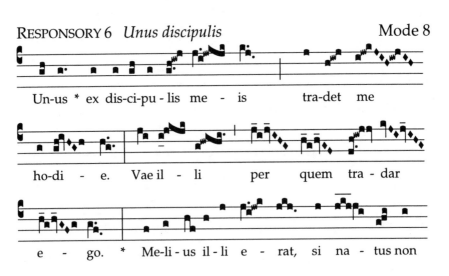

Un-us * ex dis-ci-pu - lis me - is   tra-det   me

ho-di - e. Vae il - li   per quem tra - dar

e - go. * Me-li - us il - li e - rat, si na - tus non

fu - is - set. ℣. Qui in-tin-git   me-cum ma-num

in par-op-si - de,   hic me tra-di-tur-us est   in ma-nus

pec - ca - to - - rum.   *   Me-li - us.   ℟. Un - us.

[Today one of my disciples will betray me. Woe to the one by whom I am betrayed. It had been better for him if he had not been born. ℣. One who dips his hand into the dish with mine will betray me into the hands of sinners. It had been better for that man if he had not been born.]

An alternative form of Responsory 6:

RESPONSORY 6   *Unus ex discipulis*   Anglican chant

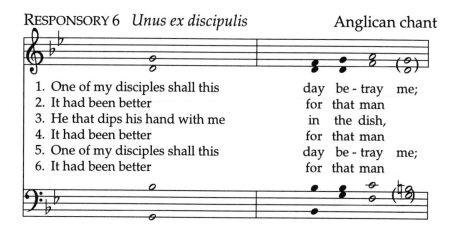

1. One of my disciples shall this   day be - tray me;
2. It had been better   for that man
3. He that dips his hand with me   in the dish,
4. It had been better   for that man
5. One of my disciples shall this   day be - tray me;
6. It had been better   for that man

woe unto that man by whom I shall	be	be -	tray - ed.
if he		had	not been born.
the same is he that shall betray me into the	hands	of	sin - ners.
if he		had	not been born.
woe unto that man by whom I shall	be	be -	tray - ed.
if he		had	not been born.

A period of silence is observed.

Matins—Nocturn III

ANTIPHON 1 *Dixi Iniquis* Mode 7

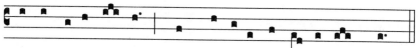

I said to the wick-ed, * speak not i - ni-qui - ty a-gainst God.

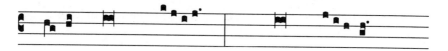

PSALM 75 *Confitebimur tibi*

1 We give you thanks, O <u>God</u>, we give⌣you thanks, *
    calling upon your Name and declaring all your <u>won</u>derful deeds.

2 "I will ap<u>point</u> a time,"⌣ says God; *
    "I will judge <u>with</u> equity.

3 Though the earth and all its inhabi⌣tants⌣are quaking, *
    I will make <u>its</u> pillars fast.

4 I will say to the <u>boast</u>ers, 'Boast⌣no more,' *
    and to the wicked, 'Do <u>not</u> toss your horns;

5 Do not <u>toss</u> your horns⌣so high, *
    nor speak <u>with</u> a proud neck.'"

6 For judgment is neither from the <u>east</u> nor from⌣the west, *
    nor yet from the wilderness <u>or</u> the mountains.

7 It is <u>God</u> who judges; *
    he puts down one and lifts <u>up</u> another.

8 For in the LORD's hand there is a cup,
    full of spiced and foaming <u>wine</u>, which he⌣pours out, *
    and all the wicked of the earth shall drink <u>and</u> drain the dregs.

9 But I will re<u>joice</u> for ever; *
    I will sing praises to the <u>God</u> of Jacob.

10 He shall break off all the <u>horns</u> of⌣the wicked; *
    but the horns of the righteous shall <u>be</u> exalted.

I said to the wick-ed, speak not i - ni-qui - ty a-gainst God.

A period of silence is observed.

ANTIPHON 2 *Terra tremuit*   Mode 8

The earth trem-bled and was still * when God a-rose in judg-ment.

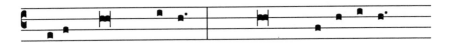

PSALM 76 *Notus in Judaea*

1 In Judah is God <u>known</u>; *
   his Name is <u>great</u> in Israel.

2 At Salem is his <u>tab</u>ernacle, *
   and his dwelling <u>is</u> in Zion.

3 There he broke the flashing <u>ar</u>rows, *
   the shield, the sword, and the wea<u>pons</u> of battle.

4 How glorious you <u>are</u>! *
   more splendid than the ever<u>last</u>ing mountains!

5 The strong of heart have been des<u>poiled</u>; †
   they sink into <u>sleep</u>; *
   none of the warriors <u>can</u> lift a hand.

6 At your rebuke, O God of <u>Jac</u>ob, *
   both horse and <u>rid</u>er lie stunned.

7 What terror you in<u>spire</u>! *
   who can stand before you when <u>you</u> are angry?

8 From heaven you pronounced <u>judg</u>ment; *
   the earth was a<u>fraid</u> and was still;

9 When God rose up to judgment *
   and to save all the oppressed of the earth.

10 Truly, wrathful Edom will give you thanks, *
    and the remnant of Hamath will keep your feasts.

11 Make a vow to the LORD your God and keep it; *
    let all around him bring gifts to him who is worthy to be feared.

12 He breaks the spirit of princes, *
    and strikes terror in the kings of the earth.

The earth trem-bled and was still   when God a-rose in judg-ment.

ANTIPHON 3 *In die tribulationis*   Mode 7

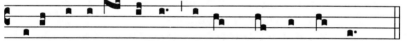

In the day of my trou-ble * I sought God with my hands.

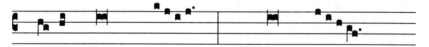

PSALM 77 *Voce mea ad Dominum*

1 I will cry aloud to God; *
   I will cry aloud, and he will hear me.

2 In the day of my trouble I sought the Lord; *
   my hands were stretched out by night and did not tire;
        I refused to be comforted.

3 I think of God, I am restless, *
   I ponder, and my spirit faints.

4 You will not let my eyelids close; *
   I am troubled and I cannot speak.

5 I consider the days of old; *
   I remember the years long past;

6 I commune with my <u>heart</u> in the night; *
   I ponder <u>and</u> search my mind.

7 Will the Lord cast me <u>off</u> for ever? *
   will he no more <u>show</u> his favor?

8 Has his loving-kindness come to an <u>end</u> for ever? *
   has his promise <u>failed</u> for ev⌣ermore?

9 Has God <u>forgotten⌣to⌣be</u> gracious? *
   has he, in his anger, withheld <u>his</u> compassion?

10 And I said, "<u>My</u> grief is this: *
   the right hand of the Most High has <u>lost</u> its power."

11 I will remember the <u>works</u> of the LORD, *
   and call to mind your <u>wonders</u> of⌣old time.

12 I will meditate <u>on</u> all your acts *
   and ponder <u>your</u> mighty deeds.

13 Your way, O <u>God</u>, is holy; *
   who is so great a <u>god</u> as our God?

14 You are the God <u>who</u> works wonders *
   and have declared your power a<u>mong</u> the peoples.

15 By your strength you have re<u>deemed</u> your people, *
   the children of <u>Jacob</u> and⌣Joseph.

16 The waters saw you, O <u>God</u>; †
the waters <u>saw</u> you⌣and trembled; *
   the very <u>depths</u> were shaken.

17 The clouds poured out water; <u>the</u> skies thundered; *
   your arrows <u>flashed</u> to and fro;

18 The sound of your thunder was in the whirl<u>wind</u>; †
your lightnings <u>lit</u> up the world; *
   the earth <u>trembled</u> and shook.

19 Your way was in the sea, and your paths in <u>the</u> great waters, *
   yet your <u>foot</u>steps were⌣not seen.

20 You led your <u>people</u> like⌣a <u>flock</u> *
   by the hand of <u>Moses</u> and⌣Aaron.

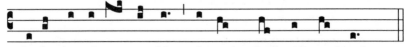

In the day of my trou-ble   I sought God with my hands.

℣. A-rise, O God.　℟. And judge thy cause.

The Lord's Prayer is said silently, standing. The M.C. may accompany the reader to the lectern. All then sit for the lesson.

LESSON 7　1 Corinthians 11:17–22

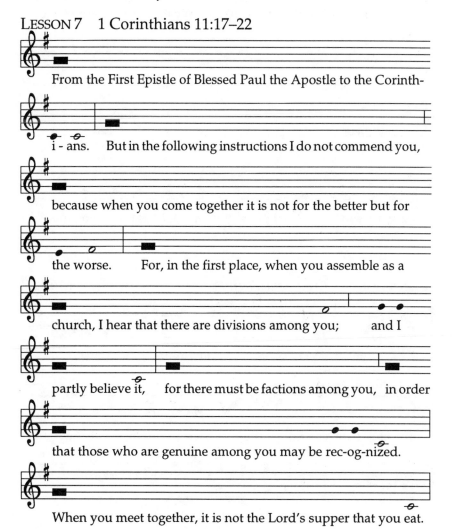

From the First Epistle of Blessed Paul the Apostle to the Corinth-

i - ans.　　But in the following instructions I do not commend you,

because when you come together it is not for the better but for

the worse.　　For, in the first place, when you assemble as a

church, I hear that there are divisions among you;　　and I

partly believe it,　for there must be factions among you,　in order

that those who are genuine among you may be rec-og-nized.

When you meet together, it is not the Lord's supper that you eat.

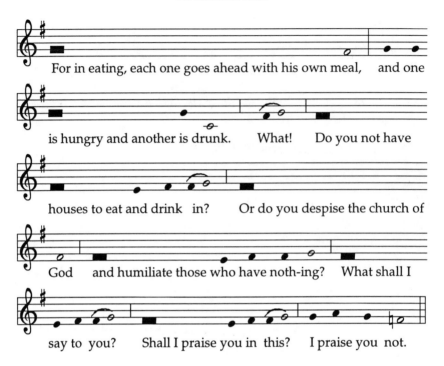

For in eating, each one goes ahead with his own meal, and one
is hungry and another is drunk. What! Do you not have
houses to eat and drink in? Or do you despise the church of
God and humiliate those who have noth-ing? What shall I
say to you? Shall I praise you in this? I praise you not.

RESPONSORY 7 *Eram quasi agnus* Mode 7

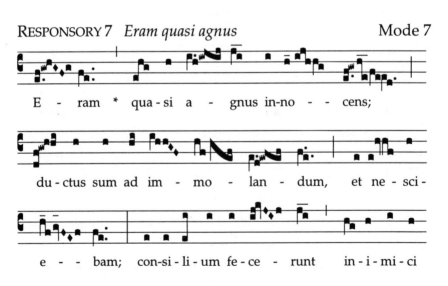

E - ram * qua-si a - gnus in-no - - cens;
du - ctus sum ad im - mo - lan - dum, et ne - sci-
e - - bam; con-si - li - um fe - ce - runt in - i - mi - ci

280

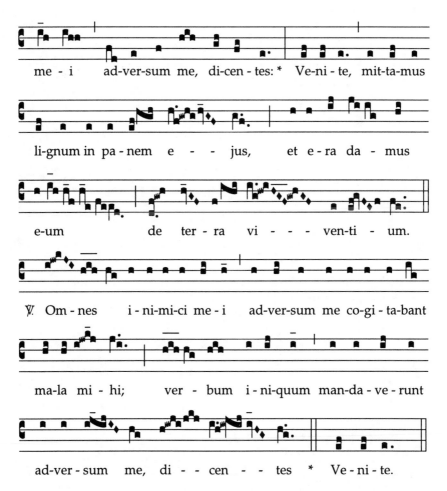

me - i ad-ver-sum me, di-cen - tes: * Ve-ni - te, mit-ta-mus

li-gnum in pa - nem e - - - jus, et e-ra da - mus

e-um de ter - ra vi - - - ven-ti - um.

℣. Om - nes i - ni-mi-ci me - i ad-ver-sum me co-gi - ta-bant

ma-la mi - hi; ver - bum i - ni-quum man-da - ve - runt

ad-ver - sum me, di - - cen - - tes * Ve - ni - te.

[I was like an innocent lamb. I was led to the slaughter and I did not know it. My enemies took counsel against me, saying, "Come, let us put wood into his bread, and remove him from the land of the living." ℣. All my enemies thought evil against me; they spoke evil against me, saying, "Come, let us put wood into his bread, and remove him from the land of the living."]

An alternative form of Responsory 7

RESPONSORY 7 *Eram quasi agnus* Anglican chant

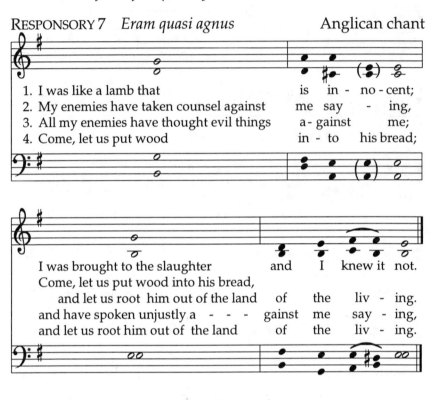

1. I was like a lamb that   is   in - no - cent;
2. My enemies have taken counsel against   me say - ing,
3. All my enemies have thought evil things   a - gainst   me;
4. Come, let us put wood   in - to   his bread;

I was brought to the slaughter   and   I   knew it not.
Come, let us put wood into his bread,
   and let us root him out of the land   of   the   liv - ing.
and have spoken unjustly a - - -   gainst me   say - ing,
and let us root him out of the land   of   the   liv - ing.

LESSON 8   1 Corinthians 11:23–26

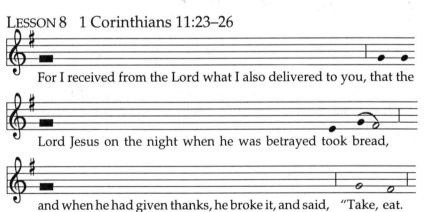

For I received from the Lord what I also delivered to you, that the

Lord Jesus on the night when he was betrayed took bread,

and when he had given thanks, he broke it, and said,   "Take, eat.

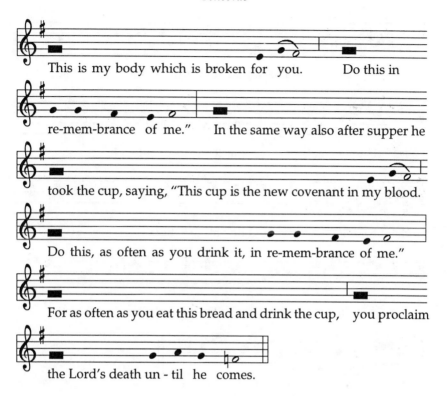

This is my body which is broken for you. Do this in re-mem-brance of me." In the same way also after supper he took the cup, saying, "This cup is the new covenant in my blood. Do this, as often as you drink it, in re-mem-brance of me." For as often as you eat this bread and drink the cup, you proclaim the Lord's death un - til he comes.

RESPONSORY 8   *Una hora*   _Mode 7

U - na ho - ra   *   non po - tu - i - - stis vi-gi-la - re   me - cum, qui ex-hor-ta-ba - mi - ni   mo - ri   pro me? * Vel Ju - dam non vi -

de - tis, quo-mo-do non dor - mit, sed

fes-ti - - nat tra-de - re me Ju -

dae - is? ℣. Quid dor-mi - tis? sur-gi-te et

o-ra - te, ne in tre-tis in ten - ta-ti-

o - nem. * Vel Ju - dam.

[Are you not able to watch with me one hour, you who were ready to die for me?
Or do you not see Judas, who does not sleep, but hastens to betray me to the Jews?
℣. Why are you sleeping? Arise and pray, that you enter not into temptation. Or
do you not see Judas, who does not sleep, but hastens to betray me to the Jews?]

An alternative form of Responsory 8

RESPONSORY 8 *Una hora* Anglican chant

1. Could you not watch with me one hour;
2. Do you not see Judas, how he sleeps not;
3. Why are you sleeping? a - rise and pray;
4. Do you not see Judas, how he sleeps not;

who were rea - dy to die for me?
but hastens to deliver me into the hands of sin - ners.
that you enter not in - to temp - ta - tion.
but hastens to deliver me into the hands of sin - ners.

LESSON 9 1 Corinthians 11:27–34

Whoever, therefore, eats the bread or drinks the cup of the Lord

in an unworthy manner will be guilty of profaning the body

and blood of the Lord. Let each one examine him-self, and so

eat of the bread and drink of the cup.   For any one who eats and

drinks without discerning the body, eats and drinks judgment

up-on him-self.   That is why many of you are weak and ill, and

some have died.   But if we judged ourselves truly, we should

not be judged.   But when we are judged by the Lord, we are

chastened so that we may not be condemned along with

the world. So then, my brethren, when you come together to eat,

wait for one a-noth-er; if any one is hungry, let him eat at home;

lest you come together to be con - demned. And concerning the

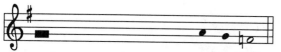

rest I will give directions when I come.

RESPONSORY 9 *Seniores populi*   Mode 1

Sen - i - o - res * po - pu - li con - si - li - um

fe - ce - - runt, * Ut Je-sum do-lo te - ne - rent, et

oc - ci - de - - rent. Cum gla - di-is et fu - sti-bus ex-

i - e - runt tam-quam ad la-tro - nem.

℣. Col - le - ge - runt pon - ti - fi - ces et pha - ri - sae - i

con - ci - li - um. * Ut Je - sum. ℟. Sen - i - o - res.

[The elders of the people took counsel how they might take Jesus by deceit and put him to death. They went out as against a thief, with swords and staves. ℣. The priests and pharisees took counsel, how they might take Jesus by deceit and put him to death. ℟. They went out as against a thief, with swords and staves.]

287

An alternative form of Responsory 9:

RESPONSORY 9 *Seniores populi*   Anglican chant

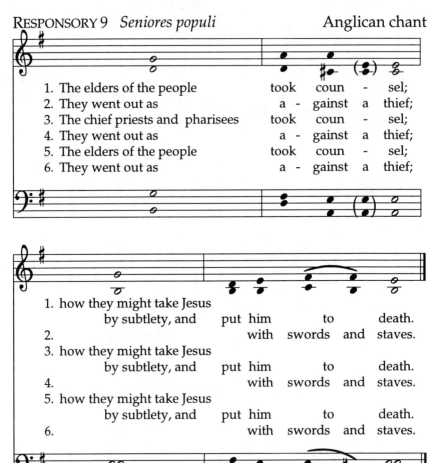

1. The elders of the people   took   coun - sel;
2. They went out as   a - gainst a thief;
3. The chief priests and pharisees   took   coun - sel;
4. They went out as   a - gainst a thief;
5. The elders of the people   took   coun - sel;
6. They went out as   a - gainst a thief;

1. how they might take Jesus
    by subtlety, and   put him   to   death.
2.   with swords and staves.
3. how they might take Jesus
    by subtlety, and   put him   to   death.
4.   with swords and staves.
5. how they might take Jesus
    by subtlety, and   put him   to   death.
6.   with swords and staves.

Matins ends. A period of silence is observed.

At Lauds

ANTIPHON 1 *Justificeris*   Mode 8

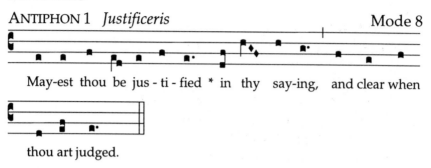

May-est thou be jus - ti - fied * in thy say-ing, and clear when

thou art judged.

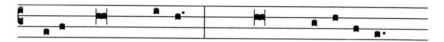

PSALM 51 *Miserere mei, Deus*

1 Have mercy on me, O God, according to your loving-<u>kind</u>ness; *
   in your great compassion blot out <u>my</u> offenses.

2 Wash me through and through from my <u>wick</u>edness *
   and cleanse <u>me</u> from my sin.

3 For I know my trans<u>gres</u>sions, *
   and my sin is <u>ev</u>er before me.

4 Against you only have I <u>sinned</u> *
   and done what is <u>ev</u>il in your sight.

5 And so you are justified when you <u>speak</u> *
   and upright <u>in</u> your judgment.

6 Indeed, I have been wicked from my <u>birth</u>, *
   a sinner from <u>my</u> mother's womb.

7 For behold, you look for truth deep with<u>in</u> me, *
   and will make me understand <u>wis</u>dom secretly.

8 Purge me from my sin, and I shall be <u>pure</u>; *
   wash me, and I shall <u>be</u> clean indeed.

9 Make me hear of joy and <u>glad</u>ness, *
   that the body you have bro<u>ken</u> may rejoice.

10 Hide your face from my <u>sins</u> *
    and blot out all <u>my</u> iniquities.

11 Create in me a clean heart, O <u>God</u>, *
    and renew a right sp<u>ir</u>it within me.

12 Cast me not away from your <u>pre</u>sence *
    and take not your holy <u>S</u>pirit from me.

13 Give me the joy of your saving help ag<u>ain</u> *
    and sustain me with your boun<u>ti</u>ful Spirit.

14 I shall teach your ways to the <u>wick</u>ed, *
    and sinners <u>shall</u> return to you.

15 Deliver me from death, O <u>God</u>, *
    and my tongue shall sing of your righteousness, O God of <u>my</u>
    salvation.

16 Open my lips, O <u>Lord</u>, *
    and my mouth shall <u>pro</u>claim your praise.

17 Had you desired it, I would have offered <u>sac</u>rifice, *
    but you take no delight <u>in</u> burnt-offerings.

18 The sacrifice of God is a troubled <u>spi</u>rit; *
    a broken and contrite heart, O God, you <u>will</u> not despise.

19 Be favorable and gracious to <u>Zion</u>, *
    and rebuild the walls <u>of</u> Jerusalem.

20 Then you will be pleased with the appointed sacrifices, with
    burnt-offerings and o<u>bla</u>tions; *
    then shall they offer young bullocks up<u>on</u> your altar.

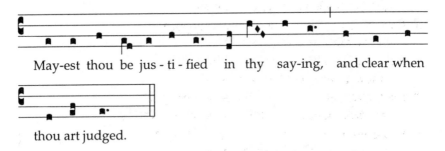

May-est thou be jus-ti-fied in thy say-ing, and clear when

thou art judged.

A period of silence is observed.

ANTIPHON 2 *Dominus tanquam ovis*   Mode 2

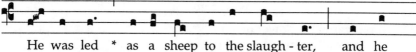

He was led   *   as   a   sheep   to   the slaugh - ter,   and   he

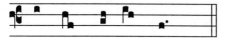

o - pened   not   his   mouth.

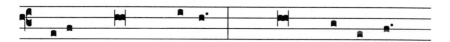

PSALM 90 *Domine, refugium*

1 Lord, you have been our <u>ref</u>uge *
   from one generation to a<u>no</u>ther.

2 Before the mountains were brought forth, or the land
         and the earth were <u>born</u>, *
   from age to age <u>you</u> are God.

3 You turn us back to the dust and <u>say</u>, *
   "Go back, O <u>child</u> of earth."

4 For a thousand years in your sight are like yesterday when it is <u>past</u> *
   and like a watch <u>in</u> the night.

5 You sweep us away like a <u>dream</u>; *
   we fade away suddenly <u>like</u> the grass.

6 In the morning it is green and <u>flour</u>ishes; *
   in the evening it is dried up <u>and</u> withered.

7 For we consume away in your dis<u>plea</u>sure; *
   we are afraid because of your wrathful in<u>dig</u>nation.

8 Our iniquities you have set be<u>fore</u> you, *
   and our secret sins in the light of <u>your</u> countenance.

9 When you are angry, all our days are <u>gone</u>; *
   we bring our years to an end <u>like</u> a sigh.

10 The span of our life is seventy years, perhaps in strength even <u>eigh</u>ty; *
       yet the sum of them is but labor and sorrow, for they pass away
           quickly and <u>we</u> are gone.

11 Who regards the power of your <u>wrath</u>? *
       who rightly fears your in<u>dig</u>nation?

12 So teach us to number our <u>days</u> *
       that we may apply our hearts <u>to</u> wisdom.

13 Return, O LORD; how long will you <u>tar</u>ry? *
       be gracious to <u>your</u> servants.

14 Satisfy us by your loving-kindness in the <u>morn</u>ing; *
       so shall we rejoice and be glad all the days <u>of</u> our life.

15 Make us glad by the measure of the days that you af<u>flic</u>ted us *
       and the years in which we suffered <u>ad</u>versity.

16 Show your servants your <u>works</u> *
       and your splendor to <u>their</u> children.

17 May the graciousness of the LORD our God be up<u>on</u> us; *
       prosper the work of our hands; prosper <u>our</u> handiwork.

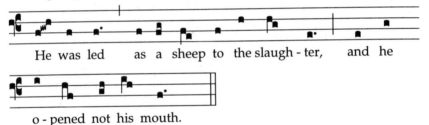

He was led   as a sheep to the slaugh - ter,   and he

o - pened not his mouth.

A period of silence is observed.

ANTIPHON 3 *Contritum est*   Mode 8

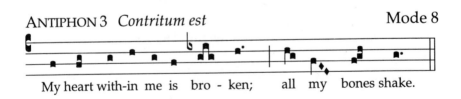

My heart with-in me is bro - ken;   all my bones shake.

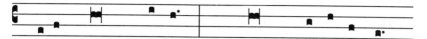

PSALM 36 *Dixit injustus*

1 There is a voice of rebellion deep in the heart of the <u>wick</u>ed; *
   there is no fear of God <u>be</u>fore his eyes.

2 He flatters himself in his own <u>eyes</u> *
   that his hateful sin will <u>not</u> be found out.

3 The words of his mouth are wicked and de<u>ceit</u>ful, *
   he has left off acting wisely <u>and</u> doing good.

4 He thinks up wickedness upon his bed
          and has set himself in no good <u>way</u>; *
   he does not abhor that <u>which</u> is evil.

5 Your love, O LORD, reaches to the <u>heav</u>ens, *
   and your faithful<u>ness</u> to the clouds.

6 Your righteousness is like the strong mountains,
          your justice like the great <u>deep</u>; *
   you save both man <u>and</u> beast, O LORD.

7 How priceless is your love, O <u>God</u>! *
   your people take refuge under the sha<u>dow</u> of your wings.

8 They feast upon the abundance of your <u>house</u>; *
   you give them drink from the river <u>of</u> your delights.

9 For with you is the well of <u>life</u>, *
   and in your <u>light</u> we see light.

10 Continue your loving-kindness to those who <u>know</u> you, *
   and your favor to those who <u>are</u> true of heart.

11 Let not the foot of the proud come <u>near</u> me, *
   nor the hand of the wicked <u>push</u> me aside.

12 See how they are fallen, those who work <u>wick</u>edness! *
   they are cast down and shall not be <u>a</u>ble to rise.

My heart with-in me is bro - ken; all my bones shake.

A period of silence is observed.

ANTIPHON 4 *Exhortatus es*   Mode 4

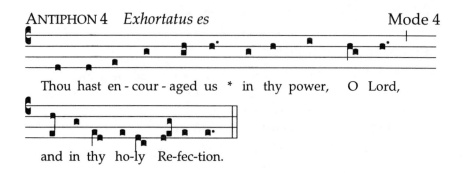

Thou hast en - cour - aged us * in thy power, O Lord,

and in thy ho-ly Re-fec-tion.

THE SONG OF MOSES *Cantemus Domino*

1 I will sing unto the Lord, for he hath triumphed gloriously; *
   the horse and his rider hath he thrown into the sea.

2 The Lord is my strength and song; *
   and he is become my salvation.

3 He is my God, and I will prepare him a habitation; *
   my father's God, and I will exalt him.

4 The Lord is a man of war; *
   —the Lord is his Name.

5 Pharaoh's chariots and his host hath he cast into the sea; *
   his chosen captains also are drowned in the Red Sea.

6 The depths have covered them; *
   they sank into the bottom as a stone.

7 Thy right hand, O Lord, is become glorious in power; *
   thy right hand, O Lord, hath dashed in pieces the enemy.

8 And in the greatness of thine excellency thou hast
           overthrown them that rose up against thee; *
   thou sentest forth thy wrath, which consumed them as stubble.

9 And with the blast of thy nostrils the waters were
           gathered together; *
   the floods stood upright as a heap; and the depths
           were congealed in the heart of the sea.

10 The enemy said I will pursue, I will overtake, I will di<u>vide</u> the spoil; *
   my lust shall be sa<u>tis</u>fied upon them.

11 I will <u>draw</u> my sword; *
   my <u>hand</u> shall destroy them.

12 Thou didst blow with thy wind and <u>the</u> sea covered them; *
   they sank as lead in <u>the</u> mighty waters.

13 Who is like unto thee, O Lord, a<u>mong</u> the gods; *
   who is like unto thee; glorious in holiness;
            fearful in pra<u>ises</u>, doing wonders?

14 Thou stretch'dst <u>out</u> thy right hand; *
   —<u>the</u> earth swallowed them.

15 Thou in thy mercy hast led forth the people which
            thou <u>hast</u> redeemed; *
   thou hast guided them in thy strength unto thy ho<u>ly</u> habitation.

16 The people shall hear, and <u>be</u> afraid; *
   sorrow shall take hold of the inhabitants <u>of</u> Palestina.

17 Then the dukes of Edom shall <u>be</u> amazed; *
   the mighty men of Moab, trembling shall take hold
   upon them; all the inhabitants of <u>Can</u>aan shall melt away.

18 Fear and dread shall fall upon <u>them</u>; †
   by the greatness of thine arm they shall be as still <u>as</u> a stone; *
   till thy people pass over, O Lord; till the people
            pass over, <u>which</u> thou hast purchased.

19 Thou shalt bring them in and plant them in the
            mountains of <u>thine</u> inheritance; *
   in the place, O Lord, which thou hast made for thee to dwell in;
            in the sanctuary, O Lord, which thy <u>hands</u>
            have established.

20 The <u>Lord</u> shall reign; *
   for <u>ev</u>er and ever.

21 For the horse of Pharaoh went in with his chariots,
            and with his horsemen in<u>to</u> the sea; *
   and the Lord brought again the waters of <u>the</u>
            sea upon them.

22 But the children of Israel went <u>on</u> dry land; *
   in <u>the</u> midst of the sea.

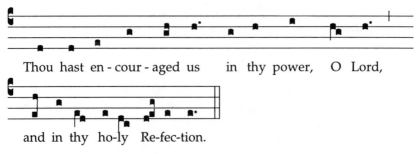

Thou hast en - cour - aged us   in thy power, O Lord,

and in thy ho-ly Re-fec-tion.

A period of silence is observed.

ANTIPHON 5 *Oblatus est*   Mode 2

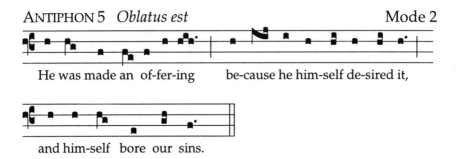

He was made an of-fer-ing   be-cause he him-self de-sired it,

and him-self bore our sins.

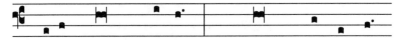

PSALM 147 *Laudate Dominum*

1 How good it is to sing praises to our <u>God</u>! *
    how pleasant it is to honor <u>him</u> with praise!

2 The LORD rebuilds Je<u>ru</u>salem; *
    he gathers the exiles <u>of</u> Israel.

3 He heals the broken<u>heart</u>ed *
    and binds <u>up</u> their wounds.

4 He counts the number of the <u>stars</u> *
    and calls them all <u>by</u> their names.

5 Great is our LORD and mighty in <u>power</u>; *
    there is no limit to <u>his</u> wisdom.

6 The LORD lifts up the l<u>ow</u>ly, *
   but casts the wicked <u>to</u> the ground.

7 Sing to the LORD with thanks<u>giv</u>ing; *
   make music to our God up<u>on</u> the harp.

8 He covers the heavens with <u>clouds</u> *
   and prepares rain <u>for</u> the earth;

9 He makes grass to grow upon the <u>moun</u>tains *
   and green plants to <u>serve</u> mankind.

10 He provides food for flocks and <u>herds</u> *
   and for the young ravens <u>when</u> they cry.

11 He is not impressed by the might of a <u>horse</u>; *
   he has no pleasure in the strength <u>of</u> a man;

12 But the LORD has pleasure in those who <u>fear</u> him, *
   in those who await his gra<u>cious</u> favor.

13 Worship the LORD, O Je<u>ru</u>salem; *
   praise your God, <u>O</u> Zion;

14 For he has strengthened the bars of your <u>gates</u>; *
   he has blessed your children <u>with</u>in you.

15 He has established peace on your <u>bor</u>ders; *
   he satisfies you with the <u>fin</u>est wheat.

16 He sends out his command to the <u>earth</u>, *
   and his word runs ve<u>ry</u> swiftly.

17 He gives snow like <u>wool</u>; *
   he scatters hoarfrost <u>like</u> ashes.

18 He scatters his hail like <u>bread</u> crumbs; *
   who can stand a<u>gainst</u> his cold?

19 He sends forth his word and <u>melts</u> them; *
   he blows with his wind, and the <u>wa</u>ters flow.

20 He declares his word to <u>Ja</u>cob, *
   his statutes and his judgments <u>to</u> Israel.

21 He has not done so to any other <u>na</u>tion; *
   to them he has not revealed <u>his</u> judgments.

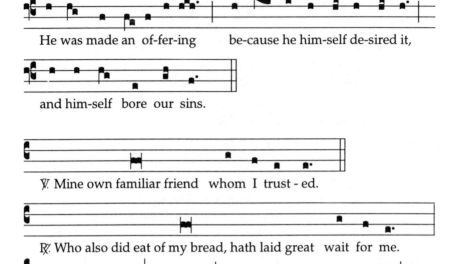

He was made an of-fer-ing   be-cause he him-self de-sired it,

and him-self bore our sins.

℣. Mine own familiar friend   whom I trust - ed.

℟. Who also did eat of my bread, hath laid great   wait   for   me.

Now he that be-trayed him   *   gave them   a   sign,   say-ing,

"Whom-so - ev-er I shall kiss,   that same is he.   Hold   him   fast."

The first three notes of the psalm tone are repeated with each verse of the following canticle. The cantor sings verse 1 alone. All join at verse 2.

THE SONG OF ZECHARIAH *Benedictus Dominus Deus*

1 Blessed be the Lord <u>God</u> of Isra͜el, *
      for he hath visited and re<u>deem</u>ed his people;

2 And hath raised up a mighty sal<u>va</u>tion for us *
      in the house of his <u>ser</u>vant David,

298

3 As he spake by the mouth of his <u>ho</u>ly prophets, *
    which have been since <u>the</u> world began:

4 That we should be <u>saved</u> from⁀our ene⁀mies, *
    and from the hand of <u>all</u> that hate us;

5 To perform the mercy <u>promised</u>⁀to⁀our forefa⁀thers, *
    and to remember his <u>ho</u>ly covenant;

6 To perform the oath which he sware to our <u>forefa</u>⁀ther Abra⁀ham, *
    that <u>he</u> would give us,

7 That we being delivered out of the <u>hand</u> of⁀our ene⁀mies *
    might serve <u>him</u> without fear,

8 In holiness and <u>righ</u>teous⁀ness⁀before him, *
    all the <u>days</u> of our life.

9 And thou, child, shalt be called the <u>prophet</u>⁀of⁀the Highest, *
    for thou shalt go before the face of the Lord to <u>pre</u>pare his ways;

10 To give knowledge of salvation <u>unto</u>⁀his people *
    for the remis<u>sion</u> of their sins,

11 Through the tender <u>mer</u>cy of⁀our God, *
    whereby the dayspring from on high hath <u>vi</u>sited us;

12 To give light to them that sit in darkness and in the <u>sha</u>dow of death, *
    and to guide our feet into <u>the</u> way of peace.

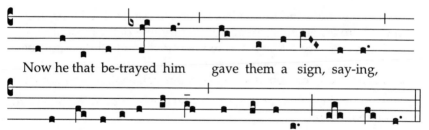

Now he that be-trayed him   gave them a sign, say-ing,

"Whom-so - ev-er I shall kiss, that same is he.   Hold him fast."

After the Benedictus antiphon has been repeated, the following is sung, all kneeling.

ENTRANCES

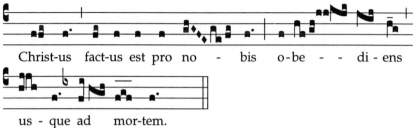

Christ-us fact-us est pro no - bis o-be - - di - ens

us - que ad mor-tem.

All sit, and OUR FATHER is said silently. PSALM 51 is then said by all in a low voice. After the psalm, the officiant says the following collect quietly but so all may hear:

Almighty God, we beseech thee graciously to behold this thy family, for which our Lord Jesus Christ was contented to be betrayed, and given up into the hands of wicked men, and to suffer death upon the cross.

The Officiant adds silently: Who now liveth and reigneth with thee and the Holy Ghost, ever one God, world without end. Amen.

The cantor now makes a knocking sound by striking a book or bench, and everyone in the choir does the same in response. The single burning Tenebrae candle is returned to view. After a period of silence, the cantor stands, and the choir leaves for the sacristy. In the sacristy, the following prayers are said by the officiant or cantor:

To the most holy and undivided Trinity, to the crucified humanity of our Lord Jesus Christ, to the fruitful virginity of the most blessed and glorious Virgin Mary, and to the company of all the saints be never ending praise, honor, power and glory from every creature, and to us also remission of all our sins, through endless ages. Amen.

℣. Blessed be the womb of the Virgin Mary, which bore the Son of the Eternal Father.

℟. And blessed be the breast which nurtured Christ the Lord.

The following are said together in a low voice:

OUR FATHER . . .

Hail Mary, full of grace, the Lord is with thee. Blessed art thou among women, and blessed is the fruit of thy womb, Jesus. Holy Mary, Mother of God, pray for us sinners, now and at the hour of our death. Amen.

All leave in silence.

Appendix 10

Compline

A NOTE ON COMPLINE

Compline disappeared from the English church in the sixteenth century, when it was absorbed into Evening Prayer. It has been re-introduced in various Anglican prayer books during the twentieth century, and first appeared in the Episcopal Church in the 1979 Book of Common Prayer. Since that introduction, it has become a favorite Office of many Episcopalians across the United States. It is short, simple, and deeply affecting as a late-evening blessing. Either said or sung, it is a perfect concluding devotion for rehearsals, retreats, and meetings as well as for individuals and families.

The order below differs slightly from the form given in the Book of Common Prayer, and so a word of explanation may be necessary. In the Benedictine (monastic) form of the opening sentences, the line, "The Lord Almighty grant us a peaceful night and a perfect end" is followed by a verse from 1 Peter: "Brothers and Sisters, be sober, be watchful; your adversary the devil prowls around like a roaring lion, seeking someone to devour. Resist him, firm in your faith" (1 Pet 5:8–9). That verse is included here as a call to inner attention ("be sober, be watchful") which is particularly appropriate to a contemplative liturgy. It is a reminder to every singer that his or her most important task in the chant is to "resist" the "devouring" force of inner distractions and egotistical desires.

In the pre-Vatican II Roman version of Compline, two of the lines given in the Book of Common Prayer as a versicle and response are the text of a short responsory to the lesson: "Into your hands, O Lord, I commend my spirit. For you have redeemed me, O Lord, O God of truth." The responsory format has been followed below because it is typical of the lesson/responsory relationship found throughout the chant repertory. If these lines are to be sung in the musical form of a short responsory, then they must be moved, as they have been here, so as to follow the lesson. As we saw in Chapter Five, the musical form of the responsory is a particularly important example of the contemplative approach to scripture. Even in the short responsories such as this one for Compline, lines of scripture are cut and recombined so as to suggest multiple contexts and meanings. (The second Compline versicle from the prayer book, "Keep us, O Lord, as the apple of your eye," remains in its place following the hymn.)

As explained in the Appendix 8 preface ("Why Vespers?"), an antiphon and prayer to the Virgin Mary may be sung after Compline. The antiphon appropriate to the season of Advent is given with Advent Vespers, above.

Compline—An Evening Blessing

If Compline is said after the Eucharist, it begins with "O God, make speed to save us." The psalms are translated from the Latin Vulgate.

THE PREPARATION

The Cantor begins:

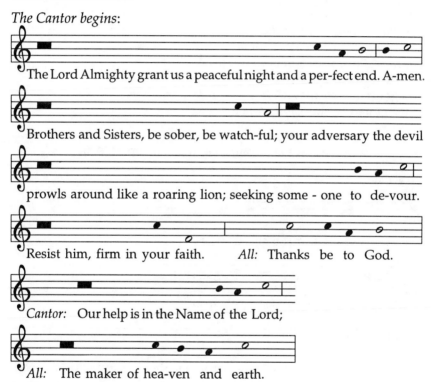

The Lord Almighty grant us a peaceful night and a per-fect end. A-men.

Brothers and Sisters, be sober, be watch-ful; your adversary the devil

prowls around like a roaring lion; seeking some - one to de-vour.

Resist him, firm in your faith.   *All:* Thanks be to God.

Cantor: Our help is in the Name of the Lord;

All: The maker of hea-ven and earth.

All kneel.

Officiant: Let us confess our sins to God.

Officiant and People (spoken):

I confess to Almighty God, * to the blessed Virgin Mary, to blessed Michael the archangel, to blessed John Baptist, to the holy apostles Peter and Paul, and to all the saints, that I have sinned exceedingly in thought, word, and deed; through my fault, through my own fault, through my own most grievous fault. Wherefore I beg blessed Mary, blessed Michael the archangel, blessed John Baptist, the holy apostles Peter and Paul, and all the saints, to pray for me to the Lord our God.

~or~

Almighty God, our heavenly Father:
We have sinned against you,
through our own fault,
in thought, and word, and deed,
and in what we have left undone.
For the sake of your Son our Lord Jesus Christ,
forgive us all our offenses;
and grant that we may serve you in newness of life,
to the glory of your Name. Amen.

Officiant: May the Almighty God grant us + forgiveness of all our sins, and the grace and comfort of the Holy Spirit. Amen.

All stand.

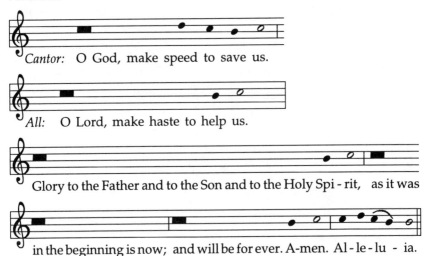

Cantor: O God, make speed to save us.

All: O Lord, make haste to help us.

Glory to the Father and to the Son and to the Holy Spi - rit,   as it was

in the beginning is now; and will be for ever. A-men. Al - le - lu - ia.

Alleluia is not sung during Lent.

THE PSALTER

Please pause at semi-colons. The Cantor sings the antiphon to the asterisk, and sings the first verse of the psalm. All sit after the antiphon.

ANTIPHON *Miserere*   Mode 8

Cantor: Have mer - cy   up - on me, O Lord, *

and heark - en un - to my pray'r.

PSALM 4   *Cum invocarem*

1 When I called upon him, the God of my justice <u>heard</u> me; *
   in distress you have enlarged me; have
       mercy on me <u>and</u> hear my prayer.

2 O mortals, how long will you be dull of <u>heart</u>? *
   why do you love emptiness and seek <u>after</u> lying?

3 Know that the Lord has made his holy one <u>wonder</u>ful; *
   when I call upon the Lord, <u>he</u> will hear me.

4 Be angry and do not <u>sin</u>; *
   be opened upon your beds to what you <u>speak</u> in your hearts.

5 Offer the sacrifice of justice, and hope in the <u>Lord</u>; *
   many are saying, Who <u>shows</u> us good things?

6 The light of your countenance, O Lord, is signed up<u>on</u> us; *
   you have given glad<u>ness</u> in my heart.

7 By the fruit of their corn, and wine, and <u>oil</u>, *
   <u>they</u> are multiplied.

8 In peace in the same I will sleep and I will <u>rest</u>; *
   for you, Lord, only, have con<u>firmed</u> me in hope.

PSALM 91 *Qui habitat*

1 He who dwells in the aid of the Most <u>High</u>, *
   shall abide in the protection of the <u>God</u> of Heaven.

2 He shall say to the Lord, You are my guardian and my <u>refuge</u>; *
   my God, I <u>will</u> hope in him.

3 For he has delivered me from the snare of the <u>hunters</u>, *
   and <u>from</u> the sharp word.

4 He will overshadow you with his <u>shoulders</u>, *
   and under his <u>wings</u> you shall hope.

5 His truth will surround you like a <u>shield</u>; *
   you shall not be afraid of any <u>terror</u> by night;

6 Of an arrow flying in the day, of trouble walking about in <u>shadows</u>; *
   of assault, and of the de<u>mon</u> at noonday.

7 A thousand shall fall at your <u>side</u>, †
              and ten thousand at your right <u>hand</u>, *
   but it shall <u>not</u> come near you.

8 But you shall consider with your <u>eyes</u>, *
   and see the reward <u>of</u> the wicked.

9 For you, O Lord, are my <u>hope</u>; *
   you have made the highest <u>place</u> your refuge.

10 Evil shall not come <u>near</u> you, *
   nor the scourge to your <u>tabernacle</u>.

11 Because he has given his angels charge <u>over</u> you, *
   to keep you <u>in</u> all your ways.

12 They shall bear you in their <u>hands</u>, *
   Lest you dash your foot <u>against</u> a stone.

13 You shall walk upon the asp and <u>basilisk</u>; *
   and trample the <u>lion</u> and dragon.

14 Because he has hoped in me I will <u>free</u> him; *
   I will protect him, because he <u>has</u> known my name.

15 He shall call upon me and I will <u>hear</u> him; *
    I am with him in distress; I will deliver him and <u>glo</u>rify him.

16 I will fill him with length of <u>days</u>; *
    and show him <u>my</u> salvation.

PSALM 134 *Ecce nunc*

1 Behold now bless the Lord, all you servants of the <u>Lord</u>, *
    who stand in the house of the Lord, in the
        courts of the <u>house</u> of our God.

2 Lift up your hands in the nights in the holy <u>place</u>, *
    <u>and</u> bless the Lord.

3 May the Lord bless you out of <u>Sion</u>, *
    who made <u>heaven</u> and earth

    Glory to the Father, and to the Son, and to the Holy <u>Spirit</u>: *
    as it was in the beginning, is now, and will be for <u>ev</u>er. Amen.

The antiphon is repeated.

All: Have mer - cy   up - on me, O   Lord, *

and heark - en un - to   my pray'r.

THE LESSON (Jeremiah 14:9,22)

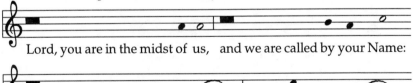

Lord, you are in the midst of us,   and we are called by your Name:

Do not forsake us, O Lord our God.   *All:* Thanks be to God.

THE SHORT RESPONSORY *In manus tuas*   Mode 6

Cantor: In - to your hands, O   Lord,   *All:* I com-mend my

spi - - rit;   In - to your hands, O   Lord,   I com-mend

my spi - - rit;   *Cantor:* You have re - deem'd me, O   Lord,

O God of truth.   *All:* I com - mend my spi - - rit.

Cantor: Glo-ry to the Fa - ther and to   the Son and to the

Ho - ly Spi - rit.   *All:* In - to your hands, O   Lord,

All: I com-mend my spi - - rit.

THE HYMN *Te lucis ante terminum* Mode 8

1. To you be- fore the close of day, * Cre - a - tor of
2. Save us from trou-bled, rest- less sleep, from all ill dreams
3. A heal - thy life we ask of you, the fire of love
4. Al - migh - ty Fa - ther, hear our cry through Je - sus Christ,

   all things, we pray that in your con- stant
   your chil - dren keep; so calm our minds that
   in us re - new; and when the dawn new
   our Lord most high whom with the Spi - rit

   clem - en - cy our guard and keep - er you would be.
   fears may cease and res - ted bod - ies wake in peace.
   light will bring your praise and glo - ry we shall sing.
   we a - dore for ev - er and for ev - er more.

A - men.

Cantor: Keep us, O Lord, as the apple of your eye;
All: And hide us under the shadow of your wings.

ENTRANCES

THE PRAYERS

All kneel.

Officiant: Lord, have mercy. *All:* Christ, have mercy. Lord, have mer-cy.

Officiant: Our Fa - ther,   ~or~   Our Father in Hea - ven

Officiant and People continue silently:

who art in heaven,	~or~	hallowed be your Name,
hallowed be thy Name,		your kingdom come,
thy kingdom come,		your will be done,
thy will be done,		on earth as in heaven.
on earth as it is in heaven.		Give us today our daily bread.
Give us this day our daily bread.		Forgive us our sins
And forgive us our trespasses,		as we forgive those
as we forgive those		who sin against us.
who trespass against us.		

Officiant:

And lead us not into temp-ta-tion, ~or~   Save us from the time of tri-al,

All:

but deliver us from e - vil.   ~or~   and deliver us from e - vil.

Officiant: Lord, hear our prayer;   *All:* And let our cry come to you.

Compline

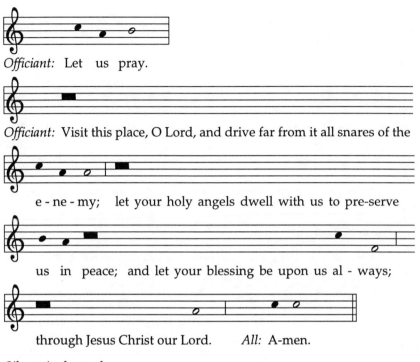

Officiant: Let us pray.

Officiant: Visit this place, O Lord, and drive far from it all snares of the

e - ne - my; let your holy angels dwell with us to pre-serve

us in peace; and let your blessing be upon us al - ways;

through Jesus Christ our Lord. *All:* A-men.

Silence is observed.

THE CANTICLE *Nunc dimittis The Song of Simeon* Mode 3

Antiphon *Salve nos*

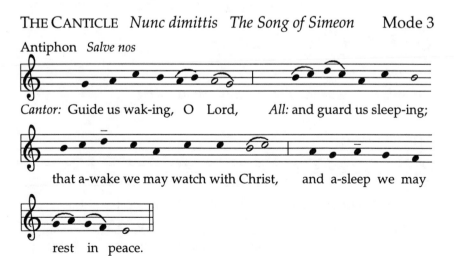

Cantor: Guide us wak-ing, O Lord, *All:* and guard us sleep-ing;

that a-wake we may watch with Christ, and a-sleep we may

rest in peace.

Cantor: Lord, now lettest thou thy ser-vant de-part in peace,

All: ac-cord-ing to thy word; For mine eyes have seen thy

sal - va - tion, which thou hast prepared before the face of all peo-ple,

To be a light to light-en the Gen-tiles, and to be the glory of thy

peo-ple Is-ra - el. Glo-ry to the Father and to the Son and to

the Ho-ly Spi - rit: as it was in the beginning is now; and will be

for e - ver. A - men.

The Antiphon is repeated, all singing: "Guide us waking . . . "

THE BLESSING

Officiant: Let us bless the Lord. *All:* Thanks be to God.

Officiant (on one note): The almighty and merciful Lord, Father, Son,
and Holy Spirit, bless us and keep us. ℟ Amen.

312

Compline

One of the following hymns to the Virgin Mary may be sung, according to the season. "Ave Maria" may be used at any time, with the collect and versicle appropriate to the season.

Compline ends with the "Concluding Versicle."

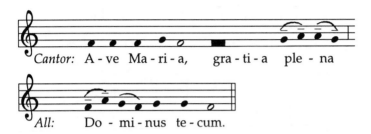

Cantor: A - ve Ma - ri - a, gra - ti - a ple - na
All: Do - mi - nus te - cum.

The above lines are repeated in full, everyone singing, then:

Cantor: Be-ne - di - cta tu in mu-li - e - ri-bus; et benedictus
fru-ctus ven-tris tu - i. All: Do - mi - nus te-cum.

The first lines are repeated in full, everyone singing (Ave Maria . . . tecum).

[Hail Mary, full of grace, the Lord is with thee. Blessed art thou among women, and blessed is the fruit of thy womb. Glory to the Father . . . Hail Mary . . .]

The following may be sung from Vespers of Saturday before the first Sunday of Advent through Second Vespers of the Presentation (February 2).

Al - - - - - ma * Re-demp-tó - ris Ma - ter, quae
pér - vi - a cae - li Por - ta ma - nes, Et stel - la

313

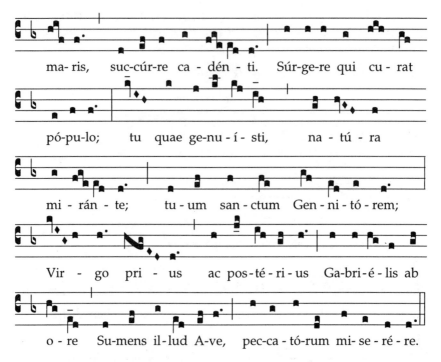

ma- ris, suc-cúr-re ca - dén - ti. Súr-ge-re qui cu - rat pó-pu-lo; tu quae ge-nu - í - sti, na - tú - ra mi - rán - te; tu - um san - ctum Gen - ni - tó - rem; Vir - go pri - us ac pos-té - ri - us Ga-bri-é - lis ab o - re Su-mens il-lud A-ve, pec-ca - tó-rum mi- se - ré - re.

[Hail, gracious Mother of our Redeemer, for ever abiding, heaven's gateway, star of the ocean. Succour those who, though falling, strive to rise, you who bore, to the wonder of all nature, your own holy Creator. O Virgin both before and after you received that greeting from the mouth of Gabriel, have mercy on us sinners.]

After the antiphon, during Advent, the following is sung:

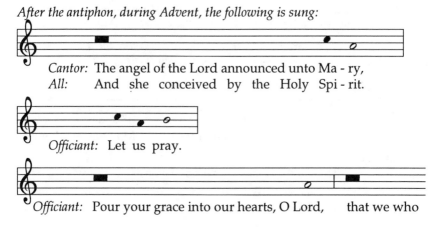

Cantor: The angel of the Lord announced unto Ma - ry,
All: And she conceived by the Holy Spi - rit.

Officiant: Let us pray.

Officiant: Pour your grace into our hearts, O Lord, that we who

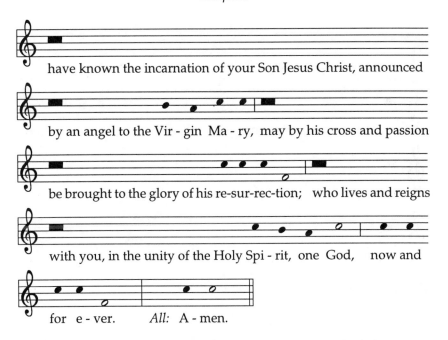

have known the incarnation of your Son Jesus Christ, announced

by an angel to the Vir - gin Ma - ry, may by his cross and passion

be brought to the glory of his re-sur-rec-tion; who lives and reigns

with you, in the unity of the Holy Spi - rit, one God, now and

for e - ver. *All:* A - men.

Compline ends with the "Concluding Versicle."

From First Vespers of Christmas through Second Vespers of the Presentation, the following is sung instead of the preceding:

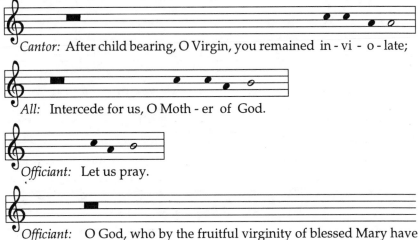

Cantor: After child bearing, O Virgin, you remained in - vi - o - late;

All: Intercede for us, O Moth - er of God.

Officiant: Let us pray.

Officiant: O God, who by the fruitful virginity of blessed Mary have

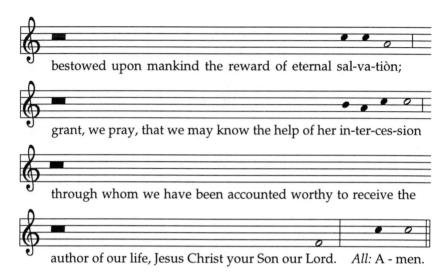

bestowed upon mankind the reward of eternal sal-va-tiòn;

grant, we pray, that we may know the help of her in-ter-ces-sion

through whom we have been accounted worthy to receive the

author of our life, Jesus Christ your Son our Lord.   *All:* A - men.

Compline ends with the "Concluding Versicle."

The following antiphon is used from the Presentation through Compline of Wednesday in Holy Week.

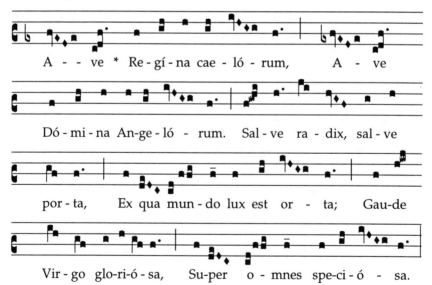

A - - ve * Re - gí - na cae - ló - rum,   A - ve

Dó - mi - na An - ge - ló - rum. Sal - ve ra - dix, sal - ve

por - ta,   Ex qua mun - do lux est or - ta;   Gau-de

Vir - go glo-ri-ó - sa,   Su-per o - mnes spe-ci - ó - sa.

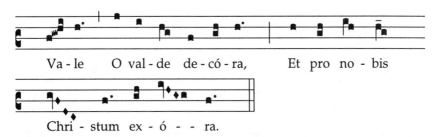

Va - le   O val - de de - có - ra,   Et pro no - bis

Chri - stum ex - ó - - ra.

[Hail, Queen of the heavens, hail, Lady of the Angels, root, door, from whom light has dawned upon the world; joy to you, Virgin glorious, beautiful beyond all others; hail, and farewell; O most gracious, plead for us to Christ.]

Cantor: Make me worthy to praise you, O Holy Vir - gin.
All: Give me strength against your e - ne - mies.

Officiant: Let us pray.

Officiant: Grant us, O merciful God, protection in our weak-ness,

that we who celebrate the memory of the holy Mother of God

may, through the aid of her in - ter - ces-sion,   rise again from

our sins.   Through the same Christ our Lòrd.

All: A - men.

Compline ends with the "Concluding Versicle."

ENTRANCES

The following antiphon is used from Compline of Easter Day through Compline of the Friday before Pentecost.

Re-gí-na cae-li * lae-tá - - - - - - re al-le-lú-ia.

Qui-a quem me-ru-ís-ti por - - - - - - tá-re

al-le- - - lú-ia. Re-sur-ré-xit, si-cut di-xit

al-le-lú-ia. O-ra pro no-bis De-um

al-le - - - - - - - - - - - - - lú-ia.

[Queen of Heaven, rejoice alleluia, for He whom you were worthy to bear alleluia has risen as he said alleluia. Pray for us to God alleluia.]

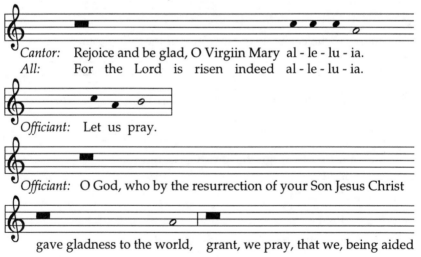

Cantor: Rejoice and be glad, O Virgiin Mary al-le-lu-ia.
All: For the Lord is risen indeed al-le-lu-ia.

Officiant: Let us pray.

Officiant: O God, who by the resurrection of your Son Jesus Christ

gave gladness to the world, grant, we pray, that we, being aided

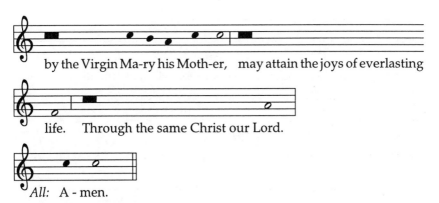

by the Virgin Ma-ry his Moth-er, may attain the joys of everlasting life. Through the same Christ our Lord.

All: A - men.

Compline ends with the "Concluding Versicle."

The following is used from Compline of the Saturday before Pentecost through Compline of the Friday before the First Sunday of Advent.

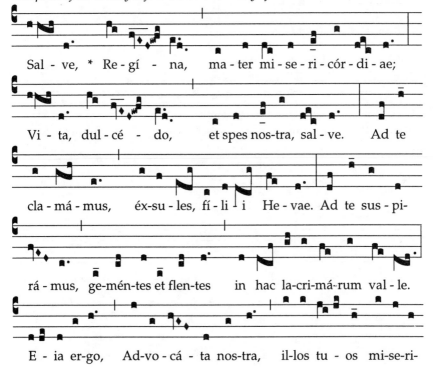

Sal - ve, * Re - gí - na, ma - ter mi - se - ri - cór - di - ae;

Vi - ta, dul - cé - do, et spes nos-tra, sal - ve. Ad te

cla - má - mus, éx-su - les, fí - li - i He - vae. Ad te sus - pi-

rá - mus, ge-mén-tes et flen-tes in hac la-cri-má-rum val - le.

E - ia er-go, Ad-vo - cá - ta nos-tra, il-los tu - os mi-se-ri-

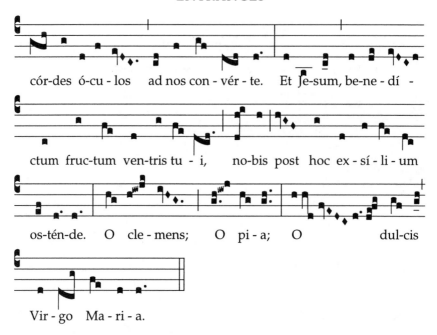

córdes ó-cu - los   ad nos con - vér - te.   Et Je-sum, be-ne - dí -

ctum fruc-tum ven-tris tu - i,   no-bis post hoc ex - sí - li - um

os-tén-de.   O cle - mens;   O pi - a;   O   dul-cis

Vir - go   Ma - ri - a.

An alternative tune for the preceding:

Sal-ve, Re-gí-na, * ma-ter mi-se-ri-cór-di-ae;   Vi-ta, dul-cé - do

Et spes nos-tra, sal - ve.   Ad te cla-má-mus,   éx-su-les, fí-li-i

He-vae.   Ad te sus-pi- rá- mus,   ge-mén-tes et flen-tes   in hac

la-cri-má- rum val-le.   E-ia er-go Ad-vo-cá-ta nos-tra,   il-los

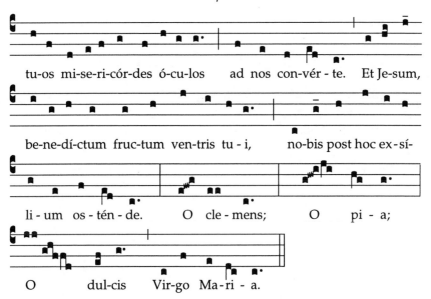

tu-os mi-se-ri-cór-des ó-cu-los   ad nos con-vér - te.   Et Je-sum,

be-ne-dí-ctum fruc-tum ven-tris tu - i,   no-bis post hoc ex-sí-

li - um os - tén - de.   O cle - mens;   O   pi - a;

O   dul-cis   Vir-go Ma-ri - a.

[Hail Queen, Mother of Mercy; Hail our life, our sweetness, our hope. To you we call, exiled children of Eve. To you we sigh, mourning and weeping in this valley of tears. Therefore, O Advocate, turn your merciful eyes toward us, and, after this our exile, show us Jesus, the blessed fruit of your womb, O gentle, O blessed, O sweet Virgin Mary.]

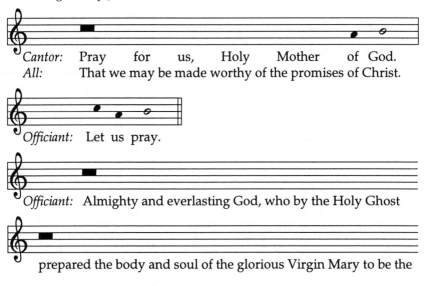

Cantor: Pray   for   us,   Holy   Mother   of God.
All: That we may be made worthy of the promises of Christ.

Officiant: Let us pray.

Officiant: Almighty and everlasting God, who by the Holy Ghost

prepared the body and soul of the glorious Virgin Mary to be the

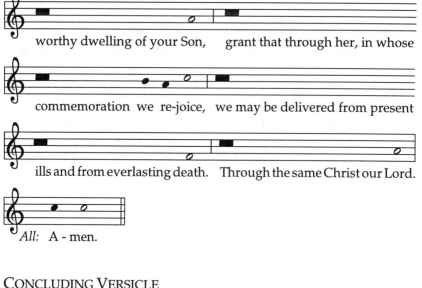

worthy dwelling of your Son,   grant that through her, in whose

commemoration we re-joice, we may be delivered from present

ills and from everlasting death.   Through the same Christ our Lord.

All: A - men.

CONCLUDING VERSICLE

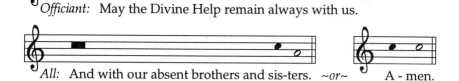

Officiant: May the Divine Help remain always with us.

All: And with our absent brothers and sis-ters.   *~or~*   A - men.

All leave the church in silence.

For personal devotions:

HAIL MARY

Ave Maria, gratia plena, Dominus tecum; benedicta tu in mulieribus, et benedictus fructus ventris tui Jesus. Sancta Maria, Mater Dei, ora pro nobis peccatoribus, nunc et in hora mortis nostrae. Amen.

[Hail Mary, full of grace, the Lord is with thee. Blessed art thou among women, and blessed is the fruit of thy womb, Jesus. Holy Mary, Mother of God, pray for us sinners now and at the hour of our death. Amen.]

THE LORD'S PRAYER

Pater noster, qui es in caelis, sanctificetur nomen tuum; adveniat regnum tuum; fiat voluntas tua, sicut caelo et in terra. Panem nostrum quotidianum da nobis hodie, et dimitte nobis debita nostra, sicut et nos dimittimus debitoribus nostris; et ne nos inducas in tentationem, sed libera nos a malo. Amen.

Appendix 11

A Eucharist in Honor of the Holy Spirit

WHAT IS A "CONTEMPLATIVE "EUCHARIST?

Of the liturgies included in this book, the Eucharist will be most thoroughly familiar to the largest number of readers. Its differences from Rite I and Rite II in the Book of Common Prayer, therefore, need to be considered. As was emphasized in Chapter Six, no one today can be certain what a "contemplative" Eucharist should look like. But its aim is clearly set out in the words of Fr. Le Saux, quoted in Chapter Six: "After such worship the faithful should go on their way fully recollected within themselves" (*Prayer* 49). Thus, the liturgy will move toward recollection and silence as it proceeds. By contrast, the Prayer Book rites conclude with a forceful "outward" movement: "Let us go forth . . ." A contemplative rite must follow a different curve. Its "call" at the end must be toward silence and individual prayer. Worshipers might be expected to remain in prayer, perhaps for a considerable time, in order to benefit from the inner preparation and openness to prayer provided by the liturgy. Further, as we saw in Chapter Six, we might expect a contemplative liturgy to be more repetitive than our naturally impatient, secular minds would wish. And so we might expect to be made uncomfortable by such a liturgy, as tension is set up within us between a deeper wish for quiet and all the expectations, opinions, and irritations we carry with us through every day of our lives. Finally, we might expect such a liturgy, as it guides us toward the stillness for which we hunger, to guide us also toward the dim perception of a different kind of meaning, beyond the literal, in the words and actions of the rite itself.

As Chapter Six tried to make clear, no one can say how these purposes might best be served in practice. The liturgy which follows is offered as a starting point. It should be considered a "teaching," or better yet, "guiding" Eucharist. It needs to be celebrated under different parish conditions, tested, no doubt altered, but altered in ways that more deeply evoke contemplative experience, not suppress it by conforming to the expectations of the secular mind. The element of "offense" to the world of the everyday in this liturgy must not be blunted. It is that very element of rebuke which, according to Origen, "denies a way and an access to the common understanding" and "calls us back to the beginning of another way," a "higher and loftier road" which "may open for us the immense breadth of divine knowledge" (*Orig/CWS* 187–188).

The language of the following liturgy is contemporary, in an effort to make its literal sense clear and avoid an archaic atmosphere. It does, however, include older prayers which help suggest the symbolic meanings of the rite. Some of these prayers, historically, were recited silently by the priest alone. They are meant to be said aloud here, in order that the insights they carry may be shared by all. Parenthetical lines of scripture and excerpts from the fathers are offered in some abundance. Worshipers are encouraged to ignore most or all of these, except for that word or phrase which may speak exactly to the moment. It is hoped that these selections will encourage individuals to bring their own scriptural meditations to the liturgy as well.

Perhaps no single aspect of the liturgy below is more illustrative of its character than the suggested reading, taken from the opening verses of John's gospel. This "Last Gospel" was common in Anglo-Catholic parishes a generation ago and in Roman Catholic parishes before Vatican II. Many congregations today will find it completely unfamiliar, and it has been criticized by liturgists as a pointless "late medieval accretion" and a liturgical "redundancy." As we have seen repeatedly, however, where the sacred is concerned, there is a fine line between repetition and redundancy. If the inner mind, the repository of the sacred in human nature, is to be opened, repetition is essential. It is recognized as essential in sacred rites across cultures and around the world. And experience teaches that the active, natural mind is quick to object to these repetitions as boring and unnecessary. On the other hand, true redundancy deadens the spirit and closes off access to the deeper intelligence. So the choices here are not simple and must be matters of discernment by the community.

If a contemplative Eucharist has been effective, so that at its conclusion worshipers are "fully recollected within themselves," then the mind in these final moments of the liturgy should be more open than it normally is to the inner sweetness of scripture. What better time to hear once again John's powerful summary of the gospel message. What better time, having just received the consecrated bread, to be offered the possibility of sensing the fundamental identity of the Body and the Word, within which lies the secret of the fundamental identity of everything created.

A Eucharist in Honor of the Holy Spirit

This liturgy is intended for weekday use. It includes only one lesson before the Gospel and does not include the Creed or Gloria. Meditations—silent or otherwise —are provided thoughout as marked with rules.

The rite conforms to the criteria for "An Order for Celebrating the Holy Eucharist" in the Book of Common Prayer of the Episcopal Church. Christians of other traditions may also find it appropriate for liturgical use.

The Liturgy of the Word

In John's Gospel, Our Lord commands that the jars at the wedding at Cana in Galilee be filled with water because first, by means of reading, our hearts are filled with sacred scripture. Our Lord turns the water to wine in us, when that same narrative, by means of the mystery of allegory, is changed in us into spiritual understanding.

–Saint Gregory the Great, 6th century

Out of the believer's heart shall flow rivers of living water.

–John 7:38

INTROIT *Spiritus Domini* (Wisdom 1:7; Psalm 68) Mode 8

All stand as the Ministers and Choir enter; the Introit is sung in procession or from the choir stalls.

You begin to go toward the altar; the angels are watching you; they have seen you begin to walk in; they have seen your appearance, which previously was wretched, suddenly become shining.

–Saint Ambrose, 4th century

Spi-ri - tus Do-mi - ni * re - ple - vit or-bem ter - ra - rum

al - le - lu - ia, Et hoc quod con - ti - net om - ni - a,

327

sci-en-ti - am   ha-bet vo - cis al - le - lu - ia al-le-lu -

ia   al - le - lu - i - a.   *Cantor:* Ex-ur-gat De-us,   et dis-si -

pen-tur i - ni - mi-ci e - jus;   *Choir:* et fu - gi-ant qui o - de-runt

e-um   a fa - ci - e   e - jus.   *Cantor:* Glo - ri - a   Pa-tri

et Fi-li-o,   et Spi-ri - tu - i San-cto;   *Choir:* si-cut e-rat in prin-

ci-pi- o,   et nunc et sem-per;   et in sae-cu - la sae-cu - lo - rum.

A - men.

All repeat "Spiritus Domini . . . alleluia."

During Lent the Introit antiphon is sung as follows. The psalm verse "Exurgat Deus" and Gloria are sung with the antiphon as above.

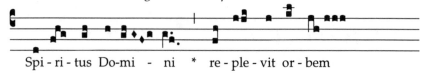

Spi - ri - tus Do-mi - ni   *   re - ple - vit or - bem

ter - - ra - rum. Et hoc quod con - ti - net om - ni - a,

sci-en-ti - am   ha-bet   vo - cis.

{The Spirit of the Lord has filled the whole world; and that which contains all things has knowledge of the voice alleluia, alleluia, alleluia. Ps. Let God arise, and let his enemies be scattered; let all who hate him flee before him. Glory to the Father . . .]

THE COLLECT FOR PURITY AND SUMMARY OF THE LAW

Celebrant The Lord be with you.

People And also with you.

Celebrant Let us pray.

Almighty God, to you all hearts are open, all desires known, and from you no secrets are hid: Cleanse the thoughts of our hearts by the inspiration of your Holy Spirit, that we may perfectly love you, and worthily magnify your holy Name; through Christ our Lord. Amen.

Celebrant Hear what our Lord Jesus Christ says. You shall love the Lord your God with all your heart, with all your soul, and with all your mind. This is the first and great commandment. And the second is like unto it: You shall love your neighbor as yourself. On these two commandments hang all the Law and the Prophets.

KYRIE ELEISON

Sung by all, still standing, led by the cantor, who sings the first "Kyrie," to the asterisk, and the last "Kyrie," to the asterisk, alone.

Ky - - ri - e   *   e - - - - le - i - son.

ENTRANCES

THE COLLECT OF THE DAY

I will lift up my hands in the holy place, and bless the Lord.

> – cf. Psalm 134:2

Celebrant The Lord be with you.

People And also with you.

Celebrant Let us pray.

Celebrant O God, who taught the hearts of your faithful people by sending to them the light of your Holy Spirit, grant us by the same Spirit to have a right judgment in all things, and evermore to rejoice in his holy comfort; through Jesus Christ your Son our Lord, who lives and reigns with you, in the unity of the Holy Spirit, one God, for ever and ever. *Amen.*

All sit.

THE LESSON (Acts 8:14–17)

There is little sweetness in the study of the literal sense of Scripture, unless there be a commentary, which is found in the heart, to reveal its inward sense.

> –Guigo II, 12th century

How sweet are your words to my taste! They are sweeter than honey to my mouth.

> –Psalm 119:103

Reader The apostles in Jerusalem now heard that Samaria had accepted the word of God. They sent off Peter and John, who went down there and prayed for the converts, asking that they might receive the Holy Spirit. For until then the Spirit had not come upon any of them. They had been baptized into the name of the Lord Jesus, that and nothing more. So Peter and John laid their hands on them and they received the Holy Spirit.

The Word of the Lord.

People Thanks be to God.

All stand.

331

THE ALLELUIA AND VERSE *Veni, Sancte Spiritus* Mode 2

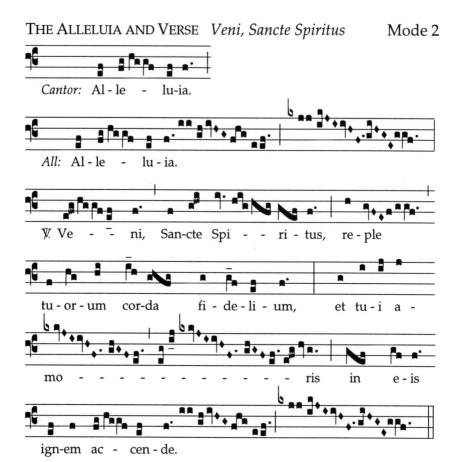

Cantor: Al - le - lu - ia.

All: Al - le - lu - ia.

℣. Ve - ni, San-cte Spi - ri - tus, re - ple

tu - or - um cor-da fi - de - li - um, et tu - i a -

mo - ris in e - is

ign-em ac - cen - de.

Repeat Alleluia from "All:".

[Alleluia. Come, Holy Ghost; fill the hearts of your faithful people; kindle in them the fire of your love.]

During Lent the Alleluia above is replaced by the following Tract:

Eucharist in Honor of the Holy Spirit

TRACT *Emitte Spiritum* (Psalm 104; Wisdom 12:1)   Mode 2

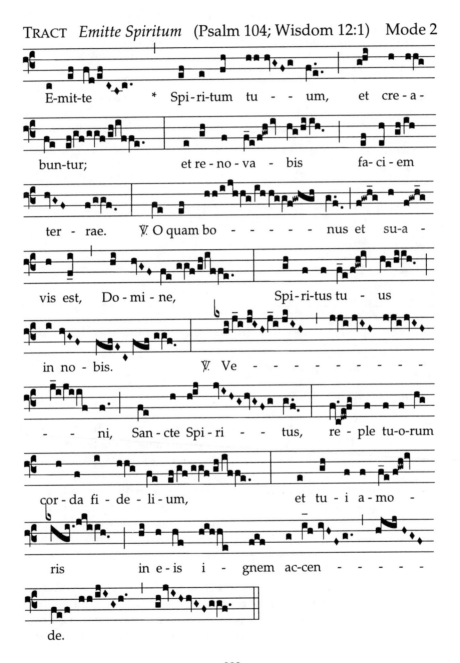

E-mit-te * Spi-ri-tum tu - - um, et cre-a-bun-tur; et re-no-va - bis fa-ci-em ter-rae. ℣. O quam bo - - - - - nus et su-a-vis est, Do-mi-ne, Spi-ri-tus tu-us in no-bis. ℣. Ve - - - - - - - - ni, San-cte Spi-ri - - tus, re-ple tu-o-rum cor-da fi-de-li-um, et tu-i a-mo-ris in e-is i-gnem ac-cen - - - - - de.

333

[Send forth your Spirit, and they shall be created, and you shall renew the face of the earth. How good and sweet, O Lord, is your Spirit within us. Come, Holy Spirit, and fill the hearts of your faithful people, and kindle in them the fire of your love.]

THE HOLY GOSPEL   (John 14:23-31)

The entrance of the Gospel signifies the coming of the Son of God and His entrance into this world.

–Saint Germanus of Constantinople, 8th century

The word is very near you; it is in your mouth and in your heart, so that you can do it.

–Deuteronomy 30:14

A deacon or priest reads the Gospel, first saying

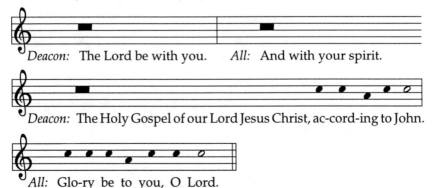

Deacon: The Lord be with you.   *All:* And with your spirit.

Deacon: The Holy Gospel of our Lord Jesus Christ, ac-cord-ing to John.

All: Glo-ry be to you, O Lord.

Deacon   Jesus said, "Anyone who loves me will heed what I say; then my Father will love him, and we will come to him and make our dwelling with him; but he who does not love me does not heed what I say. And the word you hear is not mine: it is the word of the Father who sent me. I have told you all this while I am still here with you; but your Advocate, the Holy Spirit whom the Father will send in my name, will teach you everything, and will call to mind all that I have told you. Peace is my parting gift to you, my own peace, such as the world cannot give. Set your troubled hearts at rest, and banish your fears. You heard me say, 'I am going away, and coming back to you.' If you loved me you would have been glad to hear that I was going to the Father; for the Father is greater than I. I have told you now, beforehand, so that when it happens you may have faith. I shall

334

not talk much longer with you, for the Prince of this world approaches. He has no rights over me; but the world must be shown that I love the Father, and do exactly as he commands; so up, let us go forward!"

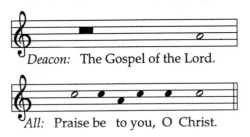

Deacon: The Gospel of the Lord.

All: Praise be to you, O Christ.

THE PRAYERS OF THE PEOPLE

When the Almighty speaks by Himself, the heart is instructed in his Word, without words and syllables; because his power is known by a kind of inward elevation . . . it is an incorporeal light, to both fill the inner parts, and circumscribe them without, when filled. It is a discourse without noise, which both opens the ears, and yet knows not to utter a sound.

–Saint Gregory the Great, 6th century

In my trouble I called upon the Lord, and he heard me. –Psalm 118:5

During the silence after each bidding, the People offer their own prayers, either silently or aloud.

I ask your prayers for God's people throughout the world; for our Bishop(s) _____ ; for this gathering; and for all ministers and people. Pray for the Church.

Silence

I ask your prayers for peace; for goodwill among nations; and for the well-being of all people. Pray for justice and peace.

Silence

I ask your prayers for the poor, the sick, the hungry, the oppressed, and those in prison. Pray for those in any need or trouble.

Silence

I ask your prayers for all who seek God, or a deeper knowledge of him. Pray that they may find and be found by him.

Silence

I ask your prayers for the departed [especially _____]. Pray for those who have died.

Silence

> *Members of the congregation may ask the prayers or the thanksgivings of those present*
>
> I ask your prayers for _____ .
> I ask your thanksgiving for _____ .
>
> *Silence*

Praise God for those in every generation in whom Christ has been honored [especially _____ whom we remember today]. Pray that we may have grace to glorify Christ in our own day.

Silence

The Celebrant adds one of the following collects.

O Lord our God, accept the fervent prayers of your people; in the multitude of your mercies, look with compassion upon us and all who turn to you for help; for you are gracious, O lover of souls, and to you we give glory, Father, Son, and Holy Spirit, now and for ever. Amen.

~or~

Almighty God, to whom our needs are known before we ask, help us to ask only what accords with your will; and those good things which we dare not, or in our blindness cannot ask, grant us for the sake of your Son Jesus Christ our Lord. Amen.

THE CONFESSION OF SIN

> The higher holy persons advance with God, the more accurately do they discover that they are unworthy; because as they come close to the light, they begin to see whatever had escaped their notice in themselves, and they appear to themselves the more deformed without, in proportion as that is very beautiful which they see within. For every one is made known to himself, when he is illumined with the touch of the true light, and by the same means as he learns what is righteousness, he is also instructed to see what is sin.
>
> –Saint Gregory the Great, 6th century

Lord, let me know my end and the number of my days, so that I may know how short my life is.

–Psalm 39:5

Deacon or
Celebrant Let us confess our sins against God and our neighbor.

Silence may be kept.

All Most merciful God,
we confess that we have sinned against you
in thought, word, and deed,
by what we have done,
and by what we have left undone.
We have not loved you with our whole heart;
we have not loved our neighbors as ourselves.
We are truly sorry and we humbly repent.
For the sake of your Son Jesus Christ,
have mercy on us and forgive us;
that we may delight in your will,
and walk in your ways,
to the glory of your Name. Amen.

Celebrant Almighty God have mercy on you, forgive you all your sins through our Lord Jesus Christ, strengthen you in all goodness, and by the power of the Holy Spirit keep you in eternal life. *Amen.*

The Holy Communion

OFFERTORY

The bread of offering signifies the superabundant riches of the goodness of our God, because the Son of God became man and gave Himself as an offering and oblation in ransom and atonement for the life and salvation of the world... The wine and the water are the blood and the water which came out from His side.

–Saint Germanus of Constantinople, 8th century

Here am I. Send me.

–Isaiah 6:8

Celebrant The Lord be with you.

People And also with you.

OFFERTORY CHANT *Confirma hoc* (Psalm 68) Mode 4

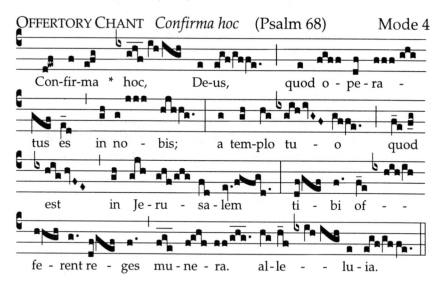

Con-fir-ma * hoc, De-us, quod o - pe - ra -

tus es in no - bis; a tem-plo tu - o quod

est in Je - ru - sa-lem ti - bi of - -

fe - rent re - ges mu - ne - ra. al-le - - lu - ia.

During Lent the Offertory Chant concludes as follows:

... re - ges mu - ne - ra.

[Establish the thing, O God, that you have made in us; at your temple, which is in Jerusalem, kings shall bring you presents alleluia.]

The people may sit.

Eucharist in Honor of the Holy Spirit

Celebrant Receive, Almighty God, this spotless host, which I, your unworthy servant, now offer unto you, for all my sins and neglect; and for all those here present; and also for all the faithful in Christ both living and dead; for their salvation and mine, unto life everlasting. *Amen.*

Celebrant We offer to you, O Lord, the cup of salvation; and pray that in your mercy it may ascend in the sight of your Divine Majesty as a sweet-smelling savor for our salvation, and that of the whole world. *Amen.*

Celebrant In a contrite heart and humble spirit, let us be accepted of you, O Lord, and let our sacrifice be well-pleasing in your sight, O Lord our God.
Come, O Sanctifier, Almighty and Everlasting God, and bless this sacrifice made ready for your Holy name.

The following is said as the Celebrant washes his or her hands (Psalm 26).

Celebrant I will wash my hands in innocence, O LORD, that I may go in procession round your altar, singing aloud a song of thanksgiving and recounting all your wonderful deeds.
LORD, I love the house in which you dwell and the place where your glory abides.
Do not sweep me away with sinners, nor my life with those who thirst for blood,
Whose hands are full of evil plots, and their right hand full of bribes.
As for me, I will live with integrity; redeem me, O LORD, and have pity on me.
My foot stands on level ground; in the full assembly I will bless the LORD.
Glory to the Father, and to the Son: and to the Holy Spirit. As it was in the beginning, is now, and will be for ever. Amen.

Celebrant Receive, O Holy Trinity, this oblation which we offer to you, in memory of the passion, resurrection and ascension of our Lord Jesus Christ; and in honor of the blessed Virgin Mary, of blessed John Baptist, of the holy Apostles Peter and Paul; of these and all the saints; that it may be to their honor and our salvation; and that as we remember them on earth, so in heaven they may plead for us. Through the same Christ our Lord. *Amen.*

All stand. The Celebrant announces the Intentions of the Eucharist.

Celebrant Pray, brothers and sisters, that my sacrifice and yours may be acceptable to God the Father Almighty.

People May the Lord receive this sacrifice at your hands, to the praise and glory of his Name; both to our benefit and that of all his holy Church.

The Sacrifice of Christ was offered once, as He entered once into the Holy of Holies. It is that same sacrifice that we offer, not one today and another tomorrow. One only Christ everywhere, entire everywhere, one only Body. As everywhere there is one Body, everywhere there is one sacrifice.
–Saint John Chrysostom, 5th century

THE GREAT THANKSGIVING

Then the priest, leading everyone into the heavenly Jerusalem, to His holy mountain, exclaims: "Let us lift up our hearts!" Then all declare: "We lift them up unto the Lord!" The priest says: "Let us give thanks unto the Lord." The people affirm: "It is right . . . " to send up hymns of thanksgiving to the Holy Trinity, to have the eye of the soul seeking the habitation of the heavenly Jerusalem.
–Saint Germanus of Constantinople, 8th century

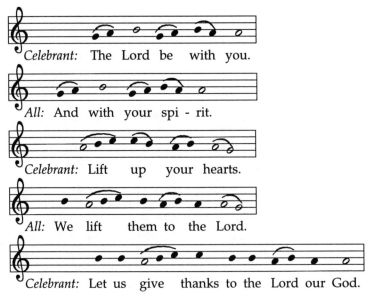

Celebrant: The Lord be with you.

All: And with your spi - rit.

Celebrant: Lift up your hearts.

All: We lift them to the Lord.

Celebrant: Let us give thanks to the Lord our God.

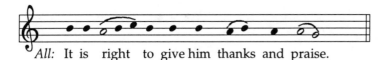

All: It is right to give him thanks and praise.

Celebrant It is right, and a good and joyful thing, always and everywhere to give thanks to you, Father Almighty, Creator of heaven and earth.

Through Jesus Christ our Lord. In fulfillment of his true promise, the Holy Spirit came down from heaven, lighting upon the disciples, to teach them and to lead them into all truth; uniting peoples of many tongues in the confession of one faith, and giving to your Church the power to serve you as a royal priesthood, and to preach the Gospel to all nations.

Therefore we praise you, joining our voices with Angels and Archangels and with all the company of heaven, who for ever sing this hymn to proclaim the glory of your Name:

SANCTUS

Sung by all, led by the cantor, who sings the first "Sanctus" and "Benedictus qui venit in nomine Domini" alone.

In the Sanctus, man is as it were transported into heaven itself. He stands near the throne of glory. He flies with the Seraphim. He sings the most holy hymn.
                                        –Saint John Chrysostom, 5th century

Dwell in the land, and you shall be fed with its riches.   –Psalm 37:3

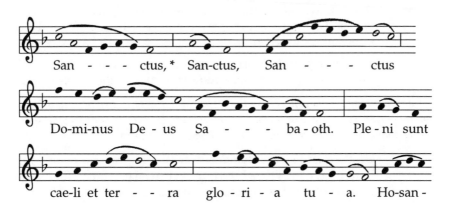

na in ex - cel - sis. *Cantor:* Be - ne - dic - tus qui

ve - nit in no - - - mi - ne Do - - - mi - ni.

All: Ho - - - - - - - - - sa - na in ex-

cel - - - - - sis.

THE EUCHARISTIC PRAYER

After we have sanctified ourselves by the Sanctus, we pray God to send
His Holy Spirit down on the offerings, so that He may make the bread His
Body and wine His Blood. And that which the Holy Spirit has touched
becomes entirely consecrated and transformed. Do not consider the bread
and wine as being ordinary things. They are the Body and the Blood of
Christ, according to His word.

–Saint Cyril of Jerusalem, 4th century

Celebrant Holy and gracious Father: In your infinite love you made us for
yourself; and, when we had fallen into sin and become subject
to evil and death, you, in your mercy, sent Jesus Christ, your
only and eternal Son, to share our human nature, to live and die
as one of us, to reconcile us to you, the God and Father of all.

He stretched out his arms upon the cross, and offered himself
in obedience to your will, a perfect sacrifice for the whole world.

*At the following words concerning the bread, the Celebrant is to hold it or lay a
hand upon it; and at the words concerning the cup, to hold or place a hand upon
the cup and any other vessel containing wine to be consecrated.*

On the night he was handed over to suffering and death, our
Lord Jesus Christ took bread; and when he had given thanks to
you, he broke it, and gave it to his disciples, and said, "Take,

342

eat: This is my Body, which is given for you. Do this for the remembrance of me."

After supper he took the cup of wine; and when he had given thanks, he gave it to them, and said, "Drink this, all of you: This is my Blood of the new Covenant, which is shed for you and for many for the forgiveness of sins. Whenever you drink it, do this for the remembrance of me."

Therefore we proclaim the mystery of faith:

All   Christ has died.
Christ is risen.
Christ will come again.

Celebrant We celebrate the memorial of our redemption, O Father, in this sacrifice of praise and thanksgiving. Recalling his death, resurrection, and ascension, we offer you these gifts.

Sanctify them by your Holy Spirit to be for your people the Body and Blood of your Son, the holy food and drink of new and unending life in him. Sanctify us also that we may faithfully receive this holy Sacrament, and serve you in unity, constancy, and peace; and at the last day bring us with all your saints into the joy of your eternal kingdom.

All this we ask through your Son Jesus Christ. By him, and with him, and in him, in the unity of the Holy Spirit all honor and glory is yours, Almighty Father, now and for ever.

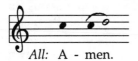

All: A - men.

THE LORD'S PRAYER

The prayer of Our Lord establishes reconciliation as a law for men, and by the fact of forgiving and being forgiven it binds nature to itself to be no longer mutilated by differences of will.

–Saint Maximus the Confessor, 7th century

Lord, teach us to pray.   –Luke 11:1

Celebrant And now, as our Savior Christ has taught us, we are bold to say:

Our Fa-ther, who art in hea-ven, hal-low - ed be thy Name. Thy King-dom come, Thy will be done, on earth as it is in hea-ven. Give us this day our dai-ly bread, and for-give us our tres-pas-ses, as we for-give those who tres-pass a-gainst us. And lead us not in-to temp-ta - tion, but de - li-ver us from e - vil. A - men.

The celebrant may add the following prayer.

Celebrant   Deliver us, O Lord, from all evils, past, present and to come:
and at the intercession of the blessed and glorious Virgin Mary,
Mother of God, with your blessed Apostles Peter and Paul, and
with Andrew, James, and with all Saints, give peace graciously
in our days, that we, sustained by your mercy, may remain free
from sin and safe from all disquiet. Through the same Jesus
Christ your Son our Lord, who lives and reigns with You, in the
unity of the Holy Spirit, one God, world without end. *Amen.*

THE FRACTION

By resorting to the perceptible, to imagery, the Celebrant makes clear that
which gives life to our minds. He shows us how Our Lord came down to
us from His own natural unity to our own fragmented level, yet without
change.

–Pseudo-Dionysius, 6th century

The Celebrant breaks the consecrated bread in silence. The mystical peace and unity of Christ proceed from the consecrated Body and Blood to all. The following prayers and chant emphasize the theme of the unity of all things in the peace of Christ.

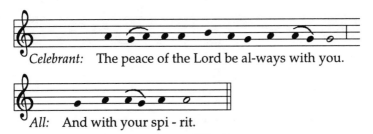

Celebrant: The peace of the Lord be al-ways with you.

All: And with your spi - rit.

Celebrant May this mingling and consecration of the Body and Blood of Jesus Christ our Lord be unto us who receive it an approach to everlasting life. *Amen.*

The people greet one another in the name of the Lord.

AGNUS DEI

Sung by all, led by the Cantor, who sings the words "Agnus Dei" each time alone. All join at each asterisk.

Cantor: A-gnus De - i * qui tol - - - lis pec - ca - ta mun - di, mi - se - re - re no - bis.

Cantor: A-gnus De - i * qui tol - lis pec - ca - ta mun - di, mi - se - re - re no - bis.

Cantor: A-gnus De - i * qui tol - - - lis pec - ca -

ta mun - di, do - na no - bis pa - cem.

PRAYER FOR THE PEACE OF THE CHURCH

Celebrant Lord Jesus Christ, you said to your apostles, "Peace I give to you; my own peace I leave with you:" Regard not our sins, but the faith of your Church, and give to us the peace and unity of that heavenly City, where with the Father and the Holy Spirit, you live and reign, now and for ever. *Amen.*

The Celebrant invites the people to communion with the following words.

Celebrant: Behold the Lamb of God; behold him who takes away the sins of the world.

All   Lord, I am not worthy that you should come under my roof, but speak the word only, and my soul shall be healed.

The Prayer of Humble Access may be said silently in preparation for communion.

We do not presume to come to this thy Table, O Merciful Lord, trusting in our own righteousness, but in thy manifold and great mercies. We are not worthy so much as to gather up the crumbs under thy Table. But thou art the same Lord, whose property is always to have mercy. Grant us therefore, gracious Lord, so to eat the flesh of thy dear Son Jesus Christ, and to drink his blood, that our sinful bodies may be made clean by his Body, and our souls washed through his most precious Blood, and that we may evermore dwell in him, and he in us. Amen.

I will go to the altar of God; to the God of my joy and gladness.

–cf. Psalm 43:4

Lord, I love the house in which you dwell and the place where your glory abides.

–Psalm 26:8

COMMUNION OF THE FAITHFUL

When the Celebrant administers the Bread, he or she says: "The Body of our Lord Jesus Christ, which was given for you, preserve your body and soul unto everlasting life." The Cup is administered with these words: "The Blood of our Lord Jesus Christ, which was shed for you, preserve your body and soul unto everlasting life." The communicant may respond "Amen" to both prayers.

By this Eucharist, we who are mortal by nature, expect to receive immortality; corruptible, we become incorruptible; from the earth and earthly evils, we pass to all the blessings and delights of heaven. By means of these kinds of figures, we have faith that we possess the realities themselves.

–Theodore of Mopsuestia, 5th century

The spirit that possesses health is the one which has no images of the things of this world at the time of prayer.

–Evagrius Ponticus, 4th century

I advise you to look for experience rather than for knowledge. Knowing often misleads us because of our pride, but mere awareness in love and humility is without deceit.

–The Cloud of Unknowing, Anonymous, 14th century

The chalice corresponds to the vessel which received the mixture which poured out from the bloodied, undefiled side and from the hands and feet of Christ. Or again, the chalice corresponds to the bowl which the Lord depicts, that is, Wisdom; because the Son of God has mixed His blood for drinking instead of that wine [Proverbs 9:2], and set it forth on His holy table, saying to all: "Drink of my blood mixed for you for the remission of sins and eternal life."

–Saint Germanus of Constantinople, 8th century

The grace of the Holy Eucharist transforms and changes each person who is found there and in fact remolds him in proportion to what is more divine in him and leads him to what is revealed through the mysteries which are celebrated.

–Saint Maximus the Confessor, 7th century

Come, eat of my bread, and drink of the wine which I [Wisdom] have mingled.

–Proverbs 9:5

The sparrow has found her a house, and the swallow a nest where she may lay her young.

–Psalm 84:2

I went down into my garden.   –Song of Songs 6:11

He shall come down like rain upon the mown field.   –Psalm 72:6

COMMUNION ANTIPHON *Spiritus Sanctus*   Mode 8

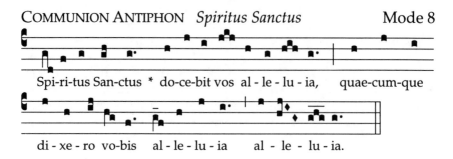

Spi-ri-tus San-ctus * do-ce-bit vos al - le - lu - ia,   quae-cum-que

di - xe - ro vo-bis   al - le - lu - ia   al - le - lu - ia.

[The Holy Spirit will teach you whatsoever I have said to you alleluia.]

THE POSTCOMMUNION PRAYER

I will give thanks to the Lord with my whole heart.   –Psalm 111:1

Celebrant Let us pray.

All   Eternal God, heavenly Father,
         you have graciously accepted us as living members
         of your Son our Savior Jesus Christ,
         and you have fed us with spiritual food
         in the Sacrament of his Body and Blood.
         Send us now into the world in peace,
         and grant us strength and courage
         to love and serve you
         with gladness and singleness of heart;
         through Christ our Lord. Amen.

The following prayer may be added.

Celebrant The Lord be with you.

People   And also with you.

Celebrant Let us pray.

        We pray, O Lord, that you would send down upon our hearts
        the quickening Spirit of your grace; pour upon us the inward
        dew of his blessing, that we may bring forth fruit for your

kingdom. Through Jesus Christ our Lord; by whom, and with whom, in the unity of the Holy Spirit, all honour and glory be unto you, O Father Almighty, world without end. *Amen.*

BLESSING AND DISMISSAL

Celebrant The Lord be with you

People And also with you.

Celebrant The Peace of God, which passes all understanding, keep your hearts and minds in the knowledge and love of God, and of his Son Jesus Christ our Lord. And the blessing of God Almighty: the Father, the Son, and the Holy Spirit, be among you, and remain with you always.

People Amen.

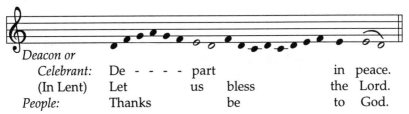

Deacon or				
Celebrant:	De - - - - part		in	peace.
(In Lent)	Let	us	bless	the	Lord.
People:	Thanks		be	to	God.

The following may be added.

THE LAST GOSPEL

Celebrant: The Lord be with you

All: And also with you.

Celebrant The Beginning of the Holy Gospel according to John.

People Glory be to you, O Lord.

Celebrant In the beginning was the Word, and the Word was with God, and the Word was God. The same was in the beginning with God. All things were made by him, and without him was not anything made that was made. In him was life, and the life was the light of men, and the light shineth in darkness, and the darkness comprehended it not. There was a man sent from God, whose name was John. The same came for a witness, to bear witness of the light, that all men through him might believe. He was not that light, but was sent to bear witness of that light. That was the true light, which lighteth every man that cometh into the world. He was in the world, and the world was made by him, and the world knew him not. He came unto his own, and his own received him not. But as many as received him, to them gave he power to become the sons of God, even to them that believe on his Name, which were born, not of blood, nor of the will of the flesh, nor of the will of man, but of God.

Here it is customary to bow or genuflect in honor of the Incarnation, the Word made flesh.

And the Word was made flesh, and dwelt among us, and we beheld his glory, the glory as of the Only-begotten of the Father, full of grace and truth.

People: Thanks be to God.

The Ministers and Choir leave in silence or a recessional chant may be sung. The Congregation is invited to remain in prayer.

MEDITATIONS

Happy are they whom you choose and draw to your courts to dwell there.
                                                                    –Psalm 65:4

Be still, then, and know that I am God.   –Psalm 46:11

A thousand years in your sight are as yesterday, which is past.
                                                                    –Psalm 90:4

May the Lord guard your coming in and your going out from now until the end of the age.
                                                                    –Psalm 121:8

Surely I come quickly; Amen. Even so, come, Lord Jesus.
                                                                –Revelation 22:20

ADDITIONAL MEDITATIONS

No one can perceive how great is the splendor of the Word, until he receives dove's eyes—that is, a spiritual understanding.
                                                        –Origen, 3rd century

350

When the mind is at rest from outward concerns, the weight of the divine teachings is more fully discerned. When the mind refuses to admit within itself the noises of worldly cares, then it penetrates the words of God in a more lively way. For the crowd of daily thoughts, when it clamors around, closes the ear of the mind.

–Saint Gregory the Great

Silence of the heart, practiced with wisdom, will see a lofty depth; and the ear of the silent mind will hear untold wonders.

–Hesychius of Jerusalem, 5th century

Fight always with your thoughts and call them back when they wander away.

–Saint John of the Ladder, 7th century

Recollection is a preparation for being able to listen, so that the soul instead of striving to engage in discourse strives to remain attentive and aware of what the Lord is working in it.

–Saint Teresa of Avila, 16th century

Let him who is thirsty come. –Revelation 22:17

Send out your light and your truth, that they may lead me, and bring me to your holy hill and to your dwelling.

–Psalm 43:3

My soul is athirst for God, athirst for the living God. –Psalm 42:2

When I awake I shall be satisfied, beholding your likeness. –Psalm 17:16

But as for me, my prayer is unto thee, O LORD, in an acceptable time: O God, in the multitude of thy mercy, hear me.

–Psalm 69:13

Your word is a lantern to my feet and a light upon my path.

–Psalm 119:105

And thine ears shall hear a word behind thee, saying, This is the way, walk ye in it.

–Isaiah 30:21

Let us through an informed study of holy scripture wisely get past its letter and rise up to the Holy Spirit in whom are found the fullness of all goodness and the treasures of knowledge and the secrets of wisdom.

–Saint Maximus the Confessor, 7th century

Blessed be the Lord God of Israel, from everlasting to everlasting. So let it be done.

–Psalm 106:48

ENTRANCES

Yet I am always with you. You hold me by my right hand. —Psalm 73:24

The Lord has turned my soul. —Psalm 23:3

O spare me a little, that I may recover my strength, before I go hence, and be no more seen.
—Psalm 39:15

My feet are standing within your gates, O Jerusalem. —cf. Psalm 122:2

Come, my beloved, let us go forth into the field. —Song of Songs 7:11

Our God shall come and not keep silence. —Psalm 50:3

The words of the Lord's Prayer point out the Father, the Father's name, and the Father's kingdom to help us learn from the source Himself to honor, to invoke, and to adore the one Trinity. For the name of God the Father is the only-begotten Son, and the kingdom of God the Father is the Holy Spirit.
—Saint Maximus the Confessor, 7th century

Your throne is prepared from of old; you are from everlasting.
—Psalm 93:2

Wake up, my spirit; awake, lute and harp. —Psalm 108:2

Blessed be the Lord, for he hath shown me his wonderful mercy in a fortified city.
—Psalm 31:22

You open your hand, O God, and fill every living creature with blessing.
—Psalm 145:16

In my life I will praise the Lord. —Psalm 146:2

Appendix 12

Where to Find Music and Texts

The best source for music with Latin texts is the Abbey of Solesmes in France. Their U.S. distributor is Paraclete Press. (Contact information is given below.) Chants for the Eucharist throughout the church year are found in Solesmes's *Graduale Romanum* and chants for the Day Office in the *Antiphonale Monasticum*. The *Graduale Triplex* contains the same chants as the *Graduale Romanum* but with neumes of two early manuscripts printed above and below the square-note lines for comparison. These two collections contain most of the music a parish choir would need, except for the Tenebrae chants, which are harder to find. Tenebrae is included in Appendix 9 of this book, and the eight psalm tones in Appendix 2. The *Liber Usualis*, a large and useful collection of the most common chants for Mass and Office is no longer available from Solesmes but has been reprinted by St. Bonaventure Publications. Software for writing chant notation on a computer, in either square or modern notation (separate programs) is available from St. Meinrad Archabbey.

The Daily Office as used in Benedictine monasteries before Vatican II was substantially the same as the medieval Office. The full text of the Office, without music, is found in a book called a "breviary." Benedictine breviaries were published in both Latin and English but are now very hard to find. A reference copy can be had in most large seminary libraries, and one of many editions is listed in the bibliography of this book. The Divine Office for non-monastics before Vatican II differed somewhat from the monastic version and was called the "secular" Office. The English *Roman Breviary* in the bibliography is the secular version. Earlier in this century an English translation of the *Roman Breviary*, called *The Anglican Breviary*, was published by the Frank Gavin Liturgical Foundation in Long Island, NY, for use by Anglo-Catholic Episcopalians, but it is long out of print. An edition of the Episcopal Book of Common Prayer with additional prayers and antiphons from the older breviaries, called *The Prayer Book Office*, is published by Church Publishing Incorporated in New York, NY.

The Douai-Rheims translation of the Latin Vulgate is published by Tan Books and is often available in Roman Catholic bookstores. The best Latin edition (*Biblia Sacra juxta Vulgatam Versionem*) is published by the Deutsche Bibelgesellschaft in Stuttgart. The two-volume, annotated edition is frequently out of print, but the single volume edition can be ordered from the American Bible Society. Identifying the biblical sources of chant texts is now easy with various online bibles. One of the best is the Brown University "Bible Browser," at:

http://goon.stg.brown.edu/

At the home page, select "Bible Browser" and follow directions. Most versions of the Bible are also available on CD-ROM. One of the better programs is QuickVerse for Windows®, but it does not include the Vulgate. The Vulgate is included on some cheaper CDs, such as the Multimedia Bible Suite from Swift Software.

The standard Latin edition of the Latin fathers is *Corpus Christianorum, Series Latina*, published by Brepols, in Belgium. The entire set is available on a very expensive series of CD-ROMs or can be consulted in large seminary libraries. Individual volumes are expensive but can be ordered from Brepols. Much more accessible for English readers is *The Classics of Western Spirituality* series, published by Paulist Press and still in print. These are excellent, readable translations with introductions by major scholars. Also important and still available are: the *Ancient Christian Writers* series from the Newman Press; and many useful volumes, including the works of Bernard of Clairvaux, from Cistercian Publications. The great missing items in this collection of English translations are the two major works of exegesis by St. Gregory the Great on Ezekiel and on Job. The homilies on Ezekiel have never been translated, but the nineteenth-century Oxford Movement translation of the *Moralia in Job (Morals on the Book of Job)* can be found in some large seminary collections.

IMPORTANT SOURCES OF THE MUSIC AND TEXTS
OF GREGORIAN CHANT:

The American Bible Society,
   1865 Broadway, New York, NY 10023-7505.
   Ph: (212) 408-8710
   Website: http://www.americanbible.org
             (Select "Catalog")
   One source for the Stuttgart (single volume) edition of the Latin Vulgate.

St. Bonaventure Publications
   324 Central Avenue, Suite 105, Great Falls, MT 59401.
   Website: http://www.mcn.net/~relbooks/liber.html
   Publishers of a reprint of the 1952 Latin chant collection *Liber Usualis*.

Brepols
   68, Steenweg op Tielen, B-2300 Turnhout, Belgium.
   Website: http://www.brepols.com
   Publishers of the standard editions of the Latin and Greek fathers in original languages.

Brown University Bible Browser
   Website: http://goon.stg.brown.edu
   An excellent online Bible search engine for the Latin Vulgate, the King James Bible, the Revised Standard Version, and other translations. From home page, select "Bible Browser."

Church Fathers: John Paul II Library Research Guides
   John Paul II Library,
   Franciscan University of Steubenville
   1235 University Blvd., Steubenville, OH 43952.
   Website: http://www.franuniv.edu/jp2/fathers.htm
      A guide to works of the fathers in English and original
      languages, in print and online.

Church Publishing Incorporated
   445 Fifth Avenue, New York, NY, 10016.
   Ph: (800) 242-1918
   Fax: (212) 779-3392
   Website: http://www.churchpublishing.org
   E-Mail: churchpublishing@cpg.org

Cistercian Publications
   St. Joseph's Abbey
   167 North Spencer Road, Spencer, MA 01562-1233.
   Ph: (508) 885-8730
   Fax: (508) 885-4687
   Website: http://www.spencerabbey.org
             (Click "Cistercian Publications")
   E-Mail: cistpub@spencerabbey.org
      Publishers of an excellent English translation of St. Bernard of
      Clairvaux's sermons on *The Song of Songs*, as well as *The Ladder
      of Monks* by Guigo II and other classics on the spiritual life by
      Cistercian writers.

The Gregorian Chant Home Page
   by Prof. Peter Jeffery of Princeton University.
   Website: http://www.music.princeton.edu/chant_html
      A center of chant information hosted by a leading musicologist.

The Choirmaster
   St. Meinrad Archabbey
   St. Meinrad, IN 47577-1010.

Ph: (812) 357 6686
Website: http://www.saintmeinrad.edu/abbey
          (Click "Liturgical Music")
Publishers of software for the writing out of chant melodies in simple modern or traditional square notation, for IBM PC or Macintosh.

Paraclete Press
P.O. Box 1568, Orleans, MA 02653
Ph: (800) 451-5006
Website: http://www.paraclete-press.com
          (Click "Chant")
American dealers for chant books published by the French monastery St. Peter of Solesmes, including a full collection of Mass chants for the year (*Graduale Romanum*), an edition of the *Graduale Romanum* with neumes written in from two early manuscript sources (*Graduale Triplex*), a missal with Mass chants for Sundays and major feasts with English translations of the texts (*The Gregorian Missal*), a full collection of chants for the hours of the Day Office (*Antiphonale Monasticum*), a useful, short collection of chants for choirs (*Liber Cantualis*), and others. Contact Paraclete to check on the availability of Solesmes titles which do not appear in their catalog.

Paulist Press
545 Island Road, Ramsey, NJ 07446.
Website: http://www.paulistpress.com
          (Click "Series")
Publishers of *The Classics of Western Spirituality*, an excellent collection of works by the fathers and other writers on the spiritual life, Christian and non-Christian.

Tan Books and Publishers, Inc.
P.O. Box 424, Rockford, IL 61105.
Ph: (800) 437-5876
Fax: (815) 226-7770

Website: http://www.tanbooks.com

E-Mail: TAN@TANBooks.com

   Publishers of the Douai-Rheims English translation of the
   Latin Vulgate.